国家社会科学基金项目
"英语专业基础阶段内容依托式课程改革研究"项目组

古希腊罗马神话

Ancient Greek and Roman Mythology

主　编：杨俊峰　黄洁芳　常俊跃
本书编校主要参与者：
　　　　范丽雅　苏晓丽　喻东　庄天赐（排名不分先后）
对本项目教材编校有贡献的其他教师：
　　　　宋杰　李莉莉　夏洋　赵秀艳
　　　　吕春媚　霍跃红　高璐璐　姚璐
　　　　李文萍　傅琼　刘晓蕖

图书在版编目(CIP)数据

古希腊罗马神话 / 常俊跃主编. — 北京:北京大学出版社,2013.1
(21世纪CBI内容依托系列英语教材)

ISBN 978-7-301-21775-7

Ⅰ. 古… Ⅱ. 常… Ⅲ. ①英语—高等学校—教材 ②神话—作品集—古希腊 ③神话—作品集—古罗马 Ⅳ. H319.4:I

中国版本图书馆CIP数据核字(2012)第300945号

书　　　名:古希腊罗马神话
著作责任者:杨俊峰　黄洁芳　常俊跃　主编
责 任 编 辑:孙　莹
标 准 书 号:ISBN 978-7-301-21775-7/H·3206
出 版 发 行:北京大学出版社
地　　　址:北京市海淀区成府路205号　100871
网　　　址:http://www.pup.cn　新浪官方微博:@北京大学出版社
电 子 邮 箱:编辑部 pupwaiwen@pup.cn　总编室 zpup@pup.cn
电　　　话:邮购部 62752015　发行部 62750672　编辑部 62754382　出版部 62754962
印　　刷　者:河北滦县鑫华书刊印刷厂
经　　销　者:新华书店
　　　　　　787毫米×1092毫米　16开本　15印张　358千字
　　　　　　2013年1月第1版　2025年1月第10次印刷
定　　　价:49.00元

未经许可,不得以任何方式复制或抄袭本书之部分或全部内容。
版权所有,侵权必究　　举报电话:010-62752024
　　　　　　　　　　　　电子邮箱:fd@pup.cn

前言

《古希腊罗马神话》是在内容依托教学理念指导下,依托国家哲学社会科学项目"英语专业基础阶段内容依托式课程改革研究"推出的系列英语内容依托教材之一,是大连外国语学院优秀教学成果一等奖、辽宁省优秀教学成果一等奖、第六届国家级优秀教学成果奖获奖成果的重要组成部分。这套系列教材和研究成果的推出具有重要的理论意义和现实意义。

随着我国英语教育的快速发展,英语专业长期贯彻的"以技能为导向"的课程建设理念及教学理念已经难以满足社会的需要。专家教师们密切关注的现行英语专业教育大、中、小学英语教学脱节,语言、内容教学割裂,单纯语言技能训练过多,专业内容课程不足,学科内容课程系统性差,高低年级内容课程安排失衡及其导致的学生知识面偏窄、知识结构欠缺、思辨能力偏弱、综合素质发展不充分等问题日益凸显。

针对上述问题,国家哲学社会科学项目"英语专业基础阶段内容依托式教学改革研究"以内容依托教学(CBI)理念为指导,确定了如下改革思路:

(一) 更新语言教学理念,改革英语专业教学的课程结构。在不改变专业总体培养目标和教学时限的前提下,对课程结构进行革命性的变革,改变传统单一的语言技能课程模式,实现内容课程与语言课程的融合,扩展学生的知识面,提高学生的语言技能。

(二) 开发课程自身潜力,同步提高专业知识和语言技能。内容依托课程本身也同时关注内容和语言,把内容教学和语言教学有机结合。以英语为媒介,系统教授专业内容;以专业内容为依托,在使用语言过程中提高语言技能,扩展学生的知识面。

(三) 改革教学方法手段,全面提高语言技能和综合素质。依靠内容依托教学在方法上的灵活性,通过问题驱动、输出驱动等方法调动学生主动学习,把启发式、任务式、讨论式、结对子、小组活动、课堂展示、多媒体手段等行之有效的活动与学科内容教学有机结合,提高学生的语言技能,激发学生的兴趣,培养学生的自主性和创造性,提升思辨能力和综合素质。

本项改革突破了我国英语专业英语教学大纲规定的课程结构,改变了英语专业基础阶段通过开设单纯的听、说、读、写四种语言技能课提高学生语言技能的传统课程建设理念,对英语课程及教学方法进行了创新性的改革。首创了有英语专业基础阶段具有我国特色的"内容·语言"融合的课程体系;率先开发了适合英语专业基础阶段的内容依托课程;系统开发了英语国家历史、地理、社会文化、欧洲文化、中国文化、跨文化交际、《圣经》与文化、古希腊罗马神话教材;以英语为媒介,系统教授专业内容;以内容为依托,全面发展学生的语言技能;扩展学生的知识面,提高学生的综合素质,以崭新的途径实现英语专业教育的总体培养目标。

经过七年的酝酿、准备、实验,内容依托教学改革取得了鼓舞人心的结果。

(一) 构建了英语专业基础阶段内容依托课程与语言课程融合的课程体系。新的课程体系改变了传统单一的听、说、读、写语言技能课程模式,实现了内容依托课程和语言技能课程两种模块的融合;语言技能课程包含综合英语、听力、语音、写作,内容课程包含了美国历史文化、美国自然人文地理、美国社会文化、英国历史文化、英国自然人文地理、英国社会文化、澳新加社会文化、欧洲文化、中国文化、跨文化交际、《圣经》与文化、古希腊罗马神话;语言技

i

能课程密切关注听、说、读、写技能的发展,内容依托课程不仅关注系统的学科内容,而且也关注综合语言技能的培养。在课程外和课程内两个层面把内容教学和语言教学有机结合,通过内容教学培养学生综合语言运用能力,扩展学生的知识面,提高学生的综合素质和多元文化意识,从根本上改变英语专业学生知识面偏窄、综合素质偏低的问题。

(二) 系统开发了相关国家的历史、地理、社会文化以及跨文化交际课程资源。在CBI教学理论的指导下,在实施内容依托教学的关键期——英语专业的第一学年,成功开出了美国和英国的历史、地理、社会文化等课程。第二学年开出澳新加社会文化、欧洲文化、中国文化、跨文化交际、《圣经》与文化、古希腊罗马神话等课程。内容依托教材改变了传统的组织模式,系统组织了教学内容,设计了新颖的栏目板块,设计的活动也丰富多样,实践教学中受到了学生的广泛欢迎。此外还开发了开设课程所需要的大量资源。在北京大学出版社的支持下,系列教材已经陆续出版。

(三) 牵动了教学手段和教学方法的改革,取得了突出的教学效果。在内容依托教学理论的指导下,教师的教学理念、教学方法、教学手段得到更新。通过问题驱动、输出驱动等活动调动学生主动学习,把启发式、任务式、讨论式、结对子、小组活动、课堂展示、多媒体手段等行之有效的活动与学科内容教学有机结合,激发学生的兴趣,培养学生自主性和创造性,提高学生的语言技能,提升思辨能力和综合素质。曾有专家教师担心取消专门的英语泛读课以及缩减基础英语精读课对阅读技能发展会产生消极影响。实验数据证明,内容依托教学不仅没有对学生的语言技能发展和语言知识的学习产生消极影响,而且还产生了多方面的积极影响;在取消专门英语阅读课的情况下,阅读能力发展迅速;内容依托教学对学科知识的学习产生了巨大的积极影响。

(四) 提高了教师的科研意识和科研水平,取得了丰硕的教研成果。项目开展以来,团队对内容依托教学问题进行了系列研究,活跃了整个教学单位的科研气氛,科研意识和科研水平也得到很大提高。课题组已经撰写研究论文30多篇,在国际、国内学术研讨会交流25篇,在国际学术期刊 World Englishes、国内外语类核心期刊《外语与外语教学》、《中国外语》、《教育理论与实践》等发表研究论文17篇。

教学改革开展以来,每次成果发布都引起强烈反响。在2008年3月的第三届中国外语教学法国际研讨会上,与会的知名外语教育专家戴炜栋教授等对这项改革给予关注,博士生导师蔡基刚教授认为本项研究"具有导向性作用"。在2008年5月的"第二届全国英语专业院系主任高级论坛"上,研究成果得到知名专家博士生导师王守仁教授和与会专家教授的高度评价。在2008年7月的中国英语教学研究会东北地区年会上,改革的系列成果引起与会专家的强烈反响,研究论文获得3个优秀论文一等奖,3个二等奖,1个三等奖。在2008年11月在中国英语教学研究会年会上,成果再次引起与会专家的强烈反响,博士生导师石坚教授等给予了高度评价。在2008年10月和12月,本项改革成果分别获得大连外国语学院教学研究成果一等奖和辽宁省优秀教学成果奖一等奖,而且还被辽宁省特别推荐参评国家教学成果奖。在2009年5月的"第三届全国英语专业院系主任高级论坛",本项改革成果再次赢得专家同行们的关注和赞誉。2009年10月"中国英语教学研究会2009年会"上,中国英语教学研究会会长、中国外语教育研究中心主任文秋芳教授和我国外语教学指导委员会主任戴炜栋教授对我们的教学研究所取得的成果给予高度肯定和赞扬。2011年5月和2012年4

月，中国教育语言学研究会专门召开了由国内外学者参加的"以内容为依托的外语教学模式探索"和"基于学科的外语教学新模式"学术研讨会，该项研究成果得到了与会专家的高度评价和广泛的赞誉。

目前，该项成果已经在全国英语专业教育领域引起广泛关注。它触及了英语专业的教学大纲，影响了课程建设的理念，引领了英语专业的教学改革，改善了教学实践，必将对未来英语专业教育的发展产生积极影响。

本项改革开展过程中得到了全国各地专家的关注、支持和帮助。衷心感谢戴炜栋教授、王守仁教授、文秋芳教授、石坚教授、蔡基刚教授、杨忠教授等前辈们给予的关注、鼓励、指导和帮助，衷心感谢大连外国语学院校长孙玉华教授、赵忠德教授、杨俊峰教授及其他各位领导的大力支持，感谢大连外国语学院教务处刘宏处长、姜凤春副处长以及工作人员们在改革实验中给予的大力支持，感谢大连外国语学院科研处张雪处长和工作人员们给予的热情帮助，感谢大连外国语学院英语学院的领导全力支持和同事们的理解、帮助以及团队成员的共同努力。同时也真诚感谢为我们内容依托教学改革提供丰富教学材料的国内外专家们。特别感谢的是北京大学出版社富有远见的张冰主任和刘强助理，没有他们对新教学理念的认同，没有他们对英语专业教育的关注和支持，这套教材不可能如此迅速地面世。

《古希腊罗马神话》针对的学生群体是具有中学英语基础的大学生。既适合英语专业基础阶段的学生，也适合具有中学英语基础的非英语专业学生和英语爱好者学习使用。总体来看，本教材具备以下主要特色：

（一）打破了传统的教材建设理念

本教材打破了"以提高语言技能为终极目的"的传统教材建设理念，在先进的内容依托教学理论指导下，改变了片面关注语言知识和语言技能却忽视内容学习的作法，围绕希腊罗马神话的主题组织素材，给学习者提供能沉浸其中的英语教材，在轻松愉悦的氛围中通过积极参与课堂教学活动达到学习使用语言的目的。

（二）涵盖了古典神话的主要内容

《古希腊罗马神话》设定了15个单元，关注了学习希腊罗马神话的意义、主要神话人物故事及其文化象征意义等生动丰富的内容。教材使用了大量真实、地道的语言材料，为学生提供了高质量的语言输入，并为他们的语言输出提供素材打下了坚实的基础。内容力求具有知识性、趣味性和启发性，引导学生关注异域文化，培养文化敏感性，树立多元文化的意识，在批判中汲取西方文化的精华，建构合理的人文知识结构，提高人文修养水平。

（三）突出了学生的主体地位

本教材设计了新颖的活动板块，每一单元的主体内容均包括Before You Read、Start to Read、After You Read、Read More四大板块，突出以学生为中心的思想，而且也方便教师借助教材开展生动有趣的教学活动。在Before You Read部分，学生通过自测了解自己的不足，激发学习热情；在Start to Read部分获得主要知识内容，拓展知识面；在After You Read部分通过练习检测对单元内容的掌握情况；Read More提供的两或三篇辅助阅读材料是对单元内容的延伸。这种设计理念，从学生的要求和实际情况出发，培养他们的自主学习能力。

（四）设计了多样的训练活动

在强调内容学习的同时，教材也关注培养学生的语言技能和综合素质。教材精心设计了生动多样的综合练习。这些练习有关注丰富文化知识的，也有专门训练语言技能的，还有培养学生主动思考，比较中西文化异同的活动，这些活动学生参与度极高，可在课内和课外进行。多样化的活动打破了传统教材单调的训练程式，使得课堂教学得以延伸。

  作为一项探索，我们团队成员虽然为打造这套精品教材做出了巨大努力，但由于水平所限，教材中难免存在疏漏和不足，希望全国各地的同仁不吝赐教，希望亲自体验内容依托教学的同学积极提出改进意见和建议，以期不断完善教材，为提高英语专业教育的质量共同努力。

编者

2012年7月于大连外国语学院

Contents

Unit 1	Why Mythology?	1
	Text A Why Mythology	2
	Text B What Is a Myth?	9
	Text C Myths and Mythology	11
Unit 2	The Olympian Gods (I)	15
	Text A The Olympian Gods (I)	15
	Text B Zeus' Consorts and Some of Their Tribulations	24
	Text C Athena	27
Unit 3	The Olympian Gods (II)	30
	Text A The Olympian Gods (II)	31
	Text B Artemis and Actaeon	40
	Text C Venus and Adonis	41
Unit 4	The Gods of the Underworld	43
	Text A The Gods of the Underworld	44
	Text B Persephone	52
	Text C Cerberus: Three Headed Dog in Greek Mythology	55
Unit 5	Other Gods	57
	Text A Other Gods	58
	Text B The Wood-Folk	66
	Text C The Judgement of Midas	68
Unit 6	Myths of Origin	71
	Text A Myths of Origin	72
	Text B The Vampire Origin Story	79
	Text C The Mythology Chiron—the Wounded Healer	83
Unit 7	Gods and Mortals	85
	Text A Gods and Mortals	85
	Text B Atalanta and the Golden Apples	94
	Text C Orpheus and Eurydice	95

Unit 8	The Age of Heroes (I)	100
	Text A The Age of Heroes (I)	101
	Text B Hercules: An Ageless Icon	110
	Text C Perseus and Medusa	113
Unit 9	The Age of Heroes (II)	115
	Text A The Age of Heroes (II)	116
	Text B Jason and the Argonauts	126
	Text C Oedipus Complex	128
Unit 10	The Trojan War	131
	Text A The Trojan War	132
	Text B Troy	141
	Text C Helen of Troy	144
Unit 11	After the Trojan War	147
	Text A After the Trojan War	148
	Text B Odysseus	157
	Text C Rome	159
Unit 12	Apollo and Daphne	163
	Text A Apollo and Daphne	164
	Text B Apollo	170
	Text C Apollo and Delphi	173
Unit 13	Echo and Narcissus	177
	Text A Echo and Narcissus	178
	Text B Echo and Narcissus' Story in Metamorphoses	184
	Text C Understanding Narcissism	185
Unit 14	Pygmalion	188
	Text A Pygmalion	189
	Text B Bernard Shaw's Pygmalion	195
	Text C The City of Paphos	196
Unit 15	Eros/Cupid and Psyche	199
	Text A Eros/Cupid and Psyche	200
	Text B Voluptas and The Kharites	206
	Text C Beauty and Beast	208
Key to Exercises		211
Bibliography		230

Unit 1
Why Mythology?

> A myth is story that has never happened and is always happening.
> — Howard Sasportas
>
> Myth is an eternal mirror in which we see ourselves.
> — J.F. Bierlein, *Parallel Myths*

Unit Goals

- To know the basic definition of "myth"
- To understand the significance of learning classical myths
- To have some knowledge of Greco-Roman mythology
- To learn the useful words and expressions that describe myths and mythology
- To improve language skills and critical thinking through the content of this unit

Before You Read

1. What is a myth? The following is a list of stories that you are very familiar with. Are they myths, fables, legends or fairy tales?

Cinderella	The Wolf in Sheep's Clothing	
The Hare and the Tortoise	King Arthur and the Knights of the Round Table	
Pandora's Box	Beauty and Beast	
Robin Hood	King Midas and the golden touch	

2. Do you understand the following words or phrases? They are all derived from classical mythology. Please work in pairs to find out their meanings.

Words from mythology	Meaning
chaotic	
hypnotic	
narcissistic	
the Trojan Horse	

Ancient Greek and Roman Mythology

Pandora's box	
Apple of discord	
Achilles' heel	

Start to Read

Text A Why Mythology

"*Myth may be defined as those paradigmatic events, conditions, deeds outside ordinary human life yet basic to it. Set in a time different from historical time, often at the beginning of creation or at an early stage of prehistory, Myth provides models of human behavior, institutions or universal conditions.*"

—Octavio Paz, *The Labyrinth of Solitude*

"*…myths evolved because people needed a way to explain where fire came from and why there was evil in the world.*"

—Sharon Creech, *Walk Two Moons*

"*Contemporary man has rationalized the myths, but he has not been able to destroy them.*"

—Tom Wolfe, *The Electric Kool-Aid Acid Test*

"Hey, Thompson, I read your thing," said Emilie.

"My thing?"

"Yeah," she replied. "You know, that thing you wrote on the Internet about why we have to study English."

"Wow!" I said, surprised that a ninth grader would willingly, and for no reward, read a seven-page treatise written by one of her teachers.

"But I still want to know why we have to do mythology!" The word mythology came out with the utter distaste of vomit. We had recently completed an extensive unit on Greek mythology, and it was apparent that Emilie still had not forgiven me. "Why do we have to learn mythology?! What good will that ever do us?"

Why is it important for students to understand mythology? Are they ever going to be tested on it? If so, does the test relate to anything even remotely connected to real life? Will knowing it ever help them get a job? Or, does any of that even matter?

There are different reasons people learn. One is purely to graduate from school and move on with life. That is the least important one. The second is to "succeed" in everyday life. The most important reason people learn is to spiritually uplift, to motivate, and to help us find purpose in our lives. The study of mythology does all these things.

Why do we have to study mythology? (The Academic Response)

Knowing Greek mythology is necessary to understand the countless allusions that appear in poetry and literature throughout your schooling and in the reading that you will do every day for the rest of your life. If you have ever been tantalized, if you have ever looked in an atlas or known someone who had the **Midas** touch or an **Achilles** heel, if you've ever seen the movie *Titanic* or listened to an old rock band called **Styx**, if you have ever been in a panic after reading *Frankenstein* (the Modern *Prometheus*), if you have ever opened **Pandora's box**, if you have ever been on an Odyssey or heard a siren, if you have ever made a Herculean effort to complete a Sisyphean task, or slept in a procrustean bed, you can thank mythology. Modern language is suffused with so many mythological references that it would be almost impossible to communicate without them. To fully understand and appreciate the richness of powerful literature, you must understand mythology. Shakespeare's plays are full of mythological references. **Mercutio**, the quick-witted rabble-rouser in *Romeo and Juliet* who calls **Dido** a Dowdy, is aptly named after the god **Mercury**, and Juliet reminds her young husband, "...at lovers' perjuries they say **Jove** laughs...." Later in the play, she wishes **Phaeton**'s chariot would move the sun more quickly across the sky so that night (and her Romeo) would arrive. If you do not know Mercury, Dido, Jove, or Phaeton, you don't fully understand the content of the play or the richness of the language. Part of the reason young audiences struggle so much with Shakespeare is not because they cannot understand the words, but rather that they can't understand the mythological allusions. There are countless such references throughout all literature. In fact, Emilie's favorite book even contains a chapter called "Pandora's Box."

Why do we have to study mythology? (The Everyday Life Response)

Myths are still relevant. Although it is true you are not likely to see **Zeus** casting lightning bolts down Main Street, it is also true that the human condition is reflected in the characters presented in mythology, and we can learn from those characters. Pride is not a quality unique to **Agamemnon**, nor is sulkiness unique to Achilles. The disastrous consequences of these qualities are personified in these mythological characters, and if we see those qualities in ourselves or in those around us, we might learn from their example. The infidelity of Zeus and the suspicion of **Hera** do not make a good marriage. But was this true only in ancient Greece? Nope. It is still true today, and in a society where more than half the marriages end in divorce, it cannot hurt to study these ancient examples and try to improve upon them in our own relationships. Yes, we are part of the modern world and myths are ancient, but if we continue making the same foolish mistakes that Zeus made, are we truly any more civilized?

Although today we no longer need magical explanations for why the sun shines, why winter comes once a year, or why there is evil in the world, we can benefit from understanding human nature. Regardless of what job you end up doing, who you end up marrying, where you end up living, you will have to deal with other people. The characters in mythology all represent human qualities, the virtues and flaws that make us real. How then do myths help us in everyday life? They illustrate for us those virtues we would do well to develop in ourselves and the idiosyncrasies we would do well to beware of in others. Understanding human nature is a key to success in any venture that involves people, and myths help us do that.

Why do we have to study mythology? (The Cosmic and Most Important Response)

Myths challenge us to question ourselves. If you do not think this is a good thing, then you aren't very secure in your own beliefs and philosophies. If you are a student of **the Old Testament**, you will find that much of what is there is similar to the stories of mythology. In fact, a fairly clear argument can be made that much of the Bible is based on mythology. The Christian story of creation, offerings and animal sacrifices to God, and the idea that God once was directly involved in human affairs and regularly communicated with humanity (the burning bush, **the Ten Commandments**, Moses' miracles) are all ideas which appeared in classical mythology 2500 years before any Christian scriptures were written down. That is hard for most of us in the Judeo-Christian world to stomach because it implies that our scriptures are the works of a bunch of ancient poets. And what if they are?

It is a dynamic world we live in, but many of our greatest stories, fondest entertainments, and legendary traditions started with mythology. Myths serve to show us that although the world and our knowledge of it may change, humanity remains the same. We are still searching for answers to unanswerable questions: What happens when we die? What is our purpose for being? Why are we here? Just as the ancient myths answered such questions for ancient peoples, modern religion and spirituality attempts to answer them for us now. Mythology was once considered religion just as Catholicism, Judaism, and **Mormonism** are now. Mythology was as firmly believed as modern faiths. We may scoff at that, but does it trouble you to consider that human progress may one day turn our modern scriptures into myths that future generations will scorn? The study of mythology reminds us that we, as individuals, must think clearly about who we are and what we believe. Mythology challenges us to ask the difficult questions, and if we rise to the challenge, we find the answers within ourselves.

And if all that still does not satisfy you, Emilie, then the only other reason I can give for studying mythology is that it is fun. Even though we doubt the reality of the myths, it's fun to believe that Zeus, **Poseidon**, and **Hades** are out there somewhere making thunder and causing earthquakes, and keeping us a little bit scared of all that stuff we do not really understand. Studying mythology is a way to hang on to the magic of childhood.

Does that answer your question?

(Excerpted from http://www.davis.k12.ut.us/ffjh/thompson/whymyths.pdf)

Proper Nouns

1. **Midas** ['maidəs]: 弥达斯,希腊神话中的人物,具有点石成金的本领。

2. **Achilles** [əˈkiliːz]：阿喀琉斯，荷马史诗《伊利亚特》中最伟大的英雄。
3. **Styx** [stiks]：希腊神话中的冥河。
4. **Frankenstein**：弗兰肯斯坦，英国作家雪莱所著同名小说中的主角，是一个人形的怪物。
5. **Prometheus** [prəuˈmiːθjuːs; -θiəs]：普罗米修斯，希腊神话中的人物，因盗取火种而受到惩罚。
6. **Pandora** [pænˈdɔːrə]：潘多拉。
7. **Siren** [ˈsaiərən]：塞壬，希腊神话中的众多海妖。
8. **Mercutio**：马库修，莎士比亚戏剧《罗密欧与朱丽叶》中的人物之一，是罗密欧的好友。
9. **Dido** [ˈdaidəu]：狄朵，传说中的迦太基女王，迦太基的创建者和王后，与埃涅阿斯坠入情网，在被抛弃后自杀。
10. **Mercury** [ˈməːkjuri]：墨丘利，罗马诸神之一，在希腊神话中被称为赫耳墨斯，是众神的信使。
11. **Jove** [dʒəuv]：指罗马主神朱庇特。
12. **Phaeton** [ˈfeiətən]：法厄同（又作 Phaethon），希腊神话里的人物，为了证明自己的父亲是太阳神，他借来太阳车自己驾驶，却差点儿毁灭了大地。
13. **Zeus** [zjuːs]：宙斯，希腊神话中的主神。
14. **Agamemnon** [ˌægəˈmemnən]：阿伽门农，特洛伊战争中希腊的总统帅。
15. **Hera** [ˈhiərə]：赫拉，希腊神话中的天后，宙斯的妻子。
16. **The Old Testament**：圣经《旧约》。
17. **The Ten Commandments**：十诫，圣经中记载，摩西在西奈山上接受了上帝的十条戒律。
18. **Mormonism**：摩门教，其正式名称为耶稣基督后期圣徒教会。
19. **Poseidon** [pɔˈsaidən]：波塞冬，希腊神话中的海神。
20. **Hades** [ˈheidiːz]：哈得斯，希腊神话中的冥界之神。

After You Read

Knowledge Focus

1. Solo Work: Decide whether the following statements are true or false.

1) (   ) Knowing Greek mythology is helpful to understand the allusions that appear in English poetry and literature.
2) (   ) The most important reason why people need to study mythology is that it helps to find purpose in life.
3) (   ) Without a basic understanding of mythology, it is almost impossible to understand modern language and literature.
4) (   ) Shakespeare's plays are full of mythological references.
5) (   ) Mythological characters are often flawless, who are virtue examples of modern people.
6) (   ) The story of Zeus and Hera's marriage makes sense only in ancient Greece.
7) (   ) Myths help us in everyday life because they illustrate those virtues we would do well to develop and the idiosyncrasies we would do to beware of in others.
8) (   ) According to the author, the stories of mythology are very similar to what is written in the New Testament.
9) (   ) We can learn from myths that the world is changing, and humanity changes as well.
10) (   ) Studying mythology is a way to continue our childhood magic and fantasies.

2. Pair Work: Discuss the following questions with your partner.

1) What is Emilie's question regarding mythology? Why does she have such doubts?
2) What is the academic response for why we have to study mythology?
3) Is modern language related to classical mythology? Give examples to explain.
4) According to the author, why do young audiences today have difficulty in understanding Shakespearean language?
5) How is mythology relevant to our everyday life? Give examples to explain.
6) What lesson can we learn from Zeus and Hera?
7) Why does the author say that the characters in mythology all represent human qualities?
8) What is the most important reason for studying mythology?
9) Why does the author say that it is also fun to study mythology?
10) What is your personal reason for learning mythology? Of all the reasons given by the author, which one do you agree with more?

Language Focus

1. Please explain the following words/phrases with the help of dictionary.

New Word/Phrase	Meaning	Origin
1) tantalize		
2) a Herculean effort		
3) a Sisyphean task		
4) a Procrustean bed		
5) to open Pandora's box		
6) Midas touch		
7) Achilles heel		
8) on an Odyssey		
9) hear a siren		
10) Titanic		

2. Fill in the blanks with the words or expressions you have learned from the text.

treatise	distaste	uplift	suffuse	sulkiness
personify	infidelity	stomach	scoff at	allusion

1) In Greek myth, love is _____ by the goddess Aphrodite.
2) Her novels are packed with literary _____.
3) He cannot _____ the idea that Peter might be the next chairman.
4) Our professor asked him to write a _____ on the subject.
5) Art was created to _____ the mind and the spirit.

6) She closed her eyes to her husband's _____.
7) He could not put up with her moods, her _____, and her bad temper.
8) The evening sky was _____ with crimson.
9) Years ago, people _____ at the idea that cars would be built by robots.
10) She looked at the advertisement with _____ before walking quickly on.

3. **Fill in the blanks with the proper form of the word in the brackets.**
    1) Pluto is the _____ (mythology) king of the underworld.
    2) He becomes more _____ (appreciate) of the meaning of life and its permanent spiritual values.
    3) The New York's circulation remained the same but the number of all pages dropped _____ (disaster).
    4) She had a nagging _____ (suspect) that she might have sent the letter to the wrong address.
    5) As to how long this war will last, it is an _____ (answer) question.
    6) Saint is used as a title of respect for a person renowned for _____ (spiritual) and high-mindedness.
    7) Was King Arthur a real or a _____ (legend) character?
    8) They are openly _____ (scorn) of the new plans.
    9) The Chinese are usually described as a _____ (virtue) and hard-working people.
    10) If only he would show a little _____ (human) for once!

4. **Fill in the blanks with the proper prepositions or adverbs that collocate with the neighboring words.**
    1) Researchers are trying to relate low exam results _____ large class sizes.
    2) He was _____ a panic that he would forget his lines on stage.
    3) This book is suffused _____ Shaw's characteristic Irish humor.
    4) The new school was named _____ the famous Civil Rights leader.
    5) After working her way around the world, she ended _____ teaching English as a foreign language.
    6) For the entire last year, he was involved _____ writing his doctoral dissertation.
    7) He searched _____ his pockets _____ some change.
    8) She asked us not to be noisy _____ fear of waking the baby.
    9) In this dictionary "reality" is defined _____ "the state of things as they are, rather than as they are imagined to be".
    10) The company rewarded him _____ his years of service with a grand farewell party and several presents.

5. **Proofreading: The following passage contains ten errors. Each indicated line contains a maximum of one error. In each case, only ONE word is involved. Read the passage and correct the errors.**

    Greek mythology is the body of myths and legends belonged to the ancient   (1) _____
    Greeks, concerned their gods and heroes, the nature of the world, and the origins and   (2) _____
    significance of their own cult and ritual practice. They were a part of religion in   (3) _____
    ancient Greece. Modern scholars refer to, and study the myths for an attempt to throw   (4) _____

light in the religious and political institutions of Ancient Greece, its civilization, and gain understanding of the nature of myth-making itself.

    Greek myth attempt to explain the origins of the world, and details the lives and adventures of a widely variety of gods, goddesses, heroes, heroines, and mythological creatures. It has exerted an intensive influence on the culture, the arts, and the literature of Western civilization and remain part of Western heritage and language. Poets and artists from ancient times to the present have derived inspiration from Greek mythology and have discovered contemporary significance and relevance in these mythological themes.

(5) _____
(6) _____
(7) _____
(8) _____
(9) _____
(10) _____

Comprehensive Work

1. It Came from a Myth.

Mythology is everywhere! Daily you run across instances of words and expressions that derive from ancient myths. Study the following names/words, and discuss how they are related to classical myths.

Term	Use Today	About Which Mythological Character?	Why Does the Term Fit?
Amazon			
Atlas			
Chaos			
Iris			
Nike			
Oracle			
Phoenix			
Psyche			
Sirens			
Styx			
Titans			

2. Translating and Writing Practice

The following statement is remarked by Thomas Bulfinch, an American writer, on the significance of studying mythology.

    Our young reader will find it (mythology) a source of entertainment; those more advanced, a useful companion in their reading; those who travel, and visit museums and galleries of art, an interpreter of paintings and sculptures; those who mingle in cultivated society, a key to allusions which are occasionally made; and last of all, those in advanced life, pleasure in retracting a path of literature which leads them back to the days of their childhood and revives at every step the associations of the morning of life.

Thomas Bulfinch, *The Age of Fable*, 1855

1) Please translate the above statement into Chinese.
2) To what extent do you agree with the author? Please write a composition of about 250 words to express your opinion on this topic.

Text B What Is a Myth?

The Oxford English Dictionary defines myth as a synonym for "untruth", "falsehood", or "lie". But the word has a long history and an equally long range of meanings. The English word comes from the Greek mythos, which Liddell and Scott's Greek-English lexicon defines much more variously than OED defines myth, with most of the meanings of the Greek word corresponding to the English story. Only towards the end of the entry is the issue of truth or falsehood explicitly raised; and it is raised in such a way as to cast doubt on the possibility of making any simple, straightforward distinction between the two.

What Is Truth?

The ancient Greeks were capable of treating "truth" and "falsehood" as mere opposites; but they were also capable of seeing an intimate connection between the two categories.

The Greeks told many stories about characters who inquired after the truth, and about others who were inveterate tricksters. Achilles, the hero of the Iliad, declares that he hates like death the man who keeps one thing hidden in his heart, but speaks another (Iliad 9.310). But Achilles speaks these words to Odysseus—hero of the second great epic poem of archaic Greece, the Odyssey, a poem in which the hero tells many extravagant lies, all of which stand in complex relation to the truth.

Many people from all over the ancient world consulted oracles, and one of the most famous was the oracle of Apollo at Delphi in central Greece. This oracle was regarded by many as the most authoritative in the world; but its prophecies were typically so worded as to be completely misleading. A famous story concerns the Lydian king Croesus, who asked the oracle whether he ought to make war on the Persians. When the oracle answered that, if he did so, he would destroy a great empire, he went to war — and in the process destroyed his own empire (Herodotus 1.53).

Hesiod, one of the earliest Greek poets and the first surviving Greek mythographer, commented rather enigmatically on the complex relationship between truth and falsehood in his own craft (Theogony 25). In doing so, he gave early expression to what remained in later times as well a very uncertain relationship between "truth" the representation of truths in stories.

These few examples illustrate the complexity of the relationship between truth and falsehood in Greek thought generally, and locate this relationship especially in the telling and interpretation of stories.

Who Owns a Myth?

One of the reasons that the truth-value of myth is so urgently questioned is that myths and bodies of myth often have to do with identity: people who tell the same stories tend to feel that they have something in common with one another, and that they differ from people who tell different stories. The early Greek historian Herodotus of Halicarnassus said that it was the even earlier Greek poets, Hesiod and Homer, who gave the Greeks their gods: i.e. by virtue of their mythic storytelling, they contributed to determining the national identity of their people (Herodotus 2.53). Subsequent cultures have to an extent modelled their own storytelling on that of the Greeks — presumably on the assumption that the stories themselves carry with them something of value, and that by adopting the stories one takes on qualities that one associates with and admires in the ancient Greeks. This is most obviously true of the Romans at the height of their power; and it is strange enough that the greatest empire of antiquity should have refashioned its own mythology to make it conform with that of a conquered people, even if the two systems shared certain features to begin with. But even after the

pagan culture of classical antiquity began to give way before the Christian culture of the Middle Ages, the classical myths maintained a certain importance down into early modern times. And even in this century, in which various sciences and technologies are often said to have replaced myth and religion in setting the parameters of our attempts to make sense of the world, mythology is continually invoked, even by the inventors of these sciences and technologies themselves. The most outstanding example is perhaps that of Sigmund Freud and the "Oedipus Complex", a supposedly universal human impulse that both explains and is explained by the power of the Oedipus myth.

The myths we will study in this course are primarily those of the ancient Greeks; but as this brief summary suggests, we will be concerned with these myths both in their ancient applications, and in later adaptations. These myths, like all myths, are often thought of as containing "universal" messages: though they may be regarded as literally false, they may nevertheless felt to be true on a more fundamental level; and at the same time, while the particular form that a myth may take in a given culture may be thought of as somehow defining that culture, myths are just as frequently held to offer access to insights that transcend any one culture. In this course we will consider the cultural significance of the Greek myths in their historical dimension, as they have been continually adapted to various purposes since antiquity.

How Do Myths Work?

The correct question might really be "How Are Myths Used". Because myth is credited with providing access to some of the fundamental truths about the human condition, it is often, perhaps normally regarded, as something to be taken very seriously. This impression is reinforced by the fact that mythology provides the subject matter for some of our most famous and revered works of art — not just literary art, but sculpture, painting, and other forms as well. But historically, all myths — including, but not limited to, the Greek myths — have been a significant part of popular culture as well. The ancient Greek satyr plays parodied what we think of as the more typical, high-minded treatment of the same stories in tragic drama. In Christian Europe the Greek myths afforded an opportunity to indulge a taste in frivolous and risqué stories under the guise of an interest in the Classics. In contemporary culture, it is primarily Norse mythology that informs the popular genre of "adult fantasy literature" (Conan the Barbarian and his ilk), but Greek mythology is represented as well. A single production company currently produces a pair of television series — *Hercules: The Legendary Journeys and Xena, Warrior Princess* — that loosely borrow their basic concepts and some of their material from Greek mythology. Another typical but more ambitious example of how the idea of mythology can be found in a certain episode of *Star Trek: The Next Generation* that first aired in October 1991. In this episode, which is entitled "Darmok", the hero involuntarily finds himself in a dangerous situation and in the company of an alien being whose language he cannot understand. Gradually, he discovers that the alien speaks in phrases that recall events in the mythology of his (the alien's) culture, and that the situation in which the two find themselves parallels a particular myth from the alien culture. The hero is able to turn this insight into an understanding of how much his own culture actually shares with that of his counterpart, and encourages him to learn more about the "root metaphors" of Earth's culture — which prove to be, the stories found in Greek mythology!

A basic knowledge of Greek mythology and an informed critical approach to how they have been used in various times and places thus has an obvious value. What is important to remember, however, is that when we try to focus our attention on these myths we are aiming at a moving target. The myths did not mean any one thing to the Greeks themselves, but took on different meanings depending on who was telling the story to whom, when and where the telling took place, in what form and for what purpose. This is all the more true of later adaptations. Our task will be not so much to unlock the meaning of these myths, as to come to grips with the protean nature.

(Excerpted from http://ccat.sas.upenn.edu/~jfarrell/courses/myth/topics/what_is_myth.html)

Questions for Reflection
1. How did ancient Greeks comprehend the relationship between "truth" and "myth"?
2. What sources do myths come from?
3. How do classical myths work and influence the life and culture of modern people?

Text C Myths and Mythology

Primitive people, as they have looked out on the world about them, on the sea and the trees, on the sky and the clouds, and as they have felt the power of natural forces, the heat of the sun, the violence of the wind, have recognized in these things the expression and action of some being more powerful than themselves. Able to understand only those motives and sensations that are like their own, they have conceived these beings more or less after their own nature. The Hebrews, indeed, at an early time recognized one supreme God, who had created and who directed all the world according to his will, but most other early people have seen living, willing beings in the forms and powers of nature, and have worshiped these beings as gods or feared them as devils. Physical events, such as the rising and setting of the sun, or the springing and ripening of the grain, are to them actions of the beings identified with sun or grain. In accounting for these acts, whether regularly recurring, as the rising of the sun, or occasionally disturbing the ordinary course of nature, as earthquakes, eclipses, or

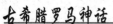

Ancient Greek and Roman Mythology

violent storms, stories more or less complete grow, are repeated, and believed. These stories told of superhuman beings and believed by a whole people are myths, and all these myths together form a mythology.

The Interest of Greek Mythology

The mythology of any people is interesting because it reflects their individual nature and developing life; that of the Greeks is more interesting to us than any other, first, because it expresses the nature of a people gifted with a peculiarly fine and artistic soul; secondly, because our own thought and art are, in great part, a heritage from the civilization of Greece. Much of this heritage comes to us quite directly from the Greek writers and artists whose works have been preserved. The dramas of Sophocles and Euripides hold an audience in America as they held those in Athens, because their art is true and great; the noble youth of the Hermes of Praxiteles, or the gallant action of the horsemen in the frieze of the Parthenon satisfy us in the twentieth century as they did the Greeks in the fifth and fourth centuries B. C. but more of this heritage comes down to us through the Romans, whose genius taught them to conquer and govern without destroying and who learned from the nations that they conquered, Egypt, Asia, and Greece, all that centuries of rich civilization had to give. The civilization of the modern world, America as well as Europe, is rooted deeply in the civilization of Rome, and through Rome in that of Greece. Greek thought and Greek principles run through our law, our government, our standards of taste, our art, and our literature. The very personages of Greek mythology are familiarly known today in the United States, divorced from religious meaning but set up before our

eyes as symbols of truths that are in the very nature of things. The winged Mercury (the god of travelers, whose Greek name was Hermes) waves his magic wand above the main entrance to the Grand Central Station in New York; the noble head of Minerva (the Greek Athena, the goddess of wisdom) is set above the doors of our libraries and colleges, and the adventures of Ulysses (or Odysseus) and of many other Greek heroes are painted on the walls of our Congressional Library. Even in our daily language there is still a hint of mythology; our troops still march to martial music, the music of the war-god Mars, and we eat at breakfast cereals, the gift of the corn-goddess Ceres; the Muses of Pieria are not too far away to inspire the music of our western world.

Classical Mythology Is Truly Greek

These beliefs and stories have been handed down through so many ages and modified in so many ways that confusion as to their real origin has naturally arisen. It is Greek, not Roman. The Roman did not develop an original mythology but took over stories from the Greeks and others and told them of their own gods. It was the Greek Zeus, not the Roman Jupiter, who had so many love adventures; it was the Greek Aphrodite, not the Roman Venus, who received the golden apple from Trojan Paris. Classical mythology is the expression of the nature and thought of the Greeks, not that of the Romans. For the Greeks were by nature artistic; they instinctively expressed their ideals, the truth as they saw it, in poetry, story, and sculpture, and because imagination, insight, and love of beauty were united in them, their stories and their art have an appeal that is universal.

The Development of Greek Mythology

The religion and mythology of the Greeks was not a fixed and unchanging thing; it varied with different localities and changed with changing conditions. For when we speak of Greece we do not speak of a nation in the strict sense — that is, a people under one central government — but of the Greek race: "Wherever the Greeks are, there is Greece." So the mythological stories grew and changed as they passed from Asia Minor to Greece, or from Greece to the islands of the Aegean Sea, to Italy and Sicily. Moreover, the independence of the individual in the Greek states, where men thought for themselves, and no autocratic government or powerful priesthood exerted undue restraint, fostered variety and permitted artists and poets so to modify tradition as to express something of their individual ideas. This added infinitely to the richness of mythology and art. Local conditions, too, and local pride, in a country broken both geographically and politically into small divisions, added variety to religious customs. In mountain districts the god of the sky and storms was most feared and worshiped, in the fertile plains, the gods of earth and harvest, while on the coast men needed the favor of the gods who were powerful over the sea and protected commerce. Local heroes gathered stories about themselves, and local pride led people to place important events, such as the birth of a god or some important manifestation of his power, in their own localities. Many different places claimed to be the birthplace of Apollo, and the fires of Hephaestus burned within many a volcano (called after his Latin name, Vulcan). Furthermore, as they came in contact with other peoples and became familiar with their religious stories and ceremonial, they incorporated much that was of foreign origin into their own religion. The stories connected with Dionysus, or Bacchus, and the extravagant rites celebrated in his honor were imported from the East, and the Aphrodite of Asia Minor was far more Asiatic and sensual in character than the Aphrodite of Greece. Finally, since mythology is not based on authority but grows from the soul of the people, it necessarily follows that as Greek life and thought grew and developed, as social conditions changed, as art was perfected and poetry and philosophy grew less simple, the telling of the myths and their interpretation changed and developed. Mythology was a living, growing thing, impossible to seize and fix in a consistent system. It must be regarded as a mass of legend, handed down through the people and poets of generation after generation, continually reflecting the developing life and soul of a great and vital race. When different versions of a story are found, one is not necessarily more authentic than another.

(Excerpted from http://www.cyberwitch.com/Wychwood/Temple/natureOfMyth.htm)

Questions for Reflection

1. Why is mythology interesting? Please give examples.
2. Why did the author say that the classical mythology is truly Greek?
3. How did Greek mythology develop in the course of history?

Websites to Visit

http://thanasis.com/modern/

This website provides thousands of excellent examples to help to understand the influence of myths

in our daily life. It proves that we are surrounded by mythology in today's society, whether we realize it or not!

http://www.davidkabraham.com/OldWeb/Beliefs/Education/mythology.htm
You may find another article in this website regarding the significance of studying mythology.

Unit 2
The Olympian Gods (I)

> When the gods wish to punish us, they answer our prayers.
> — Oscar Wilde, Irish poet, novelist, dramatist

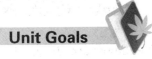
Unit Goals

- To get acquainted with the Olympian Gods
- To know the myths of Zeus, Hera, Poseidon, Demeter, Hestia and Athena
- To be able to tell the relationship among the Olympian Gods
- To learn the useful words and expressions that describe the Olympian Gods
- To improve language skills and critical thinking through the content of this unit

Before You Read

1. Do you know the meaning of the following words/phrases? Check them against a dictionary.
   Junoesque
   Argus-eyed
   mercurial
   hermetic

2. Have you ever heard of any story of the Olympian Gods/Goddesses? Please share what you know with your classmates.

Start to Read

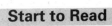
Text A The Olympian Gods (I)

  The most important Greek gods lived on the summit of **Mount Olympus**, the highest mountain in Greece, or in the clouds above it. The Greeks conceived Olympus like an ancient Greek city, with the citadel of the king (**Zeus**) on the highest peak and the homes of the other nobles/gods clustered round. Ovid in his *Metamorphoses* re-envisages it in terms of Rome's palatial Palatine Hill, and a seventeenth-century translator in turn named it the "Heaven's Whitehall".
  The principal gods were categorized by the Greeks as "the Twelve Olympians", though there was some disagreement about the composition of the list. They fall into two generations: the older generation of Zeus/Jupiter and his siblings, and the younger generation who are his children by

various mothers. The underworld god **Hades**/Pluto, who seldom sets foot on Olympus, is not counted among the Olympians; he, his consort, and his kingdom are separately dealt with later.

Zeus/Jupiter/Jove

Zeus was the supreme god and ruler of Olympus. He was known by many titles: Lord of the Sky, the Cloud-gatherer, the Rain-god and Zeus the Thunderer, all of which show which force of nature was considered to be the most important in Ancient World — rain. In most other mythologies the "ruler-god" was usually associated with the sun, but in Greece the climate is hot and dry making rain the scarce, life-giving force.

Zeus was the sixth child born to **Cronus** and **Rhea**. He is more powerful than any other god or even all the other gods combined. But, unlike many gods in other religions he was neither omnipotent nor omniscient. He could be, and in fact was, opposed, deceived and tricked by gods and men alike. His power, although great, was not boundless, Zeus had no control over The Fates and Destiny. Like all Greek divinities, Zeus was subject to pleasure, pain, grief, and anger, but he was most susceptible to the power of **Eros** — love, which often got the objects of his desire in a lot of trouble with his wife, **Hera**.

Zeus had two special attendants, **Nike** (Victoria), the goddess of victory, and his cup-bearer, **Hebe**, who was one of his numerous daughters.

Zeus was the guardian of political order and peace. He is depicted as a powerfully build bearded man of middle age. The aegis is his breastplate — so glorious and at the same time awful to behold that no human could see Zeus in all his magnificence and survive. His weapon is, of course the thunderbolt which he hurled at whoever displeased him. The thunderbolts were fashioned for him the three Cyclopes who also were the deciding power in the battle with the Titans. His bird is the Eagle, his tree — the Oak. **Dodona** was his oracle. His will was revealed by the rustling of oak leaves which was interpreted by his priests.

Hera/Juno

Hera was Zeus' wife. She was brought up by the Titans Ocean and **Tethys**, despite the nickname "cow-faced" (in some translations — "ox-eyed") which seems to have stuck with her through the ages, she was very beautiful, in fact she was one of the three contestants in the Judgment of Paris which led to the Trojan War. But her personality was not as attractive, she was petty and cruel and is most often shown administering some sort of revenge on one of Zeus' lovers. In one, and only one, myth is shown as a noble and gracious protector of heroes and inspirer of heroic deeds, the Quest of the Golden Fleece.

As might have been expected Hera's marriage to Zeus was not to her liking, after Zeus had courted her unsuccessfully for some time, he turned to trickery. Changed himself into an injured bird, Hera, feeling sorry for it, held it to her breast to warm it, Zeus, taking advantage of the situation raped her. She then married him to cover her shame.

Hera was the goddess of marriage and protector of married women. Her sandals, chariot and throne were all of pure gold, but that was not uncommon with the gods. Her animal is the cow, the peacock, and sometimes the cuckoo. Hera had her own messenger — the fleet — footed **Iris** (rainbow). **Argos** and **Sparta** were her favorite cities. She had no distinguishing features and can only be identified in artistic representations by either inscription or context.

Poseidon/Neptune

Poseidon was god of the sea and also god of earthquakes and of horses. A son of the titans, Cronus and Rhea, he was known as the Roman god of the sea, Neptune.

After aiding his brother Zeus, when they overthrew Cronus, and sent the other Titans to **Tartarus**, he received the sea as his domain. When he was not residing in Olympus, he lived with his Oceanid wife and queen, **Amphitrite**, in his underwater palace at Aegae. Poseidon was the father of the sea god **Triton**.

Poseidon was always depicted as a powerfully muscular, bearded man, carrying the mighty trident. One blow from trident could split a rock open. He drove a two-horse chariot over the waves.

Like many sea deities, he had the ability to change shape, but unlike some of them, he does not have oracular power. Poseidon amorously pursued his sister **Demeter**. When she changed her shape into a mare to hide from him, Poseidon changed himself into a stallion and mounted her.

His favorite animals were the horse and bull, and the dolphin, while pine was his sacred tree.

Demeter/Ceres

Demeter was goddess of corn or of the earth and fertility. She was also known as Deo, while the Romans called her Ceres. Demeter was a daughter of Cronus and Rhea. She is depicted as a matronly figure, sometimes rising out of the earth, with ears of grain in her hands.

She became mother of **Persephone** by her brother Zeus. One day, while Persephone was playing with her companions, Hades came and abducted her. Hades had fallen in love with Persephone's great beauty. Hades wanted to marry her and make her his queen in the Underworld.

In her grief, Demeter searched the world for nine days, trying to find out how her daughter had vanished. No one knew who abducted her until she met **Hecate** and **Helius**.

When she discovered that Hades abducted Persephone, she refused to allow plants and crops to grow. The entire world was facing starvation. Finally Zeus ruled that Persephone would spend two-thirds of a year with her mother on earth, while the rest in the Underworld with her husband.

Hestia/Vesta

Hestia was the virgin goddess of the hearth. Hestia was the eldest child of the Titans, Cronus and Rhea. The Romans called her Vesta.

Hestia was one of the children to be swallowed by her father. Later, Cronus was tricked into drinking emetic, and vomited her and her siblings out. She was the last to leave her father's belly. So,

in a way, she was both first-born (from Rhea) and last-born (disgorged from Cronus).

After the war against the Titans, Hestia managed to persuade her brothers, Poseidon and Hades, and her nephew, **Apollo**, of her wish to remain a virgin. According to the Hymn of **Aphrodite**, she sworn an oath upon the head of Zeus of not wedding to anyone and remain forever chaste and untouched by sexual love; such oath forced Poseidon and Apollo to find wives among other goddesses, or else they risk confrontation with Zeus.

Although, there is very little information about Hestia in myths and literature, Hestia was nevertheless an important goddess in both Greek and Roman religions.

In the Homeric Hymns To Hestia, she attends the house of Apollo (temple) in **Delphi**. She was held in the highest honour, both among the gods and among mortals. She was worshipped everywhere, because there are hearths in every home and temple. Each city kept a hearth that had a consecrated fire burning perpetually in a chief public building. Fire from this hearth was taken whenever they sought a new colony.

For the Romans, she was the all-important household goddess, the goddess of the hearth and the hearth fire. Her temple was situated within the Palatine in Rome, where the **Vestal Virgins** maintained the burning of the sacred fire.

Athena/Minerva

Athena was the virgin goddess of arts, craft and war. Also known as Athene, she was also identified as the Roman goddess, Minerva. Athena was daughter of Zeus and his first wife **Metis** (wisdom), who was the daughter of **Oceanus** and Tethys.

After Zeus had overthrown his father Cronus and became supreme ruler of heaven, Gaea warned her grandson that if Metis has a second child, it would be a son. Zeus was told that this son would one day overthrow him, as he had done to his own father (Cronus). Not wanting to suffer the same fate as his father, he swallowed Metis, while she was still pregnant.

Months later, Zeus suffered from a great headache. Either **Prometheus** or **Hephaestus** used an axe to split open Zeus' head. Athena leaped out of Zeus' head, wearing full armour and uttering a war cry. The gods were astonished and profoundly alarmed at this prodigy. It was only when she removed her helm, that Athena revealed herself to be less formidable in aspect. Athena became Zeus' favourite child.

Hence she is the most "masculine" of goddesses, and a sexual virgin and an incarnation of militant intelligence. She is depicted as a tall, sternly beautiful young woman, dressed in full armor with helmet and spear.

Triton, son of Poseidon, raised Athena as she was growing up. Her place of worship was not only in **Athens**, but also in Argos, Sparta and **Troy** as well. The olive tree was sacred to her, and her sacred animals were horses, sea eagles, cocks and serpents, but her favourite bird was the owl.

(Excerpted from http://www.timelessmyths.com/classical/olympians.html
http://www.zeus-publications.com/zeusgod.htm)

Unit 2 The Olympian Gods (I)

Proper Nouns

1. **Mount Olympus**: 奥林匹斯山,坐落在希腊北部,近萨洛尼卡湾,是塞萨利区与马其顿区间的分水岭。奥林匹斯山是古希腊成为欧洲文化发源地不可缺少的元素,是西方文明起源之地。也是希腊神话之源。
2. **Zeus** [zju:s] /**Jupiter** [ˈdʒu:pitə]: 宙斯,希腊神话中的主神,克洛诺斯和瑞亚之子,掌管天界;奥林匹斯的许多神祇和许多希腊英雄都是他和不同女子生下的子女。
3. **Hades** [ˈheidi:z] /**Pluto** [ˈplu:təu] /**Dis** [dis]: 哈得斯,希腊神话中的冥界之神,相对应于罗马神话的普鲁托。他是克洛诺斯和瑞亚的儿子,宙斯的哥哥。
4. **Cronus** [ˈkrəunəs] /**Saturn** [ˈsætən]: 克罗诺斯,希腊神话中提坦巨人之一,天神乌拉诺斯和地神该亚的儿子,他夺取了父亲的王位,后又被他的儿子宙斯把他的王位夺去。
5. **Rhea** [riə]: 瑞亚,丰产女神,盖亚和乌刺诺斯所生十二提坦神之一。
6. **Eros** [ˈiərɔs] /**Cupid** [ˈkju:pid]: 厄罗斯,厄洛斯,罗马神话中的爱神丘比特,希腊神话中的小爱神,是阿瑞斯和阿佛洛狄忒的儿子。
7. **Hera** [ˈhiərə]: 赫拉,希腊神话中奥林匹斯十二主神之一,是克洛诺斯之女,主神宙斯的妻子,主管婚姻和家庭。
8. **Nike** [ˈnaiki:]: 奈基,希腊神话中的胜利女神。
9. **Hebe** [ˈhi:bi]: 赫柏,希腊神话中司青春的女神。
10. **Dodona** [dəuˈdəunə]: 多多那,希腊古城。
11. **Tethys** [ˈti:θis]: 泰西丝,十二泰坦之一。
12. **Iris** [ˈaiəris]: 伊里斯,希腊神话中的彩虹女神和诸神的信使。
13. **Argos** [ˈɑ:gɔs]: 阿哥斯,希腊东南一古城。
14. **Sparta** [ˈspɑ:tə]: 斯巴达,希腊南部的古代城邦。
15. **Poseidon** [pɔˈsaidən] /**Neptune** [ˈneptju:n]: 波塞冬,希腊神话中的海神,克洛诺斯与瑞亚之子,宙斯之兄,地位仅次于宙斯,是希腊神话中的十二主神之一。
16. **Tartarus** [ˈtɑ:tərəs]: 塔耳塔洛斯,地狱底下暗无天日的深渊,为宙斯禁闭提坦之处。
17. **Amphitrite** [ˈæmfitrait]: 安菲特里忒,希腊神话里大海中的女神,海王波塞冬的妻子。
18. **Triton** [ˈtraitən]: 特里同,希腊神话中人身鱼尾的海神,波塞冬和安菲特里忒的儿子。
19. **Demeter** [diˈmi:tə] /**Ceres** [ˈsiəri:z]: 得墨忒耳,希腊神话中主管农业、结婚、丰饶的女神,是瑞亚和克罗诺斯的女儿,珀耳塞福涅的母亲。
20. **Persephone** [pəˈsefəni; pə-] /**Proserpina** [prəuˈsə:pinə] /**Proserpine** [ˈprɔsəpain]: 珀耳塞福涅,希腊神话中得墨忒耳和宙斯的女儿,她被冥神哈得斯劫持娶作冥后。
21. **Hecate** [ˈhekəti]: 赫卡忒,希腊神话中司魔法和巫术的女神。
22. **Helius** [ˈheliəs]: 赫利俄斯,太阳神。
23. **Hestia** [ˈhestiə] /**Vesta** [ˈvestə]: 赫斯提亚,宙斯的姐姐,掌管万民的家事。是希腊神话中的女灶神、家宅的保护者。罗马神话中相应的女神被称作维斯塔。
24. **Apollo** [əˈpɔləu]: 阿波罗,希腊神话中十二主神之一(在罗马神话与希腊神话同名),是主神宙斯与暗夜女神勒托所生之子,阿尔忒弥斯的孪生哥哥。阿波罗被视为司掌文艺之神,主管光明、青春、医药、畜牧、音乐等,是人类的保护神、光明之神、预言之神、迁徙和航海者的保护神、医神以及消灾弥难之神。
25. **Aphrodite** [æfrəuˈdaiti] /**Venus** [ˈvi:nəs]: 阿佛洛狄忒,希腊神话中司爱与美的神,相当于罗马

神话中的维纳斯。

26. **Delphi** [ˈdelfɑi]：特尔斐城，位于希腊中部靠近帕拿苏斯山的一座古城，其年代至少可追溯到公元前17世纪。它曾是著名的阿波罗先知所在地。

27. **Vestal Virgin** 维斯塔处女，古罗马在维斯塔神庙照料圣火的妇女之一。她们作为维斯塔的祭司，并且在她们服侍期内过着独身生活。

28. **Athena** [əˈθiːnə] /**Minerva** [miˈnəːvə]：雅典娜，希腊神话中十二主神之一，也是奥林匹斯三处女神之一，罗马名字弥涅耳瓦。在远古的神话中，雅典娜是最聪明的一位女神，是智慧与力量的完美结合。

29. **Metis** [ˈmiːtis]：墨提斯，希腊神话中宙斯的配偶泰坦女神，雅典娜的母亲。

30. **Oceanus** [əuˈsiənəs]：俄刻阿诺斯，希腊神话中的一个提坦，大洋河的河神。所谓大洋河是希腊人想象中环绕整个大地的巨大河流，代表了世界上的全部海域。

31. **Prometheus** [prəuˈmiːθjuːs]：普罗米修斯，提坦神族的神明之一，名字的意思是先觉者，能预知未来。

32. **Hephaestus** [hiˈfiːstəs] /**Vulcan** [ˈvʌlkən]：赫淮斯托斯，罗马神话中的伏尔坎，古希腊神话中的火神和匠神，阿佛洛狄忒的丈夫。他是奥林匹斯十二主神之一，是宙斯与赫拉的儿子。

33. **Athens** [ˈæθinz]：雅典，希腊的首都，位于希腊的东南部的阿提卡地区，在巴尔干半岛南端，三面环山，一面傍海，西南距爱琴海法利龙湾8公里。

34. **Troy** [trɔi]：特洛伊，小亚细亚西北部的古城。

After You Read

Knowledge Focus

1. Solo Work: Familiarize yourself with gods and goddesses by filling out the following form.

GREEK NAME	ROMAN NAME	ROLE IN MYTHOLOGY
Athena	_____	Virgin goddess of _____, craft and _____
Demeter	Ceres	Goddess of corn or of the earth and _____
_____	Juno	Goddess of _____ and protector of married women
_____	Vesta	Virgin goddess of the hearth and _____
Poseidon	_____	God of the sea and also god of _____ and of horses
Zeus	_____,	Supreme god and ruler of Olympus. Lord of the _____, the Cloud-gatherer, the _____ and Zeus the _____

Unit 2 The Olympian Gods (1)

2. **Solo Work: Match each figure with its description according to what you have learned from the text above.**

1) Zeus   A. is attended by the proud peacock, cow and sometimes cuckoo, and her messenger is Iris, the rainbow goddess

2) Hera   B. is a matronly figure, sometimes rising out of the earth, with ears of grain in her hands

3) Poseidon   C. is both first-born (from Rhea) and last-born (disgorged from Cronus)

4) Demeter   D. is the most "masculine" of goddesses, and a sexual virgin and an incarnation of militant intelligence

5) Hestia   E. a powerfully built bearded man of middle age, often grasping a thunderbolt

6) Athena   F. a powerfully muscular, bearded man, carrying the mighty trident

G. is petty and cruel, with the nickname "cow-faced" or "ox-eyed"

H. is a tall, sternly beautiful young woman, dressed in full armor with helmet and spear

I. is attended by his messenger the eagle and his sacred tree the oak

J. is attended by his wife Amphitrite, and his sacred tree pine

3. **Pair Work: Discuss the following questions with your partner.**
   1) What is Greeks' conception of Olympus?
   2) What is the relationship between the two generations of "the Twelve Olympians"?
   3) What are the titles of Zeus? List some and discuss the implication of the titles.
   4) How did Zeus trick Juno into marrying him?
   5) Zeus and Poseidon were both depicted as bearded men of middle age, how do you make a distinction between them according to their appearance?
   6) How did Demeter revenge after she discovered that Hades abducted Persephone?
   7) Why Hestia is called both the first-born child and the last-born child?
   8) Why Hestia is held in the highest honour, both among the gods and among mortals, as well as worshipped everywhere?
   9) How did Zeus give birth to Athena?
   10) Why Athena is considered the most "masculine" of goddesses?

Language Focus

1. Fill in the blanks with the words or expressions you have learned from the text.

| gracious | composition | susceptible to | distinguishing | principal |
| citadel | overthrow | categorize | omnipotent | trickery |

1) It's easy to become lost in the wilderness on the way to the _____.
2) Indeed, stress is emerging as one of the _____ contributors to poor health in modern countries.
3) One way to _____ restaurants is by the kind of service they offer.
4) Trade policies more often target the _____ of trade than its balance.
5) Infants are particularly _____ vitamin D intoxication.

6) Since God is conceived to be _____, he is a perfect being.
   7) Her soft voice and _____ smile put everyone in the room at ease.
   8) We must not fear to face the _____ of some people and expose it for what it is.
   9) Few see much benefit in trying to _____ the party: that, they fear, could cause chaos and an even bigger threat to wealth.
   10) One of my most _____ characteristics is the diversity of experiences I possess.

2. **Fill in the blanks with the proper form of the word in the brackets.**
   1) I hope this _____ (agree) will not cloud our friendship.
   2) It increases the chances of _____ (survive) and reduces the danger of brain damage.
   3) This week, when the National Governors _____ (associate) gathered inside the beltway for its winter meeting, innovation was the theme.
   4) Their faith is suffused with _____ (expect) and hope.
   5) Some _____ (recognition) others by the way they walk or by their voice.
   6) Political analysts said North-South relations still looked _____ (rock).
   7) We often read in novels how a seemingly _____ (respect) person or family has some terrible secret.
   8) Courage and _____ (religion) faith alone are not enough to win battles.
   9) The couple's marriage broke down shortly afterwards, culminating in a formal _____ (separate) in 2010.
   10) Movies and TV do not give a very accurate _____ (depict) of American culture, although Hollywood will tell you it is.

3. **Fill in the blanks with the proper prepositions or adverbs that collocate with the neighboring words.**
   1) Misleading sales may make careless buyers fall _____ financial trouble.
   2) When the scene on the ground gradually became clear, I knew I would to set foot _____ this beautiful southeast city at once.
   3) Fund managers are human too and subject _____ behavioral biases.
   4) Western investors are seeking acquisitions in Asia to take advantage _____ fast growth rates.
   5) The report claims that when women fall _____ love, they tend to eat more.
   6) We are going to bring _____ this question at the next meeting
   7) In reaction to a war that is ill conceived, we appear suspicious _____ all military action.
   8) His wedding morning would bring death to her, and she would change _____ the foam of the sea
   9) The thought was that people with low self-esteem turn _____ drinking or drugs for solace.
   10) It is a powerful reminder of how good it can feel to connect _____ others in a genuine, personal and heartfelt way.

4. Proofreading: The following passage contains ten errors. Each indicated line contains a maximum of one error. In each case, only one word is involved. Read the passage and correct the errors.

Zeus — King of the gods and ruler of the universe from his throne on Mount Olympus. Original a god of the sky and storm, thunder and lightning, he also become (1)_____ patron of kingship and government, law and custom, the patriarchal lord of the status (2)_____ quo. He is depicted like a powerfully built bearded man of middle aged, often (3)_____ grasped a thunderbolt or lightning flash, attending by his messenger the eagle and his (4)_____ sacred tree the oak. (5)_____

Zeus/Jupiter has a less exalted aspect, however. He is also an insatiable lecher, (6)_____ pursuing nymphs and mortal women and boys, and seducing or raping them in various form, thus fathering many heroes and heroines and founding many of the (7)_____ great royal and noble families of mythology. His sexual exploits have provided endlessly material for artists and poets, who tended to treat them in a lighthearted (8)_____ spirit. Ovid, observing the spectacle of the lord of the universe transformed into a bull (9)_____ and mooing his love for Europa, comments wryly that 'majesty and love go ill (10)_____ together'.

Comprehensive Work
1. Writing Practice

Now your favorite mythological character has just retired. Zeus, the father of the gods, is now accepting applications for a replacement. Please write letters of application and a brief resume or biographical sketch. List at least three reasons why you are a more competitive applicant.

2. Mythological Constellation

Jupiter is the largest of the planets, with a volume 1,400 times greater than that of the earth. The massive planet has altogether sixteen satellites, the four largest of which are Europa, Io, Callisto, and Ganymede. Search the Internet for such astronomical naming (such as the nine planets) related to mythological gods and/or goddesses and share with your partner.

◇ *What is the name?*
◇ *Where is it?*
◇ *How did it get its name?*
◇ *How long are its years and days?*
◇ *How big is it?*
◇ *Can it be seen from Earth?*
◇ *What is it made of?*
◇ *What is it like on the surface?*
◇ *Does it have any special features?*

Read More

Text B Zeus' Consorts and Some of Their Tribulations

Hera

Hera, daughter of Cronus and Rhea, was born on the island of Samos or Argos and was brought up in Arcadia by Temenus, son of Pelasgus. The Seasons were her nurses. After banishing their father Cronus, Hera's twin-brother Zeus sought her out at Cnossus in Crete or on Mount Thornax (now called Cuckoo Mountain) in Argolis, where he courted her, at first unsuccessfully. She took pity on him only when he adopted the disguise of a bedraggled cuckoo, and tenderly warmed him in her bosom. There he at once resumed his true shape and ravished her, so that she was shamed into marrying him.

All the gods brought gifts to the wedding; notably Mother Earth gave Hera a tree with golden apples, which was later guarded by the Hesperides in Hera's orchard on Mount Atlas. She and Zeus spent their wedding night on Samos, and it lasted three hundred years. Hera bathed regularly in the spring of Canathus, near Argos, and thus renewed her virginity.

To Hera and Zeus were born the deities Ares, Hephaestus, and Hebe, though some say that Ares and his twin-sister Eris were conceived when Hera touched a certain flower, and Hebe when she touched a lettuce, and that Hephaestus also was her parthenogenous child — a wonder which he would not believe until he imprisoned her in a mechanical chair with arms that folded about the sitter, thus forcing her to swear by the River Styx that she did not lie.

Ever since his marriage to Hera, Zeus began his long series of amorous adventures. He fathered the Seasons and the Three Fates on Themis; the Charities on Eurynome; the Three Muses on Mnemosyne;

some day, Persephone, the Queen of the Underworld on the nymph Styx. So many infidelities of her husband made Hera a highly jealous queen. But daunted by Zeus' fatal thunderbolt, Hera could only resort to ruthless intrigue and revenge on the objects of her husband's passion. The following though not an exhaustive list of all the stories of that nature makes interesting evidence.

Io

Hera (Juno) one day perceived it suddenly grow dark, and immediately suspected that her husband had raised a cloud to hide some of his doings that would not bear the light. She brushed away the cloud, and saw her husband on the banks of a glassy river, with a beautiful heifer standing near him. Juno suspected the heifer's form concealed some fair nymph of mortal mould—as was, indeed the case; for it was Io, the daughter of the river god Inachus, whom Jupiter had been flirting with, and, when he became aware of the approach of his wife, had changed into that form.

Juno joined her husband, and noticing the heifer praised its beauty, and asked whose it was, and of what herd. Jupiter, to stop questions, replied that it was a fresh creation from the earth. Juno asked to have it as a gift. What could Jupiter do? He was loath to give his mistress to his wife; yet how could he refuse so trifling a present as a simple heifer? Without exciting suspicion; he consented. The goddess was not yet relieved of her suspicions; so she delivered the heifer to Argus, to be strictly watched.

Now Argus had a hundred eyes in his head, and never went to sleep with more than two at a time, so that he kept watch of Io constantly. He suffered her to feed through the day, and at night tied her up with a vile rope round her neck. She would have stretched out her arms to implore freedom of Argus, but she had no arms to stretch out, and her voice was a bellow that frightened even herself. She saw her father and her sisters, went near them, and suffered them to pat her back, and heard them admire her beauty. Her father reached her a tuft of grass, and she licked the outstretched hand. She longed to make herself known to him, and would have uttered her wish; but, alas! Words were wanting. At length she bethought herself of writing, and inscribed her name—it was a short one—with her hoof on the sand. Inachus recognized it, and discovering that his daughter, whom he had long sought in vain, was hidden under this disguise, mourned over her, and, embracing her white

neck, exclaimed, "Alas! my daughter, it would have been a less grief to have lost you altogether!" While he thus lamented, Argus, observing came and drove her away, and took his seat on a high bank, from whence he could see all around in every direction.

Jupiter was troubled at beholding the sufferings of his mistress, and calling Hermes (Mercury) told him to go and dispatch Argus. Mercury made haste, put his winged slippers on his feet, and cap on his head, took his sleep-producing wand, and leaped down from the heavenly towers to the earth. There he laid aside his wings, and kept only his wand, with which he presented himself as a shepherd driving his flock. As he strolled on he blew upon his pipes. These were what are called the Syrinx or Pandean pipes. Argus listened with delight, for he had never seen the instrument before. "Young man," said he, "come and take a seat by me on this stone. There is no better place for your flocks to graze in than hereabouts, and here is a pleasant shade such as shepherds

love." Mercury sat down, talked, and told stories till it grew late, and played upon his pipes his most soothing strains, hoping to lull the watchful eyes to sleep, but all in vain; for Argus still contrived to keep some of his eyes open though he shut the rest.

Among other stories, Mercury told him how the instrument on which he played was invented. "There was a certain nymph, whose name was Syrinx, who was much beloved by the satyrs and spirits of the wood; but she would have none of them, but was a faithful worshipper of Artemis (Diana), and followed the chase. You would have thought it was Diana herself, had you seen her in her hunting dress, only that her bow was of horn and Diana's of silver. One day, as she was returning from the chase, Pan met her, told her just this, and added more of the same sort. She ran away, without stopping to hear his compliments, and he pursued till she came to the bank of the river, where he overtook her, and she had only time to call for help on her friends the water nymphs. They heard and consented. Pan threw his arms around what he supposed to be the form of the nymph, and found he embraced only a tuft of reeds! As he breathed a sigh, the air sounded through the reeds, and produced a plaintive melody. The god, charmed with the novelty and with the sweetness of the music, said, 'Thus, then, at least, you shall be mine.' And he took some of the reeds, and placing them together, of unequal lengths, side by side, made an instrument which he called Syrinx, in honor of the nymph." Before Mercury had finished his story he saw Argus's eyes all asleep. As his head nodded forward on his breast, Mercury with one stroke cut his neck through, and tumbled his head down the rocks. O hapless Argus! The light of your hundred eyes is quenched at once! Juno took them and put them as ornaments on the tail of her peacock, where they remain to this day.

But the vengeance of Juno was not yet satiated. She sent a gadfly to torment Io, who fled over the whole world from its pursuit. She swam through the Ionian sea, which derived its name from her, then roamed over the plains of Illyria, ascended Mount Haemus, and crossed the Thracian strait, thence named the Bosphorus (cowford), rambled on through Scythia, and the country of the Cimmerians, and arrived at last on the banks of the Nile. At length Jupiter interceded for her, and upon his promising not to pay her any more attentions Juno consented to restore her to her form. It was curious to see her gradually recover her former self. The coarse hairs fell from her body, her horns shrank up, her eyes grew narrower, her mouth shorter; hands and fingers came instead of hoofs to her forefeet; in fine there was nothing left of the heifer, except her beauty. At first she was afraid to speak, for fear she should low, but gradually she recovered her confidence and was restored to her father and sisters.

(Excerpted from http://www.bartleby.com/181/041.html)

Questions for Reflection

1. What was Zeus' usual way of hiding his scandals?
2. How did the musical instrument "panpipe" come into being?
3. Zeus, though all mighty and all-seeing, was such a hen-pecked husband that he had to transform himself into different forms to hide his scandals from the jealous Hera. How can you account for this inconsistency?

Text C Athena

Athena (Minerva), the goddess of wisdom, was the daughter of Jupiter (Zeus). She was said to have leaped forth from his brain, mature, and in complete armor. She presided over the useful and ornamental arts, both those of men—such as agriculture and navigation—and those of women—spinning, weaving, and needlework. She was also a warlike divinity; but it was defensive war only that she patronized, and she had no sympathy with Ares' (Mars) savage love of violence and bloodshed. Athens was her chosen seat, her own city, awarded to her as the prize of a contest with Poseidon (Neptune), who also aspired to it. The tale ran that in the reign of Cecrops, the first king of Athens, the two deities contended for the possession of the city. The gods decreed that it should be awarded to that one who produced the gift most useful to mortals. Neptune gave the horse; Minerva produced the olive. The gods gave judgment that the olive was the more useful of the two, and awarded the city to the goddess; and it was named after her, Athens.

Athena, though as modest as Artemis, is far more generous. When Teiresias, one day, accidentally surprised her in a bath, she laid her hands over his eyes and blinded him, but gave him inward sight by way of compensation. She is not recorded to have shown petulant jealousy on more than a single occasion. The following is such a story.

There was a famous contest between Athena and a mortal girl who dared to come in competition with her. That mortal was Arachne, a maiden who had attained such skill in the arts of weaving and embroidery that the nymphs themselves would leave their groves and fountains to come and gaze upon her work. It was not only beautiful when it was done, but beautiful also in the doing. To watch her, as she took the wool in its rude state and formed it into rolls, or separated it with her fingers and carded it till it looked as light and soft as a cloud, or twirled the spindle with skilful touch, or wove the web, or, after it was woven, adorned it with her needle, one would have said that Minerva herself had taught her. But this she denied, and could not bear to be thought a pupil even of a goddess. "Let Minerva try her skill with mine," said she; "if beaten I will pay the penalty." Minerva heard this and was displeased. She assumed the form of an old woman and went and gave Arachne some friendly advice. "I have had much experience," said she, "and I hope you will not despise my counsel. Challenge your fellow-mortals as you will, but do not compete with a goddess. On the contrary, I advise you to ask her forgiveness for what you have said, and as she is merciful perhaps she will pardon you." Arachne stopped her spinning and looked at the old dame with anger in her countenance. "Keep your counsel," said she, "for your daughters or handmaids; for my part I know what I say, and I stand to it. I am not afraid of the goddess; let her try her skill, if she dare venture." "She comes," said Minerva; and dropping her disguise stood confessed. The nymphs bent low in homage, and all the bystanders paid reverence. Arachne alone was unterrified. She blushed, indeed;

a sudden color dyed her cheek, and then she grew pale. But she stood to her resolve, and with a foolish conceit of her own skill rushed on her fate. Minerva forbore no longer nor interposed any further advice. They proceed to the contest. Each takes her station and attaches the web to the beam. Then the slender shuttle is passed in and out among the threads. The reed with its fine teeth strikes up the woof into its place and compacts the web. Both work with speed; their skilful hands move rapidly, and the excitement of the contest makes the labor light. Wool of Tyrian dye is contrasted with that of other colors, shaded off into one another so adroitly that the joining deceives the eye. Like the bow, whose long arch tinges the heavens, formed by sunbeams reflected from the shower, in which, where the colors meet they seem as one, but at a little distance from the point of contact are wholly different.

Minerva wrought on her web the scene of her contest with Neptune. Twelve of the heavenly powers are represented, Jupiter, with august gravity, sitting in the midst. Neptune, the ruler of the sea, holds his trident, and appears to have just smitten the earth, from which a horse has leaped forth. Minerva depicted herself with helmed head, her Aegis covering her breast. Such was the central circle; and in the four corners were represented incidents illustrating the displeasure of the gods at such presumptuous mortals as had dared to contend with them. These were meant as warnings to her rival to give up the contest before it was too late.

Arachne filled her web with subjects designedly chosen to exhibit the failings and errors of the gods. One scene represented Leda caressing the swan, under which form Jupiter had disguised himself; and another, Danaë in the brazen tower in which her father had imprisoned her, but where the god effected his entrance in the form of a golden shower. Still another depicted Europa deceived by Jupiter under the disguise of a bull. Encouraged by the tameness of the animal Europa ventured to mount his back, whereupon Jupiter advanced into the sea and swam with her to Crete. You would have thought it was a real bull, so naturally was it wrought, and so natural the water in which it swam. She seemed to look with longing eyes back upon the shore she was leaving, and to call to her companions for help. She appeared to shudder with terror at the sight of the heaving waves, and to draw back her feet from the water.

Arachne filled her canvas with similar subjects, wonderfully well done, but strongly marking her presumption and impiety. Minerva could not forbear to admire, yet felt indignant at the insult. She struck the web with her shuttle and rent it in pieces; she then touched the forehead of Arachne and made her feel her guilt and shame. She could not endure it and went and hanged herself. Minerva pitied her as she saw her suspended by a rope. "Live," she said, "guilty woman! And that you may preserve the memory of this lesson, continue to hang, both you and your descendants, to all future times." She sprinkled her with the juices of aconite, and immediately her hair came off, and her nose and ears likewise. Her form shrank up, and her head grew smaller yet; her fingers cleaved to her side and served for legs. All the rest of her is body, out of which she spins her thread, often hanging suspended by it, in the same attitude as when Minerva touched her and transformed her into a spider.

(Excerpted from http://www.bartleby.com/181/141.html)

Questions for Reflection
1. Both as warlike divinities, how did Athena differ from Mars?
2. How was Zeus able to give birth to Athena, and why did she spring out of her father's head?
3. What attitude did Arachne show towards the gods through her embroidery work?

Websites to Visit

http://www.webgreece.gr/greekmythology/olympiangods/index.html

http://www.theoi.com/greek-mythology/olympian-gods.html

If you are interested in Olympian Gods, visit these websites for more detailed information. There are also beautiful illustrations to each god/goddess.

http://en.wikipedia.org/wiki/Family_tree_of_the_Greek_gods

This website provides detailed information of family tree of the Greek gods.

Unit 3
The Olympian Gods (II)

> Myths are clues to the spiritual potentialities of the human life.
> —Joseph Campbell, American author, editor and philosopher

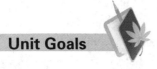
Unit Goals

- To get acquainted with the Olympian Gods
- To know the myths of Apollo, Artemis, Aphrodite, Ares, Hephaestus and Hermes
- To be able to tell the relationship among the Olympian Gods
- To learn the useful words and expressions that describe the Olympian Gods
- To improve language skills and critical thinking through the content of this unit

Before You Read

1. Mythology in business world

Mythological terms are most often found as names for companies and their products. Can you establish the connection between myths with the following companies and their products?

2. Think about how businesses are taking advantage of people's mythological knowledge to promote their products. Can you find more companies that use the mythological terms as names for products?

Start to Read

Text A The Olympian Gods (II)

Apollo

Apollo was a god of youth, music, prophecy, archery and healing. Twin brother of the goddess **Artemis** (Diana), Apollo was the son of Zeus and the Titaness, **Leto**, daughter of the titans, Coeüs (**Coeus**) and **Phoebe**.

He was popularly known as Phoebus Apollo, and therefore known as the god of light and the sun. Apollo was depicted with a perfect male body: muscular but youthful. He had always appeared beardless on statues.

Apollo was the god of archery, and he carried a silver bow like his sister. Apollo often enjoyed hunting with his sister, and sometimes with his mother. He also possessed a golden sword.

Apollo was the god of music. **Hermes** gave him the lyre that he invented, making the instrument with a tortoise shell and sheep guts for strings. No one, god or mortal, could play the lyre better than Apollo could.

Apollo was the god of prophecy and oracle. The oracle in **Delphi** was the main seat of his power, though it originally belonged to **Gaea**, then **Themis** and Phoebe, before the oracle was given to him. Delphi was only a small settlement during the Mycenaean period. It was not until the 8th century B.C., that they rebuilt the area, and it became the centre of his worship.

Apollo was also god of medicine and healing. Apollo's sacred places of worship were Delphi, **Delos** and **Tenedos**. His sacred tree was the laurel, while the animals were wolf, raven, swan, hawk, snake, mouse and grasshopper.

Artemis/Diana

Artemis was virgin goddess of childbirth and of wild animals. She was daughter of Zeus and the Titaness, Leto, offspring of the Titans, Coeüs (Coeus) and Phoebe. Artemis was the twin sister of Apollo.

She is depicted as a beautiful, athletic young woman, dressed as a huntress with bow and arrows, often wearing a small crescent moon in her hair or on her breast, and often accompanied by a deer or other wild creatures.

Artemis was the goddess of hunting and the chase. Artemis often hunts with her brother. She carried a silver bow made by **the Cyclopes**. But her arrow shafts were made out of gold. Maidens and woodland nymphs often accompanied her during her hunt.

These mortal huntresses tried to remain virgin like the goddess they worshipped. However, many of the gods, particularly her father (Zeus), often ravished her beautiful companions.

Strangely enough, Artemis was also the protectress of young

animals. She was like a game warden; she would kill any hunter who kills pregnant animals or their young.

Artemis was also the guardian of all wild animals of the forest, but the hind, bear, dog and boar were favourites. Artemis was often called the Lady of the Beasts. Her sacred tree was the laurel, like her brother.

Artemis was also the goddess of childbirth. When Leto was pregnant with the twins, **Eileithyia** refused to help Leto with labour, suffered greatly from the pain, since Eileithyia was the daughter of Hera. Leto suffered from the pang for nine days on the island of Delos, before Artemis helped her mother with the delivery of her twin Apollo.

Looking at Artemis as a whole, we find many of her functions and roles, often conflicting and contradictory. We have the goddess seen as a virgin, yet she was the goddess of childbirth and fertility. She was the huntress, yet she was protectress of wild animals.

Aphrodite/Venus

Aphrodite was the goddess of love and beauty. She was identified with the Roman goddess, Venus. There are two versions of her birth.

According to **Homer**, Aphrodite was known as the daughter of Zeus and **Dione**. Dione was either a Titaness, daughter of **Uranus** and Gaea, or an Oceanid, daughter of **Oceanus** and **Tethys**. But according to **Hesiod**, she was earlier deity than the Olympians.

When the Titan Cronus castrated his father (Uranus) and flung his genitals into the sea near the island of Cythera, the blood and semen caused foam to gather and float across the sea to the island of **Cyprus**. For this reason, Aphrodite was often called Cythereia, and Cyprian or Cypris, after her two holy islands. There, Aphrodite rose out of the sea from the foam (hence her name came from the word aphros, which means "foam"). She had experienced no infancy or childhood. She was born a grown, young woman.

Aphrodite was married to **Hephaestus** but had numerous affairs with gods and mortals. The most notorious of these affairs was her long dalliance with Ares.

She is depicted as a beautiful woman, usually naked, often accompanied by her son **Eros/Cupid**, or by a whole flock of small winged Loves or Cupids. Her favorite haunts were Cyprus and Cythera. Aphrodite's favourite animals were the dove, sparrow, swallow, swan and turtle. Her attendants were Eros, **the Graces**, and Peitho, goddess of persuasion.

Ares/Mars

Ares was god of war. He is depicted as a warrior, with armor, sword, spear, and shield. He was a son of Zeus and Hera, and was known as the Roman god, Mars. Ares was the brother of Hebe, Eileithyia and possibly of Hephaestus, though most writers say that Hephaestus was son of Hera, alone.

Though Aphrodite was married to Hephaestus, she had a long term affair with Ares. Through Aphrodite, Ares was the father of Anteros (Passion), Eros, Deimus (Fear), Phobus (Panic), and a daughter named Harmonia, wife of Cadmus of Thebes.

As a god of war, many Greek kingdoms did not worship him, because Ares personified

uncontrolled and murderous killing in war, and he engaged in bloody strife for the sheer love of combat itself. Many Greeks preferred Athena, the goddess of war, whose judgment is not clouded by the passion of fighting. She represented disciplined and cool purpose.

Even though he was god of war, Athena always seemed to be a better fighter, whenever there was a confrontation between the two. During the Trojan War, when Ares charged at Athena, brandishing his sword, the goddess coolly hurled a stone at the god of war. She left him crumbled to the ground.

Despite being a god of war, Ares was not a great fighter. He even lost to mortals in several encounters. Twice, Heracles had defeated him; he also lost to **Diomedes**, hero in the Trojan War. Both heroes seriously wounded the war god. When Ares was wounded by Diomedes, his scream was louder than thousands of men shouting.

Ares' favourite animals were the dog and the vulture. Ares had a chariot pulled by his horses: Aithon ("Red Fire"), Conabos ("Tumult"), Phlogios ("Flame") and Phobos ("Terror").

Hephaestus / Vulcan

Hephsestus was a god of fire and metalworking. He was known to the Romans as the fire-god, Vulcan.

Some say that Hephaestus was son of Zeus and Hera, but a more popular myth says that he was the son of Hera alone. When Zeus gave birth to Athena without a mother, Hera was jealous and decided to give birth to a child without a father.

There are several accounts as to how he became lame:

One said that Hephaestus was born lame.

Another account was that Hephaestus tried to protect his mother, when she angered Zeus, by wrecking Heracles' ship in Cos. It was Zeus who threw Hephaestus out of heaven, for aiding Hera. Hephaestus became crippled upon impact with the earth. The sea goddess Thetis saved Hephaestus, which was why he was later willing to make new armour for her son during the Trojan War.

Another popular version, said that Hera, upon giving birth to Hephaestus without a mate, found him ugly that she threw the infant out of Olympus. Hephaestus in anger created a golden throne and sent it to Olympus as a gift to his mother. Once Hera sat on the throne, she was bound to the chair by a golden fetter. The other gods tried to persuade Hephaestus to release his mother. Hephaestus released her either because **Dionysus** got him drunk or in return for being promised Aphrodite in marriage.

As the metal-smith of the gods, he made many pieces of armour and weapons for the gods as well as building their beautiful palaces in Olympus. He also made armour for mortals, such as Heracles, **Peleus**, husband of Thetis, and **Achilles**, the son of Peleus and Thetis. He made the armour for Achilles, at Thetis' request, because she had rescued him when he fell from heaven. Some say that the Cyclops worked under Hephaestus' supervision.

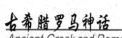

Hermes/Mercury

Hermes was herald and messenger of the gods. He was son of Zeus and **Maia** (a Pleiad), a daughter of Atlas and Pleïone (Pleione). He was identified as the Roman god, Mercury. Hermes was born in a cave within the forest near the mountain of **Cyllene**. He is depicted as a handsome, beardless youth, wearing a winged cap and sandals and carrying the caduceus.

Hermes was a god known for his invention and for theft. Before the end of his first day after his birth, he had invented the lyre made of a tortoise's shell, and he had also stolen Apollo's cattle from the mountains of Pieria.

Hermes had many skills and attributes, but his primary duty was to act as a messenger or herald for the gods. Hermes was frequently on an errand for his father (Zeus). His feminine opposite was the goddess Iris, who also often served as messenger for Zeus. Hermes often communicated to the mortals for the gods, so he was a guide. Hermes was the patron god of heralds and messengers.

Like the other younger Olympian gods, Hermes had many children from many mistresses. Like Apollo, Hermes never married. However he had many famous liaisons and children.

The only notable affair with a goddess was with Aphrodite. She was, however, not interested in Hermes. Zeus, taking pity on his son, he had his eagle steals Aphrodite's favourite sandal. She gave in to Hermes' lust in return for her sandal. Hermes became the father of **Hermaphroditus**. Obviously, Hermaphroditus was named after his parents, Hermes and Aphrodite.

(Excerpted from http://www.timelessmyths.com/classical/olympians.html)

Proper Nouns

1. **Apollo** [ə'pɔləu]: 阿波罗, 希腊神话中十二主神之一(在罗马神话与希腊神话同名), 是主神宙斯与暗夜女神勒托所生之子, 阿尔忒弥斯的孪生哥哥。阿波罗被视为司掌文艺之神, 主管光明、青春、医药、畜牧、音乐等, 是人类的保护神、光明之神、预言之神、迁徙和航海者的保护神、医神以及消灾弥难之神。

2. **Artemis** ['ɑ:timis] /Diana [daɪ'ænə]: 阿耳忒弥斯, 罗马神话中的狄安娜, 古希腊神话中的狩猎女神、月神, 奥林匹斯主神之一, 亦被视为野兽的保护神。阿耳忒弥斯为主神宙斯与暗夜女神勒托之女, 阿波罗的孪生姐姐。

3. **Leto** ['li:təu]: 勒托, 希腊神话中的黑暗女神。

4. **Coeus** ['kəuis]: 科俄斯或考伊斯, 乌拉诺斯与该亚的儿子, 十二提坦之一, 智力之神。

5. **Phoebe** ['fi:bi:]: 菲碧, 也称福伯或福碧, 十二提坦之一, 月之女神勒托与阿斯特瑞亚之母。

6. **Hermes** ['hə:mi:z] /Mercury ['mə:kjuri]: 赫耳墨斯, 希腊神话中奥林匹斯十二主神之一, 罗马名字墨丘利。宙斯与迈亚的儿子。

7. **Delphi** ['delfaɪ]: 特尔斐城, 位于希腊中部靠近帕拿苏斯山的一座古城, 其年代至少可追溯到公元前17世纪。它曾是著名的阿波罗先知所在地。

8. **Gaea** ['dʒi:ə]: 地神该亚, 希腊神话中的人物, 又称大地之母, 是希腊神话中最早出现的神, 在开天辟地时,由混沌所生。
9. **Themis** [ˈθiːmis]:忒弥斯,泰坦族女巨人,司法律和正义的女神。
10. **Delos** [ˈdiːlɔs]:提洛岛,爱琴海西南部的希腊岛屿。
11. **Tenedos** [ˈtenədɔs]:忒涅多斯岛,爱琴海岛屿。
12. **the Cyclopes** [saiˈklɔupiːz]:库克罗普斯,希腊神话中的独目巨人。
13. **Eileithyia** [aiəliˈθiə]:爱勒提亚,希腊神话中的生育女神。
14. **Aphrodite** [æfrəuˈdaiti] /**Venus** [ˈviːnəs]:阿佛洛狄忒,希腊神话中司爱与美的神,相当于罗马神话中的维纳斯。
15. **Homer** 荷马,希腊史诗作者,创作了西方文学最伟大的两部作品《伊利亚特》和《奥德赛》。
16. **Dione** [daiˈəuni]:狄俄涅,希腊神话中的女神,阿佛洛狄忒的母亲。
17. **Uranus** [ˈjuərənəs]:乌剌诺斯,从大地母亲(盖亚)的指端诞生。象征希望与未来,并代表了天空。乌刺诺斯是盖亚的儿子,也是盖亚的丈夫和十二提坦神、独眼巨人与百臂巨人的父亲。
18. **Oceanus** [əuˈsiənəs]:俄刻阿诺斯,希腊神话中的一个提坦,大洋河的河神。所谓大洋河是希腊人想象中环绕整个大地的巨大河流,代表了世界上的全部海域。
19. **Tethys** [ˈtiːθis]:泰西丝,十二泰坦之一。
20. **Hesiod** [ˈhiːsiɔd; ˈhes-]:赫西奥德,公元前8世纪末至公元前7世纪初的古希腊诗人。
21. **Cyprus** [ˈsaiprəs]:塞浦路斯,地中海东部一岛。
22. **Hephaestus** [hiˈfiːstəs] /**Vulcan** [ˈvʌlkən]:赫淮斯托斯,罗马神话中的伏尔坎,古希腊神话中的火神和匠神,阿佛洛狄忒的丈夫。他是奥林匹斯十二主神之一,是宙斯与赫拉的儿子。
23. **Eros** [ˈiərɔs] /**Cupid** [ˈkjuːpid]:厄罗斯,厄洛斯,罗马神话中的爱神丘比特,希腊神话中的小爱神,是阿瑞斯和阿佛洛狄忒的儿子。
24. **the Graces**:美惠三女神,宙斯与大洋女神欧律诺墨的女儿。
25. **Ares** [ˈɛəriːz] /**Mars** [mɑːz]:阿瑞斯,希腊神话中的战神,奥林匹斯十二主神之一,被视为尚武精神的化身,是宙斯和赫拉的儿子。
26. **Hercules** [ˈhəːkjuliːz]:赫拉克勒斯,海格立斯,罗马神话中称为赫耳枯勒斯,希腊神话中宙斯与阿尔克墨涅之子,力大无比的英雄,因完成赫拉要求的十二项任务而获得永生。
27. **Diomedes** [daiəˈmiːdiːz]:戴奥米底斯,荷马史诗 Illiad 中之英雄。
28. **Dionysus** [daiəˈnaisəs]:狄俄尼索斯,希腊神话中的酒神。
29. **Peleus** [ˈpiːljus]:珀琉斯,色萨利地方密尔弥冬人的国王,阿喀琉斯的父亲。
30. **Achilles** [əˈkiliːz]:阿喀琉斯,是荷马史诗《伊利亚特》中的英雄,是海洋女神忒提斯和凡人英雄珀琉斯所生。
31. **Maia** [ˈmeijə; ˈmaiə]:迈亚,希腊神话中的女神,普勒阿得斯七姊妹中最年长者。
32. **Cyllene** [səˈlin]:库勒涅山,赫耳墨斯出生的山洞。
33. **Hermaphroditus** [həːmæfrəˈdaitəs]:赫马佛洛狄忒斯,赫耳墨斯和阿佛洛狄忒之子。

After You Read

Knowledge Focus

1. **Solo Work:** Familiarize yourself with gods and goddesses by filling out the following form.

Ancient Greek and Roman Gods

GREEK NAME	ROMAN NAME	ROLE IN MYTHOLOGY
Aphrodite	_____	Goddess of love and _____
Apollor	Apollo	God of youth, _____, prophecy, _____ and healing
_____	Mars	God of _____
Artemis	_____	Virgin goddess of _____ and of wild animals; goddess of _____ and the chase
Hephaestus	_____	God of fire and _____
_____	Mercury	herald and _____ of the gods, known for his invention and for _____

2. **Solo Work:** Match each figure with its description according to what you have learned from the text above.

   1) Apollo
   2) Artemis
   3) Aphrodite
   4) Ares
   5) Hephaestus
   6) Hermes

   A. a beautiful woman, usually naked, often accompanied by her son Eros/Cupid, or by a whole flock of small winged Loves or Cupids
   B. is ugly and lame; makes houses and furniture, weapons and armor for the gods
   C. a warrior, with armor, sword, spear, and shield
   D. a beautiful, athletic young woman, dressed as a huntress with bow and arrows
   E. a handsome, beardless youth, wearing a winged cap and sandals and carrying the caduceus
   F. a beardless young man of perfect male body: muscular but youthful
   G. is often wearing a small crescent moon in her hair or on her breast, and often accompanied by a deer or other wild creatures

3. **Pair Work:** Discuss the following questions with your partner.

   1) Like his father, Apollo also has many titles, list the titles you know about Apollo and the relevant story.
   2) What is the relationship between Artemis and Apollo? How did Artemis help her mother to give birth to Apollo?
   3) Why do we say Artemis' functions and roles are often conflicting and contradictory?

4) What are the two versions of Aphrodite's birth?
5) Who is a better fighter, god of war, Ares or goddess of war, Athena? And give your reasons.
6) Why being a god of war, Ares cannot win the worship from many Greeks?
7) What are the accounts as to how Hephaestus became lame? Can you retell them?
8) Why is it said that Hermes was a god known for his invention and for theft?
9) How many virgin goddesses are there in "the Twelve Olympians"? And who are they?
10) Do you have a clear idea of the relationship among "the Twelve Olympians"? Try to draw a family tree based on what you know.

Language Focus
1. Fill in the blanks with the words or expressions you have learned from the text.

archery	chase	guardian	delivery	notorious
murderous	crumble	attribute	notable	infancy

1) So all we have to do now is finalize the _____ arrangements.
2) More generally, however, Japanese house prices are unlikely to _____.
3) No one knew at what moment, or in what place, a secret and _____ enemy might unmask himself.
4) The issue has gained importance as the ECB has taken on a more political role as _____ of the embattled single currency.
5) The first World _____ Championships were held in 1931.
6) The story is similar in much of the rest of Asia, with the _____ exceptions of India and Hong Kong.
7) Rarity is the _____ of a vast number of species of all classes, in all counties.
8) The Yellow River once _____ for flooding the Chinese landscape.
9) Boys are slightly more likely to die in _____ than girls.
10) Maslow believed that humans have the need to increase their intelligence and thereby _____ knowledge.

2. Fill in the blanks with the proper form of the word in the brackets.
1) They should rejoice in all its abundant fruits of daring and _____ (invent).
2) Naturally, the _____ (original) of Species was seen as a book written against religion.
3) Each and every difference contains _____ (contradict).
4) In the past 200 years, _____ (number) schools and celebrated performers have emerged.
5) His powers of _____ (persuade) calmed the confusion of the crowd.
6) The power of humor to dissolve a hostile _____ (confront) often lies in its unspoken promise.
7) This does not mean, however, that judicial _____ (supervise) of the rulemaking process has become insignificant.
8) Larry can play many _____ (music) instruments, including the violin and saxophone.
9) Masters in management degrees are growing in _____ (popular) in China.
10) But is it possible to explain the _____ (beautiful) of a human face using math?

3. **Fill in the blanks with the proper prepositions or adverbs that collocate with the neighboring words.**

   1) Florida can be known _____ energy and green industry leaders throughout the world.
   2) Such speculations no longer belong _____ the realm of science.
   3) Spring is the season sowing seeds. It is pregnant _____ life and green.
   4) Many of those affected also have learning disabilities or suffer _____ depression.
   5) Even those who identify _____ a particular party do so less strongly than they used to.
   6) One morning he drove a pickup truck into town _____ an errand.
   7) The villagers take pity _____ the hungry traveler and give them hot food.
   8) What if they give _____ to Western political pressure and allow a modest currency rise?
   9) My attitude _____ the banking industry is not a prejudice.
   10) The paper is the resource of recycling; please do not optionally throw _____.

4. **Proofreading: The following passage contains ten errors. Each indicated line contains a maximum of one error. In each case, only ONE word is involved. Read the passage and correct the errors.**

   Plato, in the *Symposium*, declared that there are two Aphrodites: "Common Aphrodite", god of ordinary love and sex, and "Heaven Aphrodite", Aphrodite   (1) _____
   Urania, a potent spiritual force. This is a philosopher's concept rather a genuine myth,   (2) _____
   but it does suggest the goddess's range of personalities. On one extreme is the   (3) _____
   goddess of the universal cycle of life. Common Aphrodite, on the other hand, is the   (4) _____
   embodiment of human love, and can be regarded in many ways as love can be: as   (5) _____
   something rapturous, or kind and cared, or wantonly lustful, or elegantly frivolous, or   (6) _____
   cruel. She married to Hephaestus/Vulcan, but continually unfaithful to him; her   (7) _____
   principle lover is Ares/Mars, but she also has human lovers, with whom Adonis is the   (8) _____
   most famous. The opposite in most ways of chaste Artemis/Diana, she is like her in   (9) _____
   her harsh punishment of those who offend on her and her values; the most famous   (10) _____
   example is the tragedy of Hippolytus and Phaedra.

Comprehensive Work

1. **Biopoems**

   After becoming somewhat familiar with Olympian gods and their relationships, let's write biopoems about each of them.

   Format:
   1) Greek Name.
   2) Four Traits of Character.
   3) Relative of _____ (1—3 people).
   4) Lover of _____ (1—3 things or people).
   5) Who needs _____ (1—3 things).
   6) Who fears _____ (1—3 things).
   7) Who gives _____ (1—3 things).
   8) Resident of _____ .
   9) Roman Name.

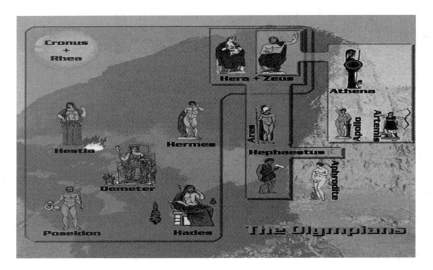

Example:

1) Aphrodite
2) Goddess of Love! Beauty and Fertility.
3) A daughter of Zeus and Dione; wife of Hephaestus.
4) Lover of sons Aeneas and Cupid and brother Ares.
5) Who needs a chariot.
6) Who fears War, Athena and Hera.
7) Who gives Helen to Paris, a magic girdle to Hera, and Medea to Jason.
8) Resident of Mt. Olympus.
9) Venus.

2. Myth Interpretation

In some myths, Eros was the illegitimate son of Aphrodite and Ares, and was sometimes portrayed wearing armor. What do all suggest about parallels between warfare and romance?

Venus and Mars , Sandro Botticelli (1445 — 1510)

Text B Artemis and Actaeon

Artemis (Diana), Apollo's sister, went armed with bow and arrows and, like him, had the power both to send plagues or sudden death among mortals, and to heal them. She was the protectress of little children, and of all sucking animals, but she also loved the chaste, especially that of stags. While she was still a three-year-old child, she asked Zeus, her father, for and was granted eternal virginity. Here is one story that tells how she punished a young hunter who dared to intrude though unintentionally upon her privacy.

It was midday, and the sun stood equally distant from either goal, when young Actaeon, son of King Cadmus, thus addressed the youths who with him were hunting the stag in the mountains, "Friends, our nets and our weapons are wet with the blood of our victims; we have had sport enough for one day, and tomorrow we can renew our labors. Now, while Phoebus parches the earth, let us put by our implements and indulge ourselves with rest."

There was a valley thick enclosed with cypresses and pines, sacred to the huntress queen, Diana. In the extremity of the valley was a cave, not adorned with art, but nature had counterfeited art in its construction, for she had turned the arch of its roof with stones as delicately fitted as if by the hand of man. A fountain burst out from one side, whose open basin was bounded by a grassy rim. Here the goddess of the woods used to come when weary with hunting and lave her virgin limbs in the sparkling water.

One day, having repaired thither with her nymphs, she handed her javelin, her quiver, and her bow to one, her robe to another, while a third unbound the sandals from her feet. Then Crocale, the most skilful of them, arranged her hair, and Nephele, Hyale, and the rest drew water in capacious urns. While the goddess was thus employed in the labors of the toilet, behold Actaeon, having quitted his companions, and rambling without any especial object, came to the place, led thither by his destiny. As he presented himself at the entrance of the cave, the nymphs, seeing a man, screamed and rushed towards the goddess to hide her with their bodies. But she was taller than the rest and overtopped them all by a head. Such a color as tinges the clouds at sunset or at dawn came over the countenance of Diana thus taken by surprise. Surrounded as she was by her nymphs, she yet turned

half away, and sought with a sudden impulse for her arrows. As they were not at hand, she dashed the water into the face of the intruder, adding these words: "Now go and tell, if you can, that you have seen Diana unapparelled." Immediately a pair of branching stag's horns grew out of his head, his neck gained in length, his ears grew sharp-pointed, his hands became feet, his arms long legs, his body was covered with a hairy spotted hide. Fear took the place of his former boldness, and the hero fled. He could not but admire his own speed; but when he saw his horns in the water, "Ah, wretched me!" he would have said, but no sound followed the effort. He groaned, and tears flowed down the face which had taken the place of his own. Yet his consciousness remained. What shall he do?—go home to seek the place, or lie hid in the woods? The latter he was afraid, the former he was ashamed, to do. While he hesitated the dogs saw him.

First Melampus, a Spartan dog, gave the signal with his bark, then Pamphagus, Dorceus, Lelaps, Theron, Nape, Tigris, and all the rest, rushed after him swifter than the wind. Over rocks and cliffs, through mountain gorges that seemed impracticable, he fled and they followed. Where he had often chased the stag and cheered on his pack, his pack now chased him, cheered on by his huntsmen. He longed to cry out, "I am Actaeon; recognize your master!" but the words came not at his will. The air resounded with the bark of the dogs. Presently one fastened on his back, another seized his shoulder. While they held their master, the rest of the pack came up and buried their teeth in his flesh. He groaned,—not in a human voice, yet certainly not in a stag's,—and falling on his knees, raised his eyes, and would have raised his arms in supplication, if he had had them. His friends and fellow-huntsmen cheered on the dogs, and looked everywhere for Actaeon, calling on him to join the sport. At the sound of his name he turned his head, and heard them regret that he should be away. He earnestly wished he was. He would have been well pleased to see the exploits of his dogs, but to feel them was too much. They were all around him, rending and tearing; and it was not till they had torn his life out that the anger of Diana was satisfied.

(Excerpted from http://www.bartleby.com/181/042.html)

Questions for Reflection
1) Please describe the cave Diana used to come when weary with hunting.
2) How does Actaeon intrude upon Diana's privacy?
3) How does Diana punish Actaeon for the intrusion?

Text C Venus and Adonis

Venus (Aphrodite), playing one day with her boy Cupid (Eros), wounded her bosom with one of his arrows. She pushed him away, but the wound was deeper than she thought. Before it healed she beheld Adonis, and was captivated with him. She no longer took any interest in her favorite resorts—Paphos, and Cnidos, and Amathos, rich in metals. She absented herself even from heaven, for Adonis was dearer to her than heaven. Him she followed and bore him company. She who used to love to recline in the shade, with no care but to cultivate her charms, now rambles through the woods and over the hills, dressed like the huntress Diana; and calls her dogs, and chases hares and stags, or other game that it is safe to hunt, but keeps clear of the wolves and bears, reeking with the slaughter of the herd. She charged Adonis, too, to beware of such dangerous animals. "Be brave towards the timid," said she; "courage against the courageous is not safe. Beware how you expose yourself to danger and put my happiness to risk. Attack not the beasts that Nature has armed with weapons. I do not value your glory so high as to consent to purchase it by such exposure. Your youth, and the beauty that charms Venus, will not touch the hearts of lions and bristly boars. Think of their terrible claws and prodigious strength! I hate the whole race of them. Do you ask me why?" Then she told him the story of Atalanta and Hippomenes, who were changed into lions for their ingratitude to her.

Having given him this warning, she mounted her chariot drawn by swans, and drove away through the air. But Adonis was too noble to heed such counsels. The dogs had roused a wild boar

from his lair, and the youth threw his spear and wounded the animal with a sidelong stroke. The beast drew out the weapon with his jaws, and rushed after Adonis, who turned and ran; but the boar overtook him, and buried his tusks in his side, and stretched him dying upon the plain.

Venus, in her swan-drawn chariot, had not yet reached Cyprus, when she heard coming up through midair the groans of her beloved, and turned her white-winged coursers back to earth. As she drew near and saw from on high his lifeless body bathed in blood, she alighted and, bending over it, beat her breast and tore her hair. Reproaching the Fates, she said, "Yet theirs shall be but a partial triumph; memorials of my grief shall endure, and the spectacle of your death, my Adonis, and of my lamentations shall be annually renewed. Your blood shall be changed into a flower; that consolation none can envy me." Thus speaking, she sprinkled nectar on the blood; and as they mingled, bubbles rose as in a pool on which raindrops fall, and in an hour's time there sprang up a flower of bloody hue like that of the pomegranate. But it is short-lived. It is said the wind blows the blossoms open, and afterwards blows the petals away; so it is called Anemone, or Wind Flower, from the cause which assists equally in its production and its decay.

(Excerpted from http://www.bartleby.com/181/083.html)

Questions for Reflection
1. How did Venus come to love Adonis, a mortal youth?
2. Why did Venus advise Adonis against attacking wild animals?
3. What did Venus do to commemorate her ill-fated lover?

Websites to Visit

http://www.temple.edu/classics/olympians/index.html
This website provides detailed information about each Olympian Gods' animal and plants, objects, attributes and activities in a form.

http://gogreece.about.com/cs/mythology/a/olympiangods.html
You want to know more about the "Top Twelve"? This website provides almost every aspect you want to know about each Olympian Gods and some interesting facts!

Unit 4
The Gods of the Underworld

> Death is the wish of some, the relief of many, and the end of all.
> ——Lucius Annaeus Seneca, Roman philosopher and playwright

Unit Goals

- To have a general understanding of the underworld
- To be able to tell the myth of Hades and Persephone
- To have some knowledge of the main figures in the underworld
- To learn the useful words and expressions that describe the underworld
- To improve language skills and critical thinking through the content of this unit

Before You Read

1. Do you know the meanings of the following phrases? Check them against a dictionary.
   ◇ Charon's boat/ferry
   ◇ the Elysian Fields
   ◇ cross the Styx
   ◇ be haunted by the furies of

2. The four phrases each corresponds to one picture below, try to match them first and then explore the meaning and story in each picture.
   Sop to Cerberus   Cask of Danaides
   Task of Sisyphus   Ixion's wheel

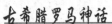

Start to Read

Text A The Gods of the Underworld

Underworld

The world of the dead or the netherworld was commonly viewed, by the ancient religions, to be a subterranean realm, ruled by a god or goddess, or both. Almost all mortals would reside in the netherworld, after their death. Few gained godhood and fewer still gained places in the Olympus, the home of the Olympian gods and goddesses.

In the Greek mythology, the rulers of the Underworld were **Hades** and Persephone, which the Romans called Pluto and Prosperina.

In classical mythology, the world of the dead or the netherworld has many different names. Though, the ruler of the Underworld was named Hades, the netherworld itself was popularly called Hades.

Hades (Underworld) was named after its ruler, Hades, who was the son of Cronus and Rhea, and brother of Zeus, Poseidon, **Hera**, **Demeter** and **Hestia**. Hades was known in the Roman myths, as Pluto. His wife and consort was **Persephone** or Prosperina (Prosperine) according to the Roman myths.

After the war between the Titans and Olympians, Hades and his two brothers decided to divide the universe between them. Zeus receive the sky or Olympus, Poseidon became lord of the sea, while Hades ruled the Underworld. The Earth was shared by all, but Zeus became the supreme ruler of the universe.

The Underworld was subterranean domain of Hades, where the sunlight never shined, and the climate was either cold or chilling. The entire domain was divided into several regions, and having several different types of landmarks.

There were five subterranean rivers flowing through the Underworld. They were called **Acheron** ("Woe"), **Cocytus** ("Wailing"), **Lethe** ("Forgetfulness"), **Phlegethon** or Pyriphlegethon ("Fiery"), and **Styx** ("Abhorrence"). The shades must cross all five rivers before they can be judged and sent to their final resting place.

The Underworld was divided into two or more main

regions. **Erebus** was the upper region, while **Tartarus** was the lowest region, where most of the Titans were imprisoned.

There were three minor gods in the Underworld, who acted as judges and presided over the souls of the dead. These three were **Minos** and **Rhadamanthys**, sons of **Europa**, and **Aeacus**, the son of **Aegina**.

Most mortals who died will find their final resting place in the Plain of Asphodel, which was part of the Erebus region. The shades that dwelled here have no memories of their former lives. The place was gray and gloomy, but the shades who populated this region will experience neither joy, nor sorrow. Only a few mortals will ever gain entry to the **Elysian** Fields. The Elysian Fields was also part of the region in Erebus.

Others, who led a wicked life, were sent down to Tartarus and punished for their crime or sin. Among the notable figures to be punished in Tartarus, were **Ixion**, **Tityus**, **Tantalus**, the Danaides and Sisyphus. Ixion, who tried to rape Hera, is tied to a turning wheel of fire; the giant Tityus, who tried to rape Leto, is tied to the ground while vultures feed on his liver. Tantalus, who tried to trick the gods into eating human flesh, is "tantalised" by hunger and thirst in the midst of plenty: he stands in water which drains away when he tries to drink, under hanging fruit which swings out of his reach when he tries to eat. **The Danaides**, the husband-killing daughters of **King Danaus**, spend their time pouring water into a leaky jar. And the trickster **Sisyphus** pushes a huge stone up a steep hill, and, every time he nears the top, sees it roll back down again.

Hades/Pluto

Hades was Lord of the Underworld. He was the son of the titans, **Cronus** and **Rhea**. Hades was the god of the dead, and ruled his world with more absolute power and authority than **Zeus**. Hades was a grim god, not an evil one.

His other name Aïdoneus (Aidoneus) means the "Unseen One". To the Romans, he was known as Pluto (wealth) and Dis Pater or Dis. Pluto is the name of the ninth planet in the solar system. **Charon** is Pluto's moon or satellite.

Hades was among the children of Cronus, to be swallowed by their father, and later disgorged. Hades was armed with the Cap of Darkness (invisibility), in which he used to aid Zeus in the war against the Titans.

After aiding brothers Zeus and **Poseidon**, in overthrowing Cronus and sending the other Titans to Tartarus, he received the world of the dead, known as Underworld, as his domain.

Hades rarely left the Underworld. He drove his chariot drawn by black horses, and abducted Persephone, daughter of Zeus and his sister, Demeter. He wanted Persephone as his wife and queen of the Underworld. He was forced to compromise with his sister, Demeter: he allowed Persephone to lived two-third of the year on earth with her mother and a third with him in the Underworld.

The Underworld was a place where the souls of human find their resting places. In the deepest region called Tartarus, it was a place of punishment for mortal who committed the worse sins or crimes. Tartarus also served as a prison for the Titans and other gods. The Underworld was guarded by a three-headed hound, named **Cerberus**. Cerberus kept the living and the dead apart. Cerberus had only allowed few of the living to pass through the gate of Hades: Heracles, **Theseus**, **Orpheus**, **Aeneas** and **Psyche**.

Hades and Persephone weren't the only one to live in the Underworld. There were **Thanatos** (Death), the winged-brother **Hypnos** (Sleep), and **Morpheus** (Dream), who was the son of Hypnos. Styx was the river goddess of one of the Underworld rivers, and the goddess **Hecate**, had also dwelled in this domain.

Persephone/Proserpina

Persephone was a goddess of the underworld. She was the daughter of Zeus and Demeter. The Romans called her Proserpina.

Before she was abducted, she was perhaps the personification of spring and goddess of corns, fruits and flowers. After her abduction, she became known as the dreaded goddess of the Underworld.

Persephone was playing in the meadow with her companions, the Oceanids (daughters of Oceanus), when Hades saw and fell in love with her.

It was said that Hades had made arrangement with his brother Zeus, over the abduction and marriage of Persephone without Demeter's prior knowledge. It was Hecate and Helius who revealed to Demeter who had abducted her daughter.

Her uncle, Hades, made Persephone his wife and queen. Hades had tricked Persephone into eating the pomegranate seeds, so that she could not leave the Underworld for very long. Since she had eaten the seeds in the Underworld, she had to stay with her husband. However, Zeus or Hermes made Hades and Demeter compromise of where and when Persephone should live. Persephone was to live a third of the year with new husband Hades, and the rest with her mother Demeter. In the Underworld, Hecate became her companion.

Hecate

Hecate was the daughter of **Perses** and **Asteria**, both of whom were offspring of the Titans. She had also been called a daughter of Demeter.

Hesiod had repeatedly said in his Theogony that Zeus had given Hecate honour above all. Hecate can bestow wealth on anyone who prayed and sacrificed to her. Hecate has shares of all the wealth in heaven (Olympus), earth and in the Underworld. This is because she have a role to play as moon-goddess, earth (fertility) goddess and goddess of the Underworld.

She was sometimes confused with **Rhea**, Demeter and

Persephone as an earth-goddess and goddess of fertility.

Again she is confused with Persephone as goddess of the Underworld. She was goddess of night and known as the invisible goddess, where she was accompanied by hell-hounds. Speaking of Persephone, Hecate tried to comfort Demeter, when Hades abducted her daughter. Hecate told Demeter that she had heard Persephone's cry, but could not identify the abductor. It was she who suggested that Demeter speak with **Helius**, the sun god who sees everything that happened below him.

Later, when Persephone was to stay with her husband for part of the year in the Underworld, Hecate would be Persephone's companion, so that Persephone would not be lonely.

Like **Artemis** and **Selene**, she was goddess of the moon, but she was associated with dark side of the moon.

(Excerpted from http://www.timelessmyths.com/classical/olympians.html)

Proper Nouns

1. **Hades** ['heidi:z] /Pluto ['plu:təu] /Dis [dis]：哈得斯，希腊神话中的冥界之神，相对应于罗马神话的普鲁托。他是克洛诺斯和瑞亚的儿子，宙斯的哥哥。
2. **Persephone** [pəˈsefəni; pə-] /Proserpina/Proserpine：珀耳塞福涅，希腊神话中得墨忒耳和宙斯的女儿，她被冥神哈得斯劫持娶作冥后。
3. **Cronus** ['krəunəs] /Saturn ['sætən]：克罗诺斯，希腊神话中提坦巨人之一，天神乌拉诺斯和地神该亚的儿子，他夺取了父亲的王位，后又被他的儿子宙斯把他的王位夺去。
4. **Rhea** [riə]：瑞亚，丰产女神，盖亚和乌剌诺斯所生十二提坦神之一。
5. **Zeus** [zju:s] /Jupiter ['dʒu:pitə]：宙斯，希腊神话中的主神，克洛诺斯和瑞亚之子，掌管天界；奥林匹斯的许多神祇和许多希腊英雄都是他和不同女子生下的子女。
6. **Poseidon** [pɔˈsaidən] /Neptune ['neptju:n]：波塞冬，希腊神话中的海神，克洛诺斯与瑞亚之子，宙斯之兄，地位仅次于宙斯，是希腊神话中的十二主神之一。
7. **Hera** ['hiərə]：赫拉，希腊神话中奥林匹斯十二主神之一，是克洛诺斯之女，主神宙斯的妻子，主管婚姻和家庭。
8. **Demeter** [diˈmi:tə] /Ceres ['siəri:z]：得墨忒耳，希腊神话中主管农业、结婚、丰饶的女神，是克洛诺斯和瑞亚的女儿，珀耳塞福涅的母亲。
9. **Hestia** ['hestiə] /Vesta ['vestə]：赫斯提亚，宙斯的姐姐，掌管万民的家事。是希腊神话中的女灶神、家宅的保护者。罗马神话中相应的女神被称作维斯塔。
10. **Acheron** ['ækərɔn]：阿刻戎，希腊神话中的冥河，痛苦之河。
11. **Cocytus** [kəuˈsaitəs]：科塞特斯河，冥河Acheron的支流。
12. **Lethe** ['li:θi:]：忘川，忘河，冥界的河流之一，饮其水者会忘掉过去。
13. **Phlegethon** ['flegəθɔn]：弗莱格桑河，系冥界五河之一。
14. **Styx** [stiks]：冥河，冥府五条河之一条，死者的灵魂渡过此河进入冥府。
15. **Erebus** ['eribəs]：厄瑞波斯，希腊神话中的古老神祇之一。他所处的位置在冥界与大地之间，据说人在死后必须穿越厄瑞波斯才能抵达冥界。
16. **Tartarus** ['ta:tərəs]：塔耳塔洛斯，地狱底下暗无天日的深渊，为宙斯禁闭提坦之处。
17. **Minos** ['mainɔs]：迈诺斯，米诺斯，希腊神话中克里特岛的王，死后做阴间的法官。
18. **Rhadamanthys** [rædəˈmænθəs]：剌达曼堤斯，拉达曼斯，希腊神话中宙斯和欧罗巴之子，生前为人公正,死后被封为冥界三判官之一。

19. **Europa** [juəˈrəupə]:欧罗巴,腓尼基王阿革诺耳之女。
20. **Aeacus** [ˈiːəkəs]:埃阿科斯,希腊神话中宙斯与埃癸娜之子,阿喀琉斯之祖父,死后成为冥界三判官之一。
21. **Aegina** [iːˈdʒainə]:埃伊娜,河神阿索波斯的女儿。
22. **Elysian** [iˈliziən] **Fields**:希腊神话中的极乐世界,至福之境。
23. **Ixion** [ikˈsaiən]:伊克西翁,希腊神话中的人物,因莽撞地追求天后赫拉的爱,而被宙斯缚在地狱永不停转的车轮上受罚。
24. **Tityus** [ˈtitiəs]:提堤俄斯,希腊神话中宙斯和厄拉瑞的儿子,因对拉托那无理而在冥界受罚,肝脏为群鹰啄食。
25. **Tantalus** [ˈtæntələs]:坦塔罗斯,希腊神话中阿耳戈斯或科斯林的国王,宙斯的儿子。因偷窃神的酒食,并把自己的儿子剁成碎块宴请众神而在冥界受罚。
26. **The Danaides** [dəˈneiidiːz]:达那伊得斯姐妹,达那俄斯的女儿们,听命于父亲,在新婚之夜杀死了她们的新郎,被罚入地狱里永不停息地用渗漏的工具取水。
27. **King Danaus** [ˈdæniːəs]:阿尔戈斯的国王达那俄斯。
28. **Sisyphus** [ˈsisifəs]:西西弗斯,希腊古时国王,因作恶多端,死后堕入地狱,被罚推石上山,但推上又滚下,永远循环不息。
29. **Charon** [ˈkɛərən]:卡戎,希腊神话中将亡魂渡到阴界去的冥府渡神。
30. **Cerberus** [ˈsəːbərəs]:刻耳柏洛斯,希腊神话中守卫冥界入口的长有三个头的狗。
31. **Hercules** [ˈhəːkjuliːz]:赫剌克勒斯,海格立斯,罗马神话中称为赫耳枯勒斯,希腊神话中宙斯与阿尔克墨涅之子,力大无比的英雄,因完成赫拉要求的十二项任务而获得永生。
32. **Theseus** [ˈθiːsjuːs; -siəs]:忒修斯,希腊神话中的雅典国王。
33. **Orpheus** [ˈɔːfiəs; -fjus]:俄耳甫斯,希腊神话中的任务,太阳神阿波罗之子,善弹竖琴,其琴声能感动草木、禽兽和顽石。
34. **Aeneas** [iˈniːəs]:埃涅阿斯,亚尼雅士,特洛伊战争中的勇士。
35. **Psyche** [ˈpsaiki]:厄洛斯(罗马神话中常说的爱神丘比特)的恋人。
36. **Thanatos** [ˈθænətɔs]:桑纳托斯,希腊神话中的死亡之神。
37. **Hypnos** [ˈhipnɔs]:许普诺斯,希腊神话中的睡眠之神。
38. **Morpheus** [ˈmɔːfiəs, -fjuːs]:墨菲斯,希腊神话中的梦神。
39. **Hecate** [ˈhekəti]:赫卡忒,希腊神话中司魔法和巫术的女神。
40. **Perses** [ˈpəːsəs]:珀耳塞斯,破坏之神,克赖伊俄斯与欧律比亚之子,智慧超群。
41. **Asteria** [æˈstiəriə]:阿斯忒瑞亚,星夜女神,暗夜女神勒托之妹。
42. **Rhea** [riə]:瑞亚,丰产女神,盖亚和乌剌诺斯所生十二提坦神之一。
43. **Helius** [ˈheliəs]:赫利俄斯,太阳神。
44. **Artemis** [ˈɑːtimis] /**Diana** [daiˈænə]:阿耳忒弥斯,罗马神话中的狄安娜,古希腊神话中的狩猎女神、月神,奥林匹斯主神之一,亦被视为野兽的保护神。阿耳忒弥斯为主神宙斯与暗夜女神勒托之女,阿波罗的孪生姐姐。
45. **Selene** [siˈliːnə]:塞勒涅,希腊神话中的月亮女神。

After You Read

Knowledge Focus

1. Solo Work: Fill in the blanks according to what you have learned from the text above.

1) In the Greek mythology, the rulers of the Underworld were _____ and _____, which the Romans called Pluto and Prosperina.
2) Hades (Underworld) was named after its ruler, Hades, who was the son of _____ and _____, and brother of Zeus, Poseidon, Hera, Demeter and Hestia.
3) There were five subterranean rivers flowing through the Underworld. They were called _____ ("Woe"), _____ ("Wailing"), _____ ("Forgetfulness"), _____ ("Fiery"), and _____ ("Abhorrence").
4) The Underworld was divided into two or more main regions. _____ was the upper region, while _____ was the lowest region, where most of the Titans were imprisoned.
5) In the underworld, there are three judges, _____, _____, and _____, who decide the fates of the dead.
6) The Underworld was guarded by a three-headed hound, named _____. It kept the living and the dead apart.
7) Hades and Persephone were not the only one to live in the Underworld. There were _____ (Death), the winged-brother _____ (Sleep), and _____ (Dream).
8) Hades had tricked Persephone into eating the _____, so that she could not leave the Underworld for very long.
9) Hecate was the daughter of _____ and _____, both of whom were offspring of the Titans.
10) Like Artemis and Selene, _____ was goddess of the moon, but she was associated with dark side of the moon.

2. Solo Work: Match each figure(s) with its description according to what you have learned from the text above.

1) Tantalus   A. is tied to a turning wheel of fire in the underworld for he tried to rape Hera

2) Aeacus   B. is the fearsome three-headed hell-hound, guard the entrance to the underworld, or the gate of Hades' palace

3) Ixion   C. is "tantalized" by hunger and thirst in the midst of plenty in the underworld for he tried to trick the gods into eating human flesh

4) Hecate   D. is tied to the ground while vultures feed on his liver in the underworld for he tried to rape Leto

5) Tityus   E. pushes a huge stone up a steep hill in the underworld, and, every time he nears the top, sees it roll back down again

6) The Danaides   F. one of the three minor gods in the Underworld, who acted as judges and presided over the souls of the dead

7) Sisyphus   G. are the husband-killing daughters of King Danaus, spend their time pouring water into a leaky jar

8) Cerberus   H. goddess of the moon and was associated with dark side of the moon

3. Pair Work: Discuss the following questions with your partner.

1) In the Greek mythology, who are the rulers of the Underworld?
2) After the war between the Titans and Olympians, how did the three sons of Cronus and Rhea divide the universe between them?
3) How many regions is the Underworld divided into? Can you name the upper region and the lowest region?
4) Where is most mortals' final resting place when they died?
5) What is Hades' compromise with his sister, Demeter about his wife, Perspehone?
6) What kind of place is Tartarus? Would you try to give a description of it according to your imagination?
7) Can you list some notable figures punished in Tartarus and the reasons for their being there?
8) Why can't Persephone leave the Underworld for very long?
9) What is the difference among Hecate, Artemis and Selene, since all are goddesses of the moon?
10) Can you list some similarities and differences about the Underworld between the Greek Mythology and Chinese Mythology after reading Text A?

Language Focus

1. Fill in the blanks with the words or expressions you have learned from the text.

| connivance | depict | possession | gloomy | conspire against |
| compromise | barren | imprison | poisonous | exceptional |

1) Ship is the place for him to protect himself and _____ himself, also isolated him with the rest of the world.
2) That _____ forecast seems all too realistic following so grave a financial crisis.
3) I am prepared to make some concession on minor details, but I cannot _____ on fundamentals.
4) The story _____ the hero as a cynical opportunist.
5) The criminals could not have escaped without your _____.
6) It is a land of great adventure where hope springs from the most _____ ground.
7) He walked carefully among the plants, as if he were walking among wild animals or _____ snakes.
8) If any force tries to _____ the people's will, we might be compelled to take that way despite our unwillingness.
9) In such _____ circumstances, a statement of the reasons why summarization is not possible must be provided.
10) Happiness lies not in the mere _____ of money; it lies in the joy of achievement, in the thrill of creative effort.

2. Fill in the blanks with the proper form of the word in the brackets.

1) There's no question that after the _____ (invade) looters did manage to pillage several

Unit 4 The Gods of the Underworld

sensitive sites.
2) It should be clear to a reader of any degree of _____ (initiate).
3) Little rain and poor soil _____ (fertile) are problems in that area, as in other parts of southern Africa.
4) Perhaps the biggest difference with the Bush era is in Obama's emphasis on US economic _____ (new).
5) This simple example is a pretty good _____ (describe) of how evolution works.
6) It would be better if there were but one _____ (inhabit) to a square mile, as where I live.
7) Half of US retailers say they will be adding fewer _____ (season) jobs this holiday season.
8) Have you confirmed your _____ (reserve) for tomorrow's flight?
9) There was general agreement that bigger was better and that the combined firm would benefit from greater _____ (geography) reach.
10) A _____ (forget) man should not trust his memory, but should write things down in a notebook.

3. **Fill in the blanks with the proper prepositions or adverbs that collocate with the neighboring words.**
   1) Be careful. They are out to trick you _____ buying something you don't need.
   2) So remember: always give your old job a chance before starting to search _____ a new one.
   3) She wanted to rage _____ him for spoiling her perfect day, but the words in her head wouldn't come out.
   4) Thanks _____ the expansion of successful firms and the entry of new ones, however, many more jobs were created than destroyed.
   5) About half of China's exports consist _____ goods that have been assembled from imported components.
   6) In reading, I usually mark _____ what I regard as important in the book.
   7) Be open _____ the possibilities that can change your life—they may bring you a greater sense of joy and fulfillment.
   8) All we need is some creativity along _____ plenty of time and practice.
   9) If we rely _____ these excessively, they can make our body functions degenerate gradually.
   10) After these three words, her strength seems to drain _____ .

4. **Proofreading: The following passage contains ten errors. Each indicated line contains a maximum of one error. In each case, only ONE word is involved. Read the passage and correct the errors.**

Later writers usually place the underworld underneath the earth, where it can be   (1) _____
reach by various passages: Orpheus ascends through a cave at Taenarus in   (2) _____
southernmost Greece, Aeneas through the sibyl's cavern near Lake Avernus in Italy.   (3) _____
Its boundary is marked on the river Styx, the "hateful river", by whose black and   (4) _____
poisonous water the gods swear their most breakable oaths. The spirits of the newly   (5) _____
dead wait on its bank to be ferried across by Charon, the filthy and churlish old   (6) _____
boatman. The fare is a obolus, a small coin; those who lack of the coin, or have not   (7) _____
been properly buried, are doomed wait in limbo on the banks of the Styx. On the

other side, the boundaries of the underworld are marked by five rivers: Styx, Acheron ("sorrowful"), Cocytus ("wailing"), Phlegethon ("fiery"), and Lethe ("forgetful"); those who drink in Lethe forget their former lives and identities. The entrance of the underworld, or the gate of Hades' palace, is guarded by the fearsome three-headed (or, more extravagantly, fifty-headed) hell-hound Cerberus.

(8) _____
(9) _____
(10) _____

Comprehensive Work

1. **Story Telling: The following three pictures depict the story happened among Hades, Persephone and Demeter. Retell the story to your partner with the words and expressions you have learned in the text.**

2. **Is there a Hell?**

Where Are The Dead? The proper answer to this question stands related to our own destiny, colors and influences our theology, and the entire trend of our lives! The correct answer gives strength, confidence, courage and assists towards the spirit of a sound mind!

For a man to declare himself uninterested in this subject would be to proclaim himself idiotic — thoughtless. If the ordinary affairs of this present life, food, raiment, finance, politics, etc., which concern us but for a few years, are deemed worthy of thought, study, how much more concern should we have in respect to the eternal future of ourselves and neighbors and mankind in general?

Discuss the question with your partner and try to find the answers from people with different religious beliefs.

Text B Persephone

When Jupiter and his brothers had defeated the Titans and banished them to Tartarus, a new enemy rose up against the gods. They were the giants Typhon, Briareus, Enceladus, and others. Some of them had a hundred arms, others breathed out fire. They were finally subdued and buried alive under Mount Aetna, where they still sometimes struggle to get loose, and shake the whole island with

earthquakes. Their breath comes up through the mountain, and is what men call the eruption of the volcano.

The fall of these monsters shook the earth, so that Hades (Pluto) was alarmed, and feared that his kingdom would be laid open to the light of day. Under this apprehension, he mounted his chariot, drawn by black horses, and took a circuit of inspection to satisfy himself of the extent of the damage. While he was thus engaged, Aphrodite (Venus), who was sitting on Mount Eryx playing with her boy Cupid, espied him, and said, "My son, take your darts with which you conquer all, even Jove himself, and send one into the breast of yonder dark monarch, who rules the realm of Tartarus. Why should he alone escape? Seize the opportunity to extend your empire and mine. Do you not see that even in heaven some despise our power? Athena (Minerva) the wise, and Artemis (Diana) the huntress, defy us; and there is that daughter of Demeter (Ceres), who threatens to follow their example. Now do you, if you have any regard for your own interest or mine, join these two in one." The boy unbound his quiver, and selected his sharpest and truest arrow; then straining the bow against his knee, he attached the string, and, having made ready, shot the arrow with its barbed point right into the heart of Hades (Pluto).

In the vale of Enna there is a lake embowered in woods, which screen it from the fervid rays of the sun, while the moist ground is covered with flowers, and Spring reigns perpetual. Here Persephone (Proserpine, Proserpina, or Kore, the "Maiden") was playing with her companions, gathering flowers in a meadow, and filling her basket and her apron with them, when Pluto saw her, loved her, and carried her off. She screamed for help to her mother and companions; and when in her fright she dropped the corners of her apron and let the flowers fall, childlike she felt the loss of them as an addition to her grief. The ravisher urged on his steeds, calling them each by name, and throwing loose over their heads and necks his iron-colored reins. When he reached the River Styx, and it opposed his passage, he struck the river-bank with his trident, and the earth opened and gave him a passage to Tartarus.

Demeter sought her daughter all the world over. Bright-haired Eos (Aurora), when she came forth in the morning, and Hesperus (Helios) when he led out the stars in the evening, found her still busy in the search. But it was all unavailing. At length, weary and sad, she sat down upon a stone, and continued sitting nine days and nights, in the open air, under the sunlight and moonlight and falling showers. It was where now stands the city of Eleusis, then the home of an old man named Celeus. He was out in the field, gathering acorns and black-berries, and sticks for his fire. His little girl was driving home their two goats, and as she passed the goddess, who appeared in the guise of an old woman, she said to her, "Mother,"—and the name was sweet to the ears of Demeter,—"why do you sit here alone upon the rocks?" The old man also stopped, though his load was heavy, and begged her to come into his cottage, such as it was. She declined, and he urged her. "Go in peace," she replied, "and be happy in your

daughter; I have lost mine." As she spoke, tears—or something like tears, for the gods never weep—fell down her cheeks upon her bosom. The compassionate old man and his child wept with her. Then said he, "Come with us, and despise not our humble roof; so may your daughter be restored to you in safety." "Lead on," said she, "I cannot resist that appeal!" So she rose from the stone and went with them. As they walked he told her that his only son, a little boy, lay very sick, feverish, and sleepless. She stooped and gathered some poppies. As they entered the cottage, they found all in great distress, for the boy seemed past hope of recovery. Metaneira, his mother, received her kindly, and the goddess stooped and kissed the lips of the sick child. Instantly the paleness left his face, and healthy vigor returned to his body. The whole family were delighted—that is, the father, mother, and little girl, for they were all; they had no servants. They spread the table, and put upon it curds and cream, apples, and honey in the comb. While they ate, Demeter mingled poppy juice in the milk of the boy. When night came and all was still, she arose, and taking the sleeping boy, moulded his limbs with her hands, and uttered over him three times a solemn charm, then went and laid him in the ashes. His mother, who had been watching what her guest was doing, sprang forward with a cry and snatched the child from the fire. Then Demeter assumed her own form, and a divine splendor shone all around. While they were overcome with astonishment, she said, "Mother, you have been cruel in your fondness to your son. I would have made him immortal, but you have frustrated my attempt. Nevertheless, he shall be great and useful. He shall teach men the use of the plough, and the rewards which labor can win from the cultivated soil." So saying, she wrapped a cloud about her, and mounting her chariot rode away.

Demeter continued her search for her daughter, passing from land to land, and across seas and rivers. One day, she met Eumolpus, a shepherd, and Eubuleus, a swineherd, who told her all that happened. They had been out in the fields, feeding their beasts, when the earth suddenly gaped open, engulfing Eubuleus's swine before his very eyes; then, with a heavy thud of hooves, a chariot drawn by black horses appeared, and dashed down the chasm. The chariot-driver's face was invisible, but his right arm was tightly clasped around a shrieking girl. Armed with this evidence, Demeter summoned Hecate. Together they approached Helios, who sees everything, and forced him to admit that Hades had been the villain.

When everything was as clear as daylight, Demeter turned her chariot towards heaven, and hastened to present herself before the throne of Jove. She told the story of her bereavement, and implored Jupiter to interfere to procure the restitution of her daughter. Jupiter consented on one condition, namely, that Persephone should not during her stay in the lower world have taken any food; otherwise, the Fates forbade her release. Accordingly, Hermes (Mercury) was sent, accompanied by Spring, to demand Persephone. The wily monarch consented; but, alas! the maiden had taken a pomegranate which Hades offered her, and had sucked the sweet pulp from a few of the seeds. This was enough to prevent her complete release; but a compromise was made, by which she was to spend three months of the year in Hades's company, as Queen of Tartarus, with the tile of Persephone, and the remaining nine in Demeter's.

Demeter allowed herself to be pacified with this arrangement, and restored the earth to her favor. Now she remembered Celeus and his family, and her promise to his infant son Triptolemus. When the boy grew up, she taught him the use of the plough, and how to sow the seed. She took him in her chariot, drawn by winged dragons, through all the countries of the earth, imparting to mankind valuable grains, and the knowledge of agriculture. After his return, Triptolemus built a magnificent temple to Demeter in Eleusis, and established the worship of the goddess, under the name of the Eleusinian mysteries, which, in the splendor and solemnity of their observance, surpassed all other religious celebrations among the Greeks.

(Excerpted from http://www.bartleby.com/181/071.html)

Questions for Reflection
1. What made Hades fall in love with Persephone?
2. Why was Venus displeased with Athena, Diana, and Persephone?
3. From what aspects can the Demeter myth be interpreted?

Text C Cerberus: Three-Headed Dog in Greek Mythology

Greek mythology comprises a huge pantheon, extensive use of anthropomorphism and mythical creatures that are symbolic. Cerberus, the three headed dog was believed to be the guardian of the realm of death, or Hades. Cerberus, it was believed, prevented those who crossed the river of death, Styx, from escaping. River Styx was supposed to be the boundary between the Underworld and Earth. Greek mythology propounded that Hades or the Underworld was encircled nine times by River Styx and that the rivers Phlegethon, Cocytus, Lethe, Eridanos and Acheron converged with Styx on the "Great Marsh". Cerberus guarded the Great Marsh.

Importance of Styx in Greek Mythology:

Hades and Persephone were believed to be the mortal portals in the Underworld. This realm was also home to Phlegyas or guardian of the River Phlegethon, Charon or Kharon, the ferryman, and the living waters of Styx. Styx was believed to have miraculous powers that could make a person immortal, resulting in the grave need for it to be guarded. This realm relates to the concept of "hell" in Christianity and the "Paradise lost", in the literary genius of "The Divine Comedy". In Greek mythology, the ferryman Charon was in charge of transporting souls across the Styx, into the Underworld. Here, it was believed that the sullen were drowned in Styx's muddy waters.

Cerberus: The Guardian

Cerberus, the mythical guardian of River Styx has been immortalized through many works of ancient Greek literature, art and architecture. Cerberus is easily recognizable among the other members of the pantheon due to his three heads. Cerberus is believed to be the sibling of the Nemean Lion, Lernaean Hydra and the Chimaera. Cerberus' parents were the half-woman-half-serpent, Echidna, and the fire-breathing giant, Typhon. Greek mythology projects Typhon as the one who even the Olympian gods feared. Cerberus had a two-headed hell hound brother called Orthrus. Cerberus, in Greek mythology, is depicted as a creature with three heads, a serpent mane like that of Medusa, a dog-like body and a dragon's tail. He is believed to have the power to look into the past, present and future with his three heads. Another theory propounds that Cerberus' heads represent birth, adulthood and old age. Cerberus has been an important part of Greek classics such as Aeneid, The Labors of Hercules, Symposium and Iliad.

Hercules and Cerberus:

This mythical creature was believed to have an eternal longing for fresh meat. This was the reason behind his being given the primary responsibility of ensuring that the souls that entered Hades remained there for fear of being torn to pieces. Hades' loyal watchdog was supposedly presented to King Eurystheus by Hercules. The story highlights that the king had given Hercules the task of capturing the guardian of Hades alive, without the use of weapons. Hercules sought Eleusinian Mysteries to enter and exit Hades alive. He was helped by Hermes to get through the entrance, and by Hestia, to get past Charon. Hercules managed to earn an audience with Hades, the God of the Underworld, and sought permission to take Cerberus to the surface. Hades agreed, but like King Eurystheus, did not permit the use of weapons. However, empowered by the magical Eleusinian Mysteries, Hercules was able to subdue Cerberus and drag the creature out of Hades, to Eurystheus. But, the frightened king begged Hercules to return the monster to the Underworld and released the muscular hero from his labors.

(Excerpted from http://www.buzzle.com/articles/cerberusthree-headed-dog-in-greek-mythology.html)

Questions for Reflection
1. What is the importance of the Styx in Greek Mythology?
2. What are the features of Cerberus?
3. How did Hercules subdue Cerberus?

Websites to Visit

http://www.igreekmythology.com/persephone.html
This website provides detailed information about the myth of Persephone.

http://www.theoi.com/Khthonios/Haides.html
This website provides detailed information about the myth of Hades.

Unit 5
Other Gods

> Myths are public dreams, dreams are private myths.
> —Joseph Campbell

Unit Goals

- To get acquainted with the lesser deities and creatures
- To know the story of God Pan and his wood
- To learn the words and phrases that describe Greek Gods
- To improve language skills and critical thinking through the content of this unit

Before You Read

1. The following pictures are telling stories in Greek Mythology. Can you identify them?

2. See if you know the right answers to the following questions. Check your answers after reading Text A.
   1) Who is the moon goddess?
      A. Hera   B. Athena   C. Selene   D. Cronus
   2) Which of the following is NOT a child of Zeus?
      A. Helios   B. Hyperion   C. Hercules   D. Athena
   3) Which of the following is in Saturn's charge?
      A. Wine   B. Agriculture   C. Wind   D. Love
   4) "Pan" can be a Greek god, and it also has an actual meaning. In "pan-African unity," pan means _____.
   5) Which of these deities can control human destinies?
      A. Zeus   B. Hera   C. Apollo   D. Fates

Start to Read

Text A Other Gods

There is a fascinating, diverse range of lesser gods (or minor deities) and creatures which personify elements of nature or spiritual concepts.

Sun, Moon, Dawn, and Winds

The gods of Sun, Moon, and Dawn are children of the Titans **Hyperion** and **Thea**.

Helios, god of the sun, is a handsome god who is responsible for giving daylight to Earth by driving his chariot of fire, pulled by four flaming steeds, across the sky from east to west. Night will fall as Helios crosses the western horizon, and it lasts as long as it takes him to return to the East. Although Helios is admired, he is also feared. No one, mortal

or immortal, can escape his eye during the day. As he crosses the sky, he looks down upon the world and sees everything. To make matters worse, Helios is a something of a gossip; he rarely keeps what he saw to himself.

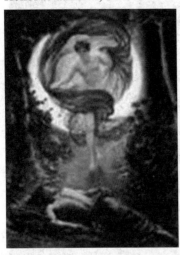

Selene, the moon, is Helios's sister. She also drives a chariot across the sky, though hers is made of silver and pulled by two horses. Selene is responsible for moonlight that shines through the night. She is beautiful and famous for her love affairs. Selene's most famous love affair is with **Endymion**, who may have been a shepherd, a hunter, or even a king. All versions of this myth agree, however, that Endymion was extremely handsome. Selene looked down upon him as he slept and fell instantly in love. She descended from the heavens and made love to him in his dreams. At Selene's request, Zeus offered Endymion one wish. He wished for eternal youth and was granted perpetual youth united with perpetual sleep.

Eos/Aurora, the dawn, is Helios's other sister. Every morning, Eos will rise from her golden throne, open the gates of heaven, and announce the coming of the sun. She also accompanies Helios in his journey across the sky. Eos's love life is even more famous than that of her sister, Selene. It will take hours to relate the tales of all her lovers. Eos's many unions result in some well known children. She is the mother of the Winds: **Boreas** (North), **Notus** (South), and **Zephyrus** (West). She also gave birth to Eosphorus (the Morning Star) and all the other stars in the heavens.

Aeolus, god of winds, is the son of Hippotes. He keeps all the winds inside a mountain, on a floating island called Aeolis or Aeolia, which is surrounded by a bronze wall. In fact, he is the king of this island, who has been made "keeper of the winds" by Zeus.

Cronus /Saturn

Cronus is the youngest of the 12 original Titans. He is also known in some myths as the god of time and agriculture. Cronus came to power by castrating his Father **Uranus.** His wife was Rhea. Their offspring were the first of the Olympians. To insure his safety Cronus ate each of the children as they were born. This worked until **Rhea**, unhappy at the loss of her children, tricked Cronus into swallowing a rock, instead of Zeus. When he grew up Zeus would revolt against Cronus and the other Titans, defeat them, and banish them to **Tartarus** in the underworld. Cronus managed to escape to Italy, where he ruled as **Saturn**. The period of his rule was said to be a golden age on earth, honored by the **Saturnalia** feast. In astrology the planet Saturn is associated with old age, disease, death, and misfortune, and those born under it are of "saturnine" or gloomy temperament.

Rhea/Ops/Cybele

Rhea is the mother of the gods, daughter of Uranus and Gaia. She is married to her brother Cronus and is the mother of Demeter, Hades, Hera, Hestia, Poseidon and Zeus. Rhea is identified with mother goddess **Cybele** from **Asia Minor** and is also known as Rhea Cybele and Magna Mater ("great mother"). She is worshipped with orgiastic rites and depicted between two lions or on a chariot pulled by lions.

Pan

He is the son of **Hermes** and **Penelope** (later married to Odysseus) in some myths and the son of Zeus and the **nymph Callisto** in others. He is the god of flocks and shepherds. He is mostly human in appearance but, with goat horns and goat feet. He is an excellent musician and plays the pipes. He is merry and playful frequently seen dancing with

woodland nymphs. He is at home in any wild place but, his favorite is **Arcady**, where he was born. He is always in pursuit of one of the nymphs but, always rejected because he is ugly.

His name is the basis for the word "panic". There are two differing explanations for this. The first is that he was present when Zeus defeated the Titans and claimed that it was his yelling that caused the Titans to flee. However, this seems at odds with his being Hermes son. The second is that he created the noises in the woods at night that scared travelers.

Nymphs, Satyrs, and Others

In Greek mythology, the Nymphs are spirits of nature. They range over beautiful groves and dwell near springs, in mountains through which rivers flow and in woods. They are portrayed as young, pretty girls, each subtype presiding over whichever aspect of nature they represent. Depending on where they reside, the Nymphs are as follows: **oceanids** and **nereids** are spirits of the sea, **oreads** of the mountains, **naiads** of lakes, streams, and fountains, **dryads** of trees. Though living for many years, Nymphs are nevertheless fated to die. A Tree Nymph lives as long as her tree, and a River Nymph likewise. Nymphs are often shown as lovers of gods and heroes, or as their mothers.

The male counterpart of a nymph is the **Satyr**. The satyrs are deities of the woods and mountains. They are half human and half beast; they usually have a goat's tail, flanks and hooves. While the upper part of the body is that of a human, they also have the horns of a goat. They can be best described as goat-men. They are the companions of **Dionysus**, the god of wine, and they spent their time drinking, dancing, and chasing nymphs.

The **Centaurs** of Greek mythology are creatures that are part human and part horse. They are usually portrayed with the torso and head of a human, and the body of a horse. Centaurs are the followers of the wine god Dionysus and are well known for drunkenness and carrying off helpless young maidens. They inhabit **Mount Pelion** in Thessaly, northern Greece. According to one myth, they are the offspring of **Ixion**, the king of Lapithae (Thessaly), and a cloud. Ixion had arranged a tryst with **Hera**, but Zeus got wind of it and fashioned a cloud into Hera's shape. Ixion slept with the

cloud and the cloud gave birth to the first Centaur. In Greek mythology they are, for the most part, savage and violent, embodiments of the animal side of human nature. An exception is the kind and wise centaur **Chiron**, the teacher of the Greek heroes Jason and Achilles.

The Fates

The **Fates,** who may be the most powerful of all, have the subtle but awesome power of deciding a man's destiny. Sometimes called the daughters of Night, sometimes of Zeus and **Themis**, they assign a man to good or evil. Their most obvious choice is choosing how long a man lives. There are three Fates: Clotho, the spinner, who spins the thread of life; Lachesis, the measurer, who choses the lot in life one will have and measures off how long it is to be; and Atropos, the inevitable, who relentlessly cuts the thread of life with her shears.

The Fates are old and predate the gods. It is not entirely clear how far their power extends. It is possible that they determine the fate of the gods as well. In any case, not even the most powerful is willing to trifle with them.

(Excerpted from http://thanasis.com/mythman/nymph.htm, http://www.pantheon.org/articles/s/satyrs.html, http://www.pantheon.org/articles/c/centaurs.html, http://www.netplaces.com/classical-mythology/out-of-chaos-creation/sun-moon-and-dawn.htm, http://www.pantheon.org/articles/r/rhea.html, http://www.legendscrolls.co.uk/greekgods)

Proper Nouns

1. **Hyperion** [haiˈpiəriən]：许珀里翁，提坦巨神之一；天神乌剌诺斯和盖亚之子。
2. **Thea** [ˈθiːə]：西娅，泰坦女神。
3. **Helios**：赫利乌斯，太阳神。
4. **Selene** [siˈliːnə]：塞勒涅，月神。
5. **Endymion** [enˈdimiən]：恩底弥翁，月之女神所爱的英俊牧童。
6. **Eos** [ˈiːɔs] / **Aurora** [ɔːˈrɔːrə]：厄俄斯/奥罗拉，黎明女神。
7. **Boreas** [ˈbɔriæs]：玻瑞阿斯，北风之神。
8. **Notus** [ˈnəutəs]：诺特斯，南风或西南风之神。
9. **Zephyrus** [ˈzefərəs]：仄费罗斯，西风之神。
10. **Aeolus** [ˈiːəuləs]：埃俄罗斯，风神。
11. **Cronus** [ˈkrəunəs]：克罗诺斯，提坦神之王。
12. **Saturn** [ˈsætən]：萨杜恩，农业之神；土星。
13. **Uranus** [ˈjuərənəs]：乌剌诺斯，天神。
14. **Rhea** [riə]：瑞亚，丰产女神，盖亚和乌剌诺斯所生十二提坦神之一。
15. **Tartarus** [ˈtɑːtərəs]：塔耳塔洛斯，地狱底下暗无天日的深渊；地狱。
16. **Saturnalia** [ˌsætəˈneiliə]：农神节（十二月中旬）。
17. **Ops** [ɔps]：俄普斯，播种和丰产女神，萨杜恩之妻，相当于希腊神话中的瑞亚。
18. **Cybele** [ˈsibəliː]：西布莉，古代小亚细亚人崇拜的自然女神，地位与瑞亚和俄普斯相当。
19. **Asia Minor**：小亚细亚。
20. **Pan**：潘，掌管树林、田地和羊群的神，有人的躯干和头，山羊的腿、角和耳朵。
21. **Hermes** [ˈhəːmiːz]：赫耳墨斯，商业、发明、灵巧之神；盗贼的保护神；众神的信使、书吏及报信者。

22. **Penelope** [piˈneləpi]：佩内洛普，奥德修斯的忠实妻子。
23. **Callisto** [kəˈlistəu]：卡利斯托，宙斯心爱的女神，被赫拉所憎恨并被她变为一只熊。
24. **Arcady** [ˈɑːkədi]：阿卡迪亚，古希腊一山区，世外桃源。
25. **Nymph** [nimf]：居于山林水泽的仙女。
26. **Oceanid** [əuˈsiːənid]：海洋女神，指俄刻阿诺斯和忒堤斯的3000个女儿中的任何一个。
27. **Nereid** [ˈniəriid]：海中仙女，海神涅柔斯的50个女儿之一。
28. **Oread** [ˈɔːriæd]：山岳女神。
29. **Naiad** [ˈnaiæd]：掌管河、泉的水泽女神。
30. **Dryad** [ˈdraiəd]：树神，又称护树神女。
31. **Satyr** [ˈsætə]：萨梯，森林之神，具部分人身和部分马、羊身，好女色。
32. **Centaur** [ˈsentɔː]：半人马座；人首马身的怪物。
33. **Dionysus** [ˌdaiəˈnaisəs]：狄俄倪索斯，丰饶之神以及酒神。
34. **Mount Pelion** [ˈpiːliən]：珀利翁山。
35. **Ixion** [ikˈsaiən]：伊克西翁，拉庇泰国王；因企图对赫拉无理，宙斯将他缚在旋转的车轮上，永久在冥土受罚。
36. **Hera** [ˈhiərə]：赫拉，天后，主神宙斯之妻。
37. **Chrion** [ˈkaiərən]：半人半马的聪明博学的怪物。
38. **The Fates**：命运三女神，掌管大地上所有人的命运。
39. **Themis** [ˈθiːmis]：忒弥斯，泰坦族女巨人，司法律和正义的女神。

After You Read

Knowledge Focus

1. Solo Work: Matching. Draw a line to match the Greek god or creature with the description.

1) Helios   a. wind god
2) Selene   b. horned and hoofed god
3) Aeolus   c. sun god
4) Cronus   d. moon goddess
5) Pan   e. father of Zeus
6) centaur   f. dawn goddess
7) nymphs   g. female spirits
8) Rhea   h. gods controlling human fates
9) Eos   i. creature with a horse's body and a human torso
10) Fates   j. wife of Cronus

2. Solo Work: True or False. Identify the following statements, please correct the false ones.

1) (　　) The gods of Sun, Moon, Dawn and Winds are siblings.
2) (　　) Cronus suffered the same punishment as he did to his father Uranus.
3) (　　) People born under Saturn are apt to have good fortune astrologically.
4) (　　) Zeus is the son of Gaia, who is known as mother of the gods.
5) (　　) Pan always fails in pursuit of lovers because he is a terrible musician.

6) (   ) Nymphs, though long-lived, will die if the place they inhabit is destroyed.
7) (   ) Nymphs are actually long-lived human women.
8) (   ) The first centaur was the child of Ixion and Hera.
9) (   ) The centaurs tend to be humane in many respects.
10) (   ) The three Fates control human destinies. Even gods might well be afraid of them.

Language Focus
1. **Fill in the blanks with the words or expressions you have learned from the text; change the form when necessary.**

associate	identify	diverse	version	grant
honor	panic	minor	immortal	descend

1) The best way to discourage pirating is to offer a _____ range of attractive, legal alternatives.
2) In one _____ of the story, a country with a lot of poor people suddenly experiences fast economic expansion, but only half of the people share in the new prosperity.
3) She _____ herself with good company.
4) He requested that the Premier _____ him an interview.
5) Never _____ wealth with happiness.
6) Happiness is not about being _____ nor having food or rights in one's hand.
7) I can teach you respect, but I cannot force you to show _____.
8) The financial _____ is indeed over, as it should be, given the scale of government guarantees.
9) To be sure there was always the next station, where one might _____ and return.
10) No one was hurt and only _____ damage was reported.

2. **Fill in the blanks with the proper form of the words in brackets.**
1) Humans' creativity should _____ (embodiment) in the natural protection not the natural destruction.
2) Gossip cheapens the one who gossips more than the one _____ (gossip) about.
3) _____ (eternal) is not a distance but a decision.
4) Medicine is her _____ (destiny) profession.
5) They say I am the smartest man in the world, but the truth is I have often felt stupid at being unable to _____ (relate) to anybody.
6) The _____ (worship) of the golden calf is the characteristic cult of modern society.
7) _____ (pursuit) a dream job is less a leap than a series of incremental steps that move you closer to your goal.
8) Whatever the man called every living _____ (create), that was its name.
9) Wisdom too often never comes, and so one ought not to _____ (reject) it merely because it comes late.
10) A true critic ought to _____ (dwell) rather upon excellencies than imperfections.

3. **Fill in the blanks with the proper prepositions or adverbs that collocate with the neighboring words.**

1) He is not a people person. He likes to keep _____ himself and when he is in a group, he does not talk so much.

2) When a patient in agony dies, then a doctor's true calling implies, one should do what is best, _____ the patient's request, for humane, quick and painless demise.

3) The sister cried her eyes out _____ the loss of a golden educational opportunity.

4) Love means identify _____ the person I love.

5) Generally speaking, young people are inclined to adore the people who excel _____ appearance, intelligence or talent.

6) The Night Stalker is _____ home at night. He attacks and moves more swiftly.

7) If you wish _____ peace, be prepared for war.

8) It is incorrect to think of creation and destruction as being _____ odds with each other.

9) Many are stubborn in pursuit _____ the path they have chosen, few in pursuit _____ the goal.

10) Men trifle _____ their business and their politics, but they never trifle _____ their games.

4. **Proofreading: The following passage contains ten errors. Each indicated line contains a maximum of one error. In each case, only ONE word is involved. Read the passage and correct the errors.**

    Aethra and her father begged Theseus to go to Athens on sea, for horrible robbers and bandits inhabited in the road, but Theseus was bold and went overland. ... Theseus started walking again. Not much farther he saw a giant man held a battle-ax on the side of the road. "I am Sciron and these are my cliffs. To pass you must wash my feet like a toll!" the man said. "What would happen if I did?" replied Theseus. "I will chop off your head with this ax, and don't think that puny little twig you're carrying will save you, you're absolutely... WRONG!!!!" Sciron yelled.

    So Theseus sat down but started to wash Sciron's feet. Theseus looked over the side of the cliff, there was a monstrous turtle on the bottom. Then Theseus knew that this was the Sciron what kicked people off the cliff which a man-eating turtle waited. Where Sciron's foot came towards him, Theseus jerked aside and hurled Sciron off the cliff.

(1) _____
(2) _____
(3) _____
(4) _____
(5) _____
(6) _____
(7) _____
(8) _____
(9) _____
(10) _____

Comprehensive Work

1. **Translation.** Read the story—The Apple of Discord, and then retell it in English.

不和果

    珀琉斯和海神忒提斯结婚时邀请了所有的神祇。但是，显然有一位女神不在邀请之列，她就是厄里斯——不和女神。由于她在所到之处播撒不和之种，很自然，人们并不希望她出席婚宴。理所当然，厄里斯为此感到愤怒。她决定嘲弄宴会上的众神。当新娘、新郎退场后，厄里斯偷偷溜进了大厅，向地上抛出了一个金苹果，上书"献给最美的人"。苹果在赫拉、雅典娜和阿佛洛狄忒三位女神间引起了激烈争执。宙斯明智地决定将她们送到爱达山上一位名叫帕里斯的牧童那里，让他来判断谁最美。赫耳墨斯作为使者，手持金苹果，领着三位女神出发了。

　　帕里斯是特洛伊国王皮安姆的儿子,由于他母亲在他出生时梦到自己正手持一根燃烧的断木,于是人们认为婴儿会给城市带来毁灭。为了挽救王朝,免受可能之灾,国王及王后把孩子扔到了爱达山上。但是,孩子幸运地逃离了死亡。在牧人们的精心抚养下,孩子长得既强壮又英俊。他偷偷地与奥诺妮,一位漂亮忠诚的山神结了婚。那一天,帕里斯正在山腰照看他的羊群,他惊奇地发现四个人正在他面前。赫耳墨斯给他布置了任务后离去了。三位美丽的女神立即互相争吵起来,并且充分向牧童显示自己的美貌。赫拉许诺要使他成为亚洲国王;雅典娜愿意帮助他在战争中得到不朽的荣誉;而阿佛洛狄忒则答应他得到世上最美丽女人的爱。男孩原始的本性被激发了出来,阿佛洛狄忒蒂得到了金苹果,而另两位女神则怒气冲冲地离去了,并成了特洛伊城最可怕的敌人。

(珀琉斯:Peleus; 忒提斯:Thetis; 厄里斯:Eris; 帕里斯:Paris; 皮安姆:Priam; 奥诺妮:Oenone)

2. **Offering Suggestions.** As queen of the Olympian gods, Hera enjoys unchallenged honor. Nonetheless, she gets much irritated by her husband's cheating after cheating. Now Hera is facing two diverged ways: to let things slide, or to leave her husband for good. Which way do you suggest her to take? Offer sound reasons to convince her.

Ancient Greek and Roman Mythology

Read More

Text B The Wood-Folk

PAN led a merrier life than all the other gods together. He was beloved alike by shepherds and countrymen, and by the fauns and satyrs, birds and beasts, of his own kingdom. The care of flocks and herds was his, and for home he had all the world of woods and waters; he was lord of everything out-of-doors! Yet he felt the burden of it no more than he felt the shadow of a leaf when he danced, but spent the days in laughter and music among his fellows. Like him, the fauns and satyrs had furry, pointed ears, and little horns that sprouted above their brows; in fact, they were all enough like wild creatures to seem no strangers to anything untamed. They slept in the sun, piped in the shade, and lived on wild grapes and the nuts that every squirrel was ready to share with them.

The woods were never lonely. A man might wander away into those solitudes and think himself friendless; but here and there a river knew, and a tree could tell, a story of its own. Beautiful creatures they were, that for one reason or another had left off human shape. Some had been transformed against their will, that they might do no more harm to their fellow men. Some were changed through the pity of the gods, that they might share the simple life of Pan, mindless of mortal cares, glad in rain and sunshine, and always close to the heart of the Earth.

There was Dryope, for instance, the lotus-tree. Once a careless, happy woman, walking among the trees with her sister Iole and her own baby, she had broken a lotus that held a live nymph hidden, and blood dripped from the wounded plant. Too late, Dryope saw her heedlessness; and there her steps had taken root, and there she had said good-bye to her child, and prayed Iole to bring him sometimes to play beneath her shadow. Poor mother-tree! Perhaps she took comfort with the birds and gave a kindly shelter to some nest.

There, too, was Echo, once a wood-nymph who angered the goddess Juno with her waste of words, and was compelled now to wait till others spoke, and then to say nothing but their last word, like any mocking-bird. One day she saw and loved the youth Narcissus, who was searching the woods for his hunting companions. "Come here!" he called, and Echo cried "Here!" eager to speak at last. "Here am I,—come!" he repeated, looking about for the voice. "I come," said Echo, and she stood before him. But the youth, angry at such mimicry, only stared at her and hastened away. From that time she faded to a voice, and to this day she lurks hidden and silent till you call.

But Narcissus himself was destined to fall in love

with a shadow. For, leaning over the edge of a brook one day, he saw his own beautiful face looking up at him like a water nymph. He leaned nearer, and the face rose towards him, but when he touched the surface it was gone in a hundred ripples. Day after day he besought the lovely creature to have pity and to speak; but it mocked him with his own tears and smiles, and he forgot all else, till he changed into a flower that leans over to see its image in the pool.

There, too, was the sunflower Clytie, once a maiden who thought nothing so beautiful as the sun god Phæbus Apollo. All the day long she used to look after him as he journeyed across the heavens in his golden chariot, till she came to be a fair rooted plant that ever turns its head to watch the sun.

Many others were there: Daphne the laurel, Hyacinthus (once a beautiful youth, slain by mischance), who lives and renews his bloom as a flower, —these and a hundred others. The very weeds were friendly…

But there were wise, immortal voices in certain caves and trees. Men called them Oracles; for here the gods spoke in answer to the prayers of folk in sorrow or bewilderment. Sometimes they built a temple around such a befriending voice, and kings would journey far to hear it speak.

As for Pan, only one grief had he, and in the end a glad thing came of it.

One day, when he was loitering in Arcadia, he saw the beautiful wood nymph Syrinx. She was hastening to join Diana at the chase, and she herself was as swift and lovely as any bright bird that one longs to capture. So Pan thought, and he hurried after to tell her. But Syrinx turned, caught one glimpse of the god's shaggy locks and bright eyes, and the two little horns on his head (he was much like a wild thing, at a look), and she sprang away down the path in terror.

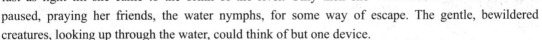

Begging her to listen, Pan followed; and Syrinx, more and more frightened by the patter of his hoofs, never heeded him, but went as fast as light till she came to the brink of the river. Only then she paused, praying her friends, the water nymphs, for some way of escape. The gentle, bewildered creatures, looking up through the water, could think of but one device.

Just as the god overtook Syrinx and stretched out his arms to her, she vanished like a mist, and he found himself grasping a cluster of tall reeds. Poor Pan!

The breeze that sighed whenever he did—and oftener—shook the reeds and made a sweet little sound, a sudden music. Pan heard it, half consoled.

"Is it your voice, Syrinx?" he said. "Shall we sing together?"

He bound a number of reeds side by side; to this day, shepherds know how. He blew across the hollow pipes and they made music!

(Excerpted from *Old Greek Folk Stories Told Anew* by Josephine Preston Peabody)

Questions for Reflection

1. Write down detailed answers for these questions.

   1) What were Pan's responsibilities?

   2) Pan was greatly burdened by his duty, wasn't he?

2. What was Pan's wood like? Describe it following the hints.

fauns & satyrs	story, human shape	Dryope, the lotus-tree
Echo, a wood nymph	Narcissus	Clytie, the sunflower
Oracles, immortal voices		Syrinx, Pan's only grief

Text C The Judgement of Midas

PAN came at length to be such a wonderful piper with his syrinx (for so he named his flute) that he challenged Apollo to make better music if he could. Now the sun god was also the greatest of divine musicians, and resolving to punish the vanity of the country-god, and so he consented to the test. For judge they chose the mountain Tmolus, since no one is so old and wise as the hills. And, since Tmolus could not leave his home, to him went Pan and Apollo, each with his followers, oreads and dryads, fauns, satyrs, and centaurs.

Among the worshippers of Pan was a certain Midas, who had a strange story. Once a king of great wealth, he had chanced to befriend Dionysus, god of the vine; and when he was asked to choose some good gift in return, he prayed that everything he touched might be turned into gold. Dionysus smiled a little when he heard this foolish prayer, but he granted it. Within two days, King Midas learned the secret of that smile, and begged the god to take away the gift that was a curse. He had touched everything that belonged to him, and little joy did he have of his possessions! His palace was as yellow a home as a dandelion to a bee, but not half so sweet. Row on row of stiff golden trees stood in his garden; they no longer knew a breeze when they heard it. When he sat down to eat, his feast turned to treasure uneatable. He learned that a king may starve, and he came to see that gold cannot replace the live, warm gifts of the Earth. Kindly Dionysus took back the

charm, but from that day King Midas so hated gold that he chose to live far from luxury, among the woods and fields. Even here he was not to go free from misadventure.

Tmolus gave the word, and Pan uprose with his syrinx, and blew on the reeds a melody so wild and yet so coaxing that the squirrels came, as if at a call, and the birds hopped down in rows. The trees swayed with a longing to dance, and the fauns looked at one another and laughed for joy. To

their furry little ears, it was the sweetest music that could be.

But Tmolus bowed before Apollo, and the sun god rose with his golden lyre in his hands. As he moved, light shook out of his radiant hair as raindrops are showered from the leaves. His trailing robes were purple, like the clouds that temper the glory of a sunset, so that one may look on it. He touched the strings of his lyre, and all things were silent with joy. He made music, and the woods dreamed. The fauns and satyrs were quite still; and the wild creatures crouched, blinking, under a charm of light that they could not understand. To hear such music cease was like bidding farewell to father and mother.

With one accord they fell at the feet of Apollo, and Tmolus proclaimed the victory his. Only one voice disputed that award.

Midas refused to acknowledge Apollo lord of music—perhaps because the looks of the god dazzled his eyes unpleasantly, and put him in mind of his foolish wish years before. For him there was no music in a golden lyre!

But Apollo would not leave such dull ears unpunished. At a word from him they grew long, pointed, furry, and able to turn this way and that (like a poplar leaf), —a plain warning to musicians. Midas had the ears of an ass, for every one to see!

For a long time the poor man hid this oddity with such skill that we might never have heard of it. But one of his servants learned the secret, and suffered so much from keeping it to himself that he had to unburden his mind at last. Out into the meadows he went, hollowed a little place in the turf, whispered the strange news into it quite softly, and heaped the earth over again. Alas! A bed of reeds sprang up there before long, and whispered in turn to the grass-blades. Year after year they grew again, ever gossiping among themselves; and to this day, with every wind that sets them nodding together, they murmur, laughing, "Midas has the ears of an ass: Oh, hush, hush!"

(Excerpted from *Old Greek Folk Stories Told Anew* by Josephine Preston Peabody)

Questions for Reflection
1. How did the story happen?
2. Where did the story happen?
3. Who was a better musician?
4. What was Midas's judgment? What led to his judgment?
5. What did Midas' judgment bring?

Websites to Visit

http://www.ecsis.net/fantasy/RealmsFantasy/Ocean/Clytie.html

The complete story of Clytie is offered here. To fall in love with someone unreachable is a tragic, yet a beautiful legend to be told. Visit this website if you have interest.

http://thanasis.com/helios.htm

To know more about Helios, the sun god, the tragedy of his son Phaethon, and other short stories, please visit this website.

Unit 6
Myths of Origin

> I believe that imagination is stronger than knowledge— myth is more potent than history—dreams are more powerful than facts—hope always triumphs over experience—laughter is the cure for grief—love is stronger than death
>
> —Robert Fulghum

Unit Goals

- To know the beginning of the Greek Pantheon
- To know what the ancient Greeks believed about how the world began
- To be able to tell the legendary origin of vampire
- To learn about the legendary Chiron
- To learn the words and phrases that describe Greek Gods
- To improve language skills and critical thinking through the content of this unit

Before You Read

1. Have you ever wondered how the world got started? Discuss how the other ancient civilizations (excluding the ancient Greece because you will learn it in Text A) made up stories to explain the world. Write your findings down in the form.

Ancient Civilization	Its Creation Myth

2. Which of these creation myths in your discussion is the most fascinating? Do you find these legends have interesting similarities or big differences?

Start to Read

Text A Myths of Origin

The Origins of the Gods

In the beginning, there was **Chaos** until **Erebus** and night came from the void. Erebus is the unknowable place where death lives. Everything else was silent endless darkness until love Eros was born bringing the beginning of order. From love came light and day. Once there was light and day, **Gaia**, the Earth appeared. Erebus and night made ether, heavenly light, and Day earthly light. Night alone made the things that come to man out of darkness doom, fate, death, sleep, dreams, and **Nemesis**. Gaia birthed **Uranus**, the sky god. Uranus was Gaia's mate because sky covers the Earth completely. Gaia and Uranus's union resulted in the three **Cyclopes**, three **Hecatoncheires** and the twelve **Titans**.

Uranus hated Hecatoncheires and pushed them into the hidden places of the earth. Gaia furious at this imprisonment of her children plotted to overthrow Uranus. She made a flint sickle and encouraged her children to attack Uranus. They were all afraid, save the youngest titan, Cronus. Cronus castrated his father with the sickle whilst he slept. There are conflicting stories of what happened to Uranus—he either died, withdrew from the earth, or exiled himself to Italy. On departing, Uranus promised that Cronus and Titans would suffer. From Uranus's spilt blood, the Giants, the Ash tree nymphs, and the **three Furies** emerged. **Aphrodite** was born from the sea foam where Uranus's genitals hit the ocean.

Cronus took the throne of the gods, imprisoning the Cyclopes and Hecatoncheires in **Tartarus**, which was deep in the Earth, even below **Hades**, and was the ultimate prison. Cronus married his sister **Rhea** and ruled the Titans, who had many children during his rule. Both Gaia and Uranus had prophesied that a son would overthrow Cronus so Cronus swallowed each of his own children as they were born. Rhea, naturally, objected to this and, when the time came for her sixth child to be born, hid from Cronus and left the child with the nymphs. She then wrapped a stone in swaddling clothes and gave to Cronus, who, thinking that it was the baby, swallowed it.

That child was **Zeus**, who grew up into a handsome young man on **Crete**. Zeus consulted **Metis**, Titaness of the fourth day and the planet **Mercury**, who governed all wisdom and knowledge, on how to overcome Cronus. She made an emetic drink for Cronus to recover Zeus's five siblings.

Rhea prevailed on Cronus to accept his son and, eventually, Cronus made Zeus his cupbearer on Mount Olympus. Being Cronus's cupbearer allowed Zeus to slip Cronus the emetic drink. The other five children emerged unharmed from Cronus, and were so grateful to Zeus that they made him their leader.

Cronus and the Titans, excepting **Prometheus**, **Epimetheus** and **Oceanus**, led by **Atlas** fought to retain power. For some time, it looked as though the young gods would lose, but Zeus went to Tartarus and freed the Cyclopes and Hecatoncheires and they along with Prometheus joined Zeus. The Cyclopes gave Zeus lightening bolts to use as weapons. Zeus then feigned a retreat, drawing the Titans into an ambush, where the Hecatoncheires were waiting to shower them furiously with boulders. The Titans, thinking the mountains were falling on them, broke and ran, giving Zeus the victory.

Victory did not bring peace, however. Gaia, mother of the Titans was angry when Zeus imprisoned her children. She gave birth to her final child, **Typhoeus**, a monster so frightening that most gods fled. Zeus was able to kill Typhoeus with lightning bolts. Typhoeus is buried under Mount Etna in Sicily.

The final challenge to The Olympians and Zeus's rule came much later, when the Giants attempted to invade mount Olympus by piling mountains up, to try to reach the summit. The Olympians, with Heracles's help defeated the giants. Zeus then imprisoned the giants in Tartarus.

The Origins of Humankind

Prometheus and Epimetheus were spared imprisonment in Tatarus because they had not fought with their fellow Titans during the war with the Olympians. They were given the task of creating man. Prometheus shaped man out of mud, and **Athena** breathed life into his clay figure.

Prometheus had assigned Epimetheus the task of giving the creatures of the earth their various qualities, such as swiftness, cunning, strength, fur, wings. Unfortunately, by the time he got to man Epimetheus had given all the good qualities out and there were none left for man. So Prometheus decided to make man stand upright as the gods did and to give them fire.

Prometheus loved man more than the Olympians, who had banished most of his family to Tartarus. So when Zeus decreed that man must present a portion of each animal to be sacrificed to the gods Prometheus decided to trick Zeus. He created two piles, one with the bones wrapped in juicy fat, and the other with the good meat hidden in the hide. He then bade Zeus to pick. Zeus picked the bones. Since he had given his word Zeus had to accept that as his share for future sacrifices. In his anger over the trick he took fire away from man. However, Prometheus lit a torch from the sun and brought it back again to man. Zeus was enraged that man again had fire. He decided to inflict a terrible punishment on both man and Prometheus.

To punish man, Zeus had **Hephaestus** create a mortal of stunning beauty. The gods gave the mortal many gifts of wealth. He then had **Hermes** give the mortal a deceptive heart and a lying tongue. This

creation was **Pandora**, the first woman. A final gift was a jar which Pandora was forbidden to open. Then Zeus sent Pandora down to Epimetheus, brother of Prometheus, who was staying amongst the men. In spite of his brother's warning not to receive any present from Zeus, Epimetheus was ensnared by Pandora's charms and took her to wife.

Eventually, Pandora's curiosity about the jar she was forbidden to open became too great. She opened the jar and out flew all manner of evils, sorrows, plagues and misfortunes, before unknown to man, and spread all over the earth. However, the bottom of the jar held one good thing—hope.

Zeus was angry at Prometheus for three things: being tricked on sacrifices, stealing fire for man, and for refusing to tell Zeus which of Zeus's children would dethrone him. Zeus had his servants, Force and Violence, seize Prometheus, take him to the **Caucasus Mountains**, and chain him to a rock with unbreakable chains. Here he was tormented day and night by a giant eagle tearing at his liver. Zeus gave Prometheus two ways out of this torment. He could tell Zeus who the mother of the child that would dethrone him was. Or meet two conditions: First, that an immortal must volunteer to die for Prometheus. Second, that a mortal must kill the eagle and unchain him. Eventually, Chiron the Centaur agreed to die for him and Heracles killed the eagle and unbound him.

As time passed, Zeus became increasingly disgusted with the hubris of the human race, and eventually, he resolved to wipe it out in a great Flood and start again. **Deucalion**, son of Prometheus, and his wife **Pyrrha**, daughter of Epimetheus, were the sole survivors. They were saved because of their piety. Prometheus advised his son to build an ark and they survived by staying on the boat. When they were finally able to get back on land, they gave thank offerings to Zeus and consulted the oracle of **Themis** how they might replenish the earth with humans once again. They were told to throw the bones of their mother behind their shoulder and the human race would reappear. Since the mother of all is Earth, they threw stones and reformed the human race. The stones thrown by Pyrrha became women; those thrown by Deucalion became men.

When talking about the mythical history of the world, the concept of the Four Ages of Man cannot be bypassed. According to **Hesiod** and **Ovid**, human history has passed through four ages—Golden, Silver, Bronze and Iron. The Golden Age was just how it sounded—Golden. This took place during the reign of Cronus. Peace and harmony prevailed during this age. Humans did not grow old, but died peacefully. Spring was eternal and people were fed on acorns from a great oak as well as wild fruits and honey that dripped from the trees. Then followed the Silver Age, when the seasons began and agriculture and work were invented. People lived for one hundred years as children without growing up, and then they suddenly aged and died. Zeus destroyed these people because of their impiety. Men of the Bronze Age were hard. War was their purpose and passion. And their tools and implements were made of bronze. Finally, in the Iron Age, in which we now live, people are warlike, greedy and impious. Truth, modesty and loyalty are nowhere to be found.

The Four Ages of Man demonstrates the descending

progression of mankind. The symbolism can be seen through the decreasing value of the metals that are associated with each period in time.

(Excerpted from http://www.brighthub.com/society/cultures-customs/articles/102041.aspx, http://www.greekmythology.com/Myths/The_Myths/Creation_of_Man_by_Prometheus/creation_of_man_by_prometheus.html)

Proper Nouns

1. **Chaos** [ˈkeiɔs]: 卡俄斯, 即"混沌", 希腊神话中最古老的神。
2. **Erebus** [ˈeribəs]: 厄瑞玻斯, 混沌之子, 永久黑暗的化身; 阳界与阴界中的黑暗界。
3. **Gaia** [geiə]: 盖亚, 大地女神。
4. **Nemesis** [ˈnemisis]: 涅墨西斯, 复仇女神。
5. **Uranus** [ˈjuərənəs]: 乌剌诺斯, 天神。
6. **Cyclopes** [saiˈklɔupiːz]: 库克罗普斯, 独眼巨人。
7. **Hecatoncheires** [hekətɔnˈkairiːz]: 百臂巨人。
8. **Titans**: 提坦诸神, 盖亚和乌剌诺斯的十二个子女; 也指这十二位子女的后代。
9. **the Furies**: 复仇女神三姐妹, 乌剌诺斯的三滴鲜血掉到地上而形成。
10. **Aphrodite** [ˌæfrəuˈdaiti]: 阿佛洛狄忒, 爱与美的女神, 相当于罗马神话中的维纳斯。
11. **Tartarus** [ˈtɑːtərəs]: 塔耳塔洛斯, 冥府底下暗无天日的深渊, 为宙斯禁闭提坦之处。
12. **Hades** [ˈheidiːz]: 冥府, 地狱; 冥神, 掌管冥界。
13. **Rhea** [riə]: 瑞亚, 众神之母。
14. **Zeus** [zjuːs]: 宙斯, 希腊众神之神, 奥林匹亚的主神。
15. **Crete** [kriːt]: 克里特岛, 地中海东部的希腊岛屿。
16. **Metis** [ˈmiːtis]: 墨提斯, 宙斯的第一位妻子。
17. **Mercury** [ˈməːkjuri]: 水星。
18. **Prometheus** [prəuˈmiːθiəs]: 普罗米修斯, 提坦神族的神明之一, 名字的意思是先觉者, 能预知未来。
19. **Epimetheus** [ˌepiˈmiːθiːəs]: 厄庇墨透斯, 普罗米修斯之弟。
20. **Oceanus** [əuˈsiənəs]: 俄克阿诺斯, 海洋之神。
21. **Atlas** [ˈætləs]: 阿特拉斯, 受罚以双肩掮天的巨人。
22. **Typhoeus** [taiˈfəujuːs]: 堤福俄斯, 百头巨怪。
23. **Hercules** [ˈhəːkjuliːz]: 赫剌克勒斯, 大力神, 宙斯之子。
24. **Athena** [əˈθiːnə]: 雅典娜, 智慧、技艺、勤俭和战争女神。
25. **Hephaestus** [hiˈfiːstəs]: 赫淮斯托斯, 司火、冶金之神。
26. **Hermes** [ˈhəːmiːz]: 赫耳墨斯, 商业、发明、灵巧之神; 盗贼的保护神; 众神的信使、书吏及报信者。
27. **Pandora** [pænˈdɔːrə]: 潘多拉, 意思为"被赋予一切天赋的"。
28. **Caucasus** ([ˈkɔːkəsəs]) Mountains: 高加索山脉。
29. **Deucalion** [djuːˈkeiljən]: 丢卡利翁。
30. **Pyrrha** [ˈpirə]: 皮拉。
31. **Themis** [ˈθiːmis]: 忒弥斯, 乌拉诺斯和盖亚之女, 司法律和正义的女神。
32. **Hesiod** [ˈhiːsiɔd]: 赫西奥德, 公元前8世纪希腊诗人。
33. **Ovid** [ˈɔvid]: 奥维德, 古罗马诗人。

Ancient Greek and Roman Mythology

After You Read

Knowledge Focus

1. Solo Work: Guess who I am in the Greek mythology?

1) I am the most ancient of gods, the personification of the infinity of space. I am _____.	2) I gave birth to the sky and the sea, and I am mother of the Titans. I am _____.
3) Our father had a fight with one of his sons, and three drops of our father's blood fell on the earth and then we were born. We are tasked to punish crime. I am _____.	4) I overthrew my father and took his place. Then I worried that my children would do the same thing to me, so I devoured them as soon as they were born. I am _____.
5) My father would have eaten me at my birth; luckily I was secretly transferred to a safe island, where I was brought up by nymphs. I am _____.	6) I love the mankind. I even created part of them. And I gave them fire. I am _____.
7) I was terribly stupid, and hence opened a box which Hermes instructed me not to open. I am _____.	8) I am the only lucky man to survive the Great Flood. On the way running away from the Flood, together with my wife, we made humans out of stones. I am _____.

2. Solo Work: Complete the family tree of Greek gods.

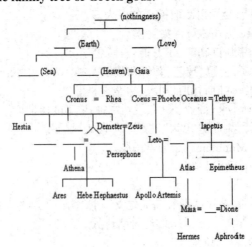

3. **Pair Work: Discuss the following questions with your partner.**
   1) How did Cronus come into power?
   2) How did Zeus come into power?
   3) Why was man given the gift of standing upright?
   4) What led to Gods' creation of Pandora?
   5) How was man created for the second time?
   6) What are the features of the Four Ages of Man?

Language Focus

1. **Fill in the blanks with the words in the bank; there's no need to change the form of any of them.**

plotted	objected	chaos	grief	save
spare	conflicting	exile	retreat	ultimate

   1) Melissa _____ that nobody had asked her opinion.
   2) Reading books provide comfortable, quiet places to _____ to and curl up with a good book.
   3) He has skillfully _____ and schemed his way to the top, using power to win power.
   4) The variations are usually random and chaotic, but there is occasionally order within the _____.
   5) They often make _____ demands that managers must struggle to reconcile.
   6) He would have gone, _____ that he had no means.
   7) Indeed, many college students do not select their _____ career path until after they graduate.
   8) Everyone is born king, and most people die in _____.
   9) Not a moment to _____. I don't even have time to breathe.
   10) Time dulls the most exquisite emotions and softens the most heartrending _____.

2. **Complete the sentences with the right verb phrases; change the form of the verbs when necessary.**
   1) Tom _____ _____ where his father left off. (take)
   2) Loyalty, some people feel it means that, no matter what, your friend will always _____ _____ _____ . (take)
   3) It is possible to _____ the brain _____ _____ (feel) romantic love in a long-term relationship by doing novel things with your partner. (trick)
   4) The actor _____ _____ admiration from the public. (feed)
   5) When one asks oneself this question, many explanations _____ _____ in the mind. We are so concerned with ourselves—that is one explanation. (spring)

3. **Fill in the blanks with the proper prepositions or adverbs that collocate with the neighboring words.**
   1) I object _____ violence because when it appears to do good, the good is only temporary. The evil it does is permanent.
   2) Without a conductive setting, a few experts and enthusiasts are not enough to breathe life _____ the language.

3) It is hard to be angry _____ such happy men.

4) It is not a time for homeowners to panic. Any price declines are unlikely to wipe _____ their gains of recent years.

5) What type of people would you least like to associate _____?

6) Faith does not feed _____ thin air but on facts.

4. **Proofreading:** The following passage contains ten errors. Each indicated line contains a maximum of one error. In each case, only ONE word is involved. Read the passage and correct the errors.

That evening when the courtiers sat feasted in the palace and the minstrel arose (1) _____
to sing, Iobates bade him tell the tale of Phaethon, which tried to equal the (2) _____
immortals by driving the chariot of the sun. Then as the minstrel's tale came to an
end, and Phaethon fell from heaven in a trail of gleaming fire, the king turned to his
chief guest and drank a toast to him, said, "Tell me, Bellerophon, do you think that (3) _____
Phaethon was wise? He aspired to like a god, and though he failed, his end was (4) _____
glorious, but he has become a hero of song. Would you not rather try some (5) _____
impossible feat and die than rest content at the knowledge that there were things you (6) _____
dared not do?"

"I dare do all things," answered the young Bellerophon, with his blue eyes (7) _____
sparkled. "I dare even mount to Olympus and battle with the gods. What matter if I
fail? I shall still die a hero because of I aimed for mighty deeds." (8) _____

"Then do a deed for me," Iobatess leaned forward quickly. "Rid me of the
monster that no man in my kingdom dares to face. Kill me the Chimera."...

As Bellerophon said goodnight to his host, both men were well pleased. To
Iobates it seemed most likely that the Chimera would kill Bellerophon and
accomplish the desire of King Proitos. If not, however, at most the kingdom of Lycia
would be rid of the dreadful beast. Bellerophon at his side was glad at the thought of (9) _____
the great adventure. In his mind was already a plan by which he might approach the (10) _____
monster. He hoped to capture first the horse, Pegasus, and with his aid to conquer
the Chimera.

Comprehensive Work

1. **Writing Practice.** Suppose you are Prometheus and write a letter to Zeus to persuade him to allow you to give fire to humans. You must give at least three reasons why Zeus should grant you the permission.

2. Debating. The myth of Pandora sheds light on the always contentious notions of hope and optimism. Look what Friedrich Nietzsche, the late German philosopher, said about this matter:

In reality, hope is the worst of all evils, because it prolongs man's torments.

Now divide the whole class into 2 groups and debate around whether hope is a good thing. The teacher will be the arbitrator. Take down the remarkable arguments on both sides that impressed you.

The Supporting Party: Hope Is Good!	The Opposing Party: Hope Is Evil!

Text B The Vampire Origin Story

Ambrogio was a young adventurer. Born and raised in Italy, he had always longed to travel to Greece to have his fortune told by the Oracle of Delphi. When he was an adult, he got on a boat and sailed to the western edge of Greece, near Astakos. He traveled east until he eventually reached the city of Delphi.

Delphi was home to a great temple of Apollo, the sun god. It was also the home of the Pythia, better known as the Oracles. The Pythia would sit in a chamber within the temple and speak of prophecies, inspired by Apollo, to those who came to seek the Oracle's wisdom.

When Ambrogio finally arrived at the temple, he went to speak to the Pythia. The Pythia, whose words were often cryptic, said only a few words: "The curse. The moon. The blood will run."

He couldn't sleep that night. He stayed awake outside of the temple, pondering the meaning of the Pythia's words. As the sun rose in the morning he realized that he had not slept. As he walked back toward the town he saw a beautiful woman dressed in white robes walking to the temple. He ran over to her and introduced himself.

Her name was Selene, and she was a maiden of the temple. Her sister was the Oracle, and so Selene tended to the temple and took care of her sister while in her entranced state.

For the next few days every morning Ambrogio met Selene at dawn before she entered the temple. They soon fell in love.

On his last day in Greece, Ambrogio asked Selene to marry him and return with him to Italy. She agreed. He said he would make the preparations then meet her at dawn the next morning at their meeting spot outside the temple.

Apollo, the sun god, had been watching. He, himself, had taken a liking to the beautiful Selene and was enraged that Ambrogio would come to his temple and take one of his maidens away. At sunset that night, Apollo appeared to Ambrogio and cursed him so that from that day forth a mere touch of Apollo's sunlight would burn Ambrogio's skin.

Ambrogio was distraught. He was set to leave with Selene in the morning, but he would not be able to meet her at sunrise as he promised because of the curse. Having nowhere else to turn, he ran to a cave that led to Hades for protection. Hades, god of the underworld, listened to his tale and made him a deal—if he could steal the sliver bow of Artemis and bring it back, Hades would grant him and Selene protection in the underworld. The deal specified that Hades would give Ambrogio a magical wooden bow and 11 arrows to hunt with. He was to offer his hunting trophies to Artemis in order to gain her favor and steal her silver bow. As collateral, Ambrogio had to leave his soul in Hades until he returned with the bow. Should he return without the silver bow, he would have to live in Hades forever, never to return to Selene. Having no other choice, Ambrogio agreed.

He had no way to contact Selene. He had parchments, but no writing implement, so he took his bow and arrow and killed a swan. Using its feather as a pen, and its blood as the ink, he wrote her a note explaining that he could not meet with her but would find a way for them to be together. He left the note in their meeting place and ran off to find a place to hide from the sunlight.

Naturally, Selene was devastated when she found the note, but she kept working at the temple as she did not want to anger Apollo any further. The next morning, Selene went back to the meeting place, but once again Ambrogio was not there. She saw another piece of parchment with writing in blood on it. It was a love poem from Ambrogio.

Before morning for 44 days Ambrogio slew a swan and used its blood to write Selene a love poem. After draining the blood and taking a single feather he offered the body of the swan as a tribute

to Artemis, the goddess of hunting and the moon, and also sister to Apollo. He hoped that even if he could not steal her bow, she would be honored by the tribute and would be able to convince her brother Apollo to remove the curse.

On the 45th night, Ambrogio had only one arrow left. He shot it at a swan and missed, the arrow sailing into the distance. He had neither the blood to write Selene's poem nor the swan to sacrifice to Artemis. He fell to the ground and wept.

Seeing how good of a hunter and how dedicated of a follower Ambrogio had been, Artemis came down to him. He begged Artemis to let him borrow her bow and an arrow so he could kill one last bird and leave one final note to Selene.

Artemis took pity on him and agreed to let him borrow her silver bow and an arrow. He took the bow, and in desperation, ran to the cave that led to Hades. Artemis realized what was happening and cast her own curse on him. The curse caused all silver burn his skin. Ambrogio dropped the silver bow and fell to the ground in pain.

Artemis was furious at his deceit, but he begged her for forgiveness. He explained the deal he was forced to make with Hades, his curse by Apollo, and his love for Selene. He apologized profusely and swore that he had no other choice.

Artemis took pity on him again and decided to give him one last chance. She offered to make him a great hunter, almost as great as she was, with the speed and strength of a god and fangs with which to drain the blood of the beasts to write his poems. In exchange for this immortality, he would have to agree to a deal. He and Selene would have to escape Apollo's temple and worship only Artemis forever. The catch was that Artemis was a virgin goddess, and all of her followers had to remain chaste and unmarried, so Ambrogio was never allowed to touch Selene again. They could never kiss, never touch, never have children.

Ambrogio agreed. At least this way he and Selene could be together. He killed another swan and left Selene a note telling her to meet him on a ship at the docks. Before dawn the next morning, she saw the note and ran away before Apollo could notice.

When Selene arrived at the dock she found Ambrogio's ship and met him down in the hull. There was a wooden coffin with a note on it, telling her to order the ship's captain to set sail, and to open the coffin only after the sun had set. She did as the note said, and after sunset she opened the coffin to find Ambrogio alive and well.

The couple sailed to Ephesus, where they lived in a cave during the day and worshiped Artemis at her grand temple every night. They lived happily together for many years, never touching, never kissing, never having children.

After a number of years, Ambrogio's immortality allowed him to stay young, but Selene continued to age as a mortal. She finally fell ill and was on her deathbed. Ambrogio was distraught, knowing that he would not join Selene in the afterlife because his soul still resided in Hades. At night, he went into the woods and found a white

swan swimming alone in a small lake. He killed the swan and offered it to Artemis, begging for her to make Selene immortal so they could stay together forever.

Artemis appeared to him. Thankful for his years of dedication and worship, she made him one last deal. Artemis told Ambrogio that he could touch Selene just once—to drink her blood. Doing so would kill her mortal body, but from then on, her blood mixed with his could create eternal life for any who drink of it. If he did this, Artemis would see to it that they stayed together forever.

Ambrogio wanted to refuse, but after telling Selene what happened, Selene begged him to do it. After much convincing, he bit her neck and took her blood into his body. As he set her limp body down, Selene began to radiate with light, and raise up to the sky. Ambrogio watched as Selene's glowing spirit lifted to meet Artemis at the moon. When she arrived, the moon lit up with a brilliant light.

Selene became the goddess of moonlight, and every night she would reach down with her rays of light to the earth and finally touch her beloved Ambrogio as well as all of their children—the newly created vampires who carried the blood of Ambrogio and Selene, together.

(Excerpted from http://www.gods-and-monsters.com/vampire-origin.html)

Questions for Reflection

1. Make a name card for the hero and heroine.

Ambrogio

_____

_____

Selene

_____

_____

2. How did the three powerful gods intervene in the two mortals' love affair?

Apollo	
Hades	
Artemis	

3. How did the vampire family come into being?

_____

_____

Text C The Mythology Chiron—the Wounded Healer

The Greek mythology encircling the figure of Chiron, the Wounded Healer, is of great assistance in helping us acquire a deeper understanding of the archetypal energies reflected by the Chiron in our sky.

Chiron, a centaur, was known as a wise teacher, healer and prophet. Chiron's father was the Greek god Cronus (Saturn) and his mother was a beautiful nymph named Philyra. Cronus was a cruel and devouring father god—and he met the nymph Philyra during one of his many searches for his (then) baby son, Zeus. Cronus was hoping to have some "baby Zeus kabob" for supper that night. However, upon seeing Philyra, Cronus managed to get sidetracked—instantly getting a serious case of the hots for the nymph. Problem is—though—that the nymph Philyra did not share in his lusty desires. So Philyra turned herself into a mare in the attempt to flee the unwelcome desirous advances of Cronus. But Cronus likewise transformed himself into a stallion and thus was able to consummate his overwhelming desire to mate with Philyra. Satisfied, Cronus left, never to return.

But here comes the dreadful tearjerker (pull on your heart strings) part of the story. Philyra, upon seeing her newborn son Chiron (obviously a centaur), is so disgusted and appalled that she rejects and abandons her child. That is the really bad, tragic news for young Chiron...a child born of a violent rape, is abandoned and rejected by both his parents, the very ones who should have been there to love and nurture young Chiron.

The really good news is that Chiron was later adopted by the Greek sun god Apollo. Upon becoming Chiron's foster parent, Apollo (god of music, prophecy, poetry and healing) taught Chiron all that he knew. As a result, Chiron later in life became a powerful mentor to the sons of kings and many of the most famous Greek heroes, including Jason (of the original Jason and the Argonauts), Asclepius (that became a famous healer in his own right), Achilles and Hercules.

Speaking of Hercules... Hercules plays a starring role in the continuing saga of Chiron becoming a wounded healer. Good old Herc always seemed to be at odds with the centaurs (and it was eventually to be a centaur that did him in). During a skirmish with a rowdy bunch of centaurs who were all scattering and heading for the hills—Hercules carelessly, accidentally wounded his friend and mentor, Chiron, in the knee with one of his arrows.

The arrows Hercules had chosen to use on this particular day were arrows coated with the blood of the monster Hydra. Arrows coated with the blood of the Hydra were known to cause painful wounds that would never heal. And being an immortal, Chiron having a wound that would never heal was a way serious problem. Chiron would never be able to heal from the wound caused by Hercules, and being immortal he could never die...

A seriously bad Catch 22...

And so after a long passing of time, with no relief, the wound caused Chiron much severe pain...

The Titan god Prometheus had been chained to a rock by Zeus, the chief Olympian god. Being chained to the rock was to be his (Prometheus') punishment for having previous stolen fire from Olympia as a gift to mortals. Each day, some versions say every other day, Zeus's eagle would come and eat Prometheus' liver. Each night the liver would heal itself. Then the eagle would come again for his liver snacks.

As stipulated by Zeus—Prometheus could only be released if (and when) an immortal offered to go to Tartarus and take his place. Going to Tartarus would mean the immortal was giving up his status as an immortal and would die.

Chiron, being the son of Cronus and half-brother of Zeus, agreed to take the place of Prometheus, and then eventually died. Upon his death, he was then released from his wound that would never heal.

Chiron was then honored with the constellation of Centaurus.

(Excerpted from http://thezodiac.com/chiron2.htm)

Questions for Reflection

1. Judging by the first paragraph, the writer of this story is most likely a/an _____.
   A. doctor   B. astrologist   C. psychologist   D. parapsychologist
2. In paragraph 7, the underlined words "catch 22" means_____; it originates from _____.
3. Complete the form with detailed information you get from the story.

Chiron's Identity	
Chiron's Origin	
Chiron's Major Miseries	

Websites to Visit

http://www.pagebypagebooks.com/Nathaniel_Hawthorne/Tanglewood_Tales/index.html
You may know Nathaniel Hawthorne for his most prominent work *The Scarlet Letter*, but please note that his *Tanglewood Tales*, a collection of rewrite of Greek myths in modern language, is not any less attractive or fascinating. Visit this website to enjoy the beautiful reading experience.

http://www.livescience.com/11316-top-10-intelligent-designs-creation-myths.html
Every culture has its own creation myth. And all creation myths speak to deeply meaningful questions held by the society that shares them, revealing of their central worldview and the framework for the self-identity of the culture and individual in a universal context. Visit this website to see the top 10 creation myth presented by LiveScience.

Unit 7
Gods and Mortals

> Of mortals there is no one who is happy. If wealth flows in upon one, one may be perhaps luckier than one's neighbor, but still not happy.
> —Euripides

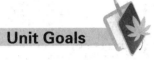
Unit Goals

- To get a general view of the myths involving gods and humans
- To explore the relationship between gods and humans
- To know the story of Atalanta and the Golden Apples
- To learn about the myth of Orpheus and Eurydice
- To learn the words and phrases that describe Greek Gods
- To improve language skills and critical thinking through the content of this unit

Before You Read

1. Read and respond to the quote below.
   Immortals are mortal, mortals immortal, living the others' death, dead in the others' life.
   —Heraclitus

2. Think on your own.

After reading the Greek myths, including the following one (Text A), you find the Greek Gods are_____.

Start to Read

Text A Gods and Mortals

Bridging the age when gods lived alone and the age when divine interference in human affairs was limited was a transitional age in which gods and men moved together. These were the early days of the world when the groups mingled more freely than they did later. Most of these tales were later told by Ovid's *Metamorphoses* and they are often divided in two thematic groups: tales of love, and tales of punishment.

Tales of Love

Tales of love often involve incest, or the seduction or rape of a mortal woman by a male god, resulting in heroic offspring. The stories generally suggest that relationships between gods and mortals are something to avoid; even consenting relationships rarely have happy endings. In a few cases, a female divinity mates with a mortal man, as in the Homeric Hymn to Aphrodite, where the goddess lies with **Anchises** to produce **Aeneas**. The marriage of **Peleus** and **Thetis**, which yielded Achilles, is another such myth.

Zeus had numerous love affairs before he married Hera, but marriage did nothing to end his philandering. In spite of Hera's jealousy and consequences that this jealousy might have on the victims, Zeus continued to have love affairs, many of them with mortal women. Many of his love affairs took place with Zeus disguised as an animal or in some other form. In the shape of eagle he seduced the Nymph **Aegina**. With her sister **Antiope**, he took the form of a Satyr, surprised her while she was asleep. Transformed into a shower of gold, Zeus loved **Danae**. He approached **Europa** in the shape of bull, **Leda** as a swan, and **Alcmene** by taking her husband's shape. Zeus also took as a lover the Trojan prince **Ganymede**, who  was abducted by an eagle sent by Zeus (some legends believe it was Zeus disguised as an eagle). The prince was taken to Mount Olympus, where he became Zeus's cup-bearer. Another Zeus's passionate love was **Io**. Disguised into a cloud, Zeus made love to her. Hera learnt about this relationship and turned Io into a cow and drove her from place to place by the stinging of a monstrous gadfly. Io finally found shelter in Egypt, where, in some accounts, she became the Egyptian cow-goddess **Isis**. **Callisto**, who was the companion of **Artemis** and had vowed to remain a virgin, Zeus took by a trick. He transformed himself into Artemis and raped her. Hera, Zeus's wife, then turned Callisto into a bear out of revenge. Later, Arcas, the son of Callisto and Zeus, nearly killed her in a hunt but Zeus placed them both in the sky as the constellations of the Great and Little Bear. The list of Zeus's love affairs is countless. They say that there was hardly a region in the Greek world that didn't have a hero who was either a son or descendant of Zeus.

 Apollo, though a handsome youthful god, was seldom lucky in his relationships with the female. **Cassandra**, daughter of King Priam of Troy, Apollo fell in love with her and gave her the gift of prophecy to win her favor. When she rejected him anyway, Apollo punished her by declaring that her prophecies would be accurate but that no one would believe her. In another story, he courted the nymph Sinope, who asked him to grant her a favor before she accepted his proposal. When Apollo agreed, she asked to remain a virgin until her death. Perhaps the most famous tale of Apollo's unfulfilled love involved his pursuit of **Daphne**, who, to escape his advances, turned into a laurel tree, which Apollo adopted as his sacred emblem. Apollo had more male lovers

than all the other Greek gods combined. Many of his young male lovers died in accidents. A famous one is **Hyacinthus**, a Spartan prince and athlete. The wind god Zephyr also loved Hyacinthus and in a jealous rage blew a discus off course and killed the prince. Apollo used Hyacinthus's blood to create the flower that is named after him.

Tithonus, lover of the dawn goddess Aurora, was a mortal, and would age and die. Wanting to be with her lover for all eternity, **Aurora** asked Zeus to grant him immortality but she failed to ask for eternal youth for him and he wound up aging eternally until Aurora turned him into a grasshopper. **Endymion**, lover of the moon goddess **Selene**, had a perhaps happier fate: in a state of perpetual sleep, he kept both his youth and his good looks, and the everlasting love of the goddess. The story of Pan and **Syrinx** resembles that of Apollo and Daphne: Syrinx was pursued by the amorous goat-god and to avoid his embrace was transformed into a bunch of reed, out of which Pan crafted his famous pan-pipes. Another ill-fated story is about Narcissus and Echo. **Narcissus** was a beautiful youth who rejected the love of the nymph **Echo** and was condemned to fall in love with his own reflection in a pool. He pined away and in the place where he died a flower sprang up that was named after him.

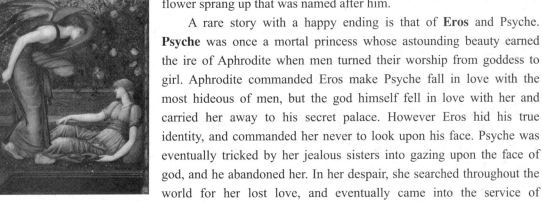

A rare story with a happy ending is that of **Eros** and Psyche. **Psyche** was once a mortal princess whose astounding beauty earned the ire of Aphrodite when men turned their worship from goddess to girl. Aphrodite commanded Eros make Psyche fall in love with the most hideous of men, but the god himself fell in love with her and carried her away to his secret palace. However Eros hid his true identity, and commanded her never to look upon his face. Psyche was eventually tricked by her jealous sisters into gazing upon the face of god, and he abandoned her. In her despair, she searched throughout the world for her lost love, and eventually came into the service of Aphrodite. The goddess commanded her perform a series of difficult labors which culminated in a journey to the Underworld. In the end Psyche was reunited with Eros and the couple wed in a ceremony attended by the gods. This story is frequently interpreted as an allegory of spiritual quest, with Eros representing Love and Psyche the soul.

Tales of Punishment

In many myths, mortals who display arrogance and hubris end up learning, in quite brutal ways, the folly of this overexertion of ego. The Greek concept of hubris refers to the overweening pride of humans who hold themselves up as equals to the gods. Hubris is one of the worst traits one can exhibit in the world of ancient Greece and invariably brings the worst kind of destruction.

Some of those who directly challenged the god's power would be placed into Tartarus, like **Tantalus**, who killed his son and fed him to the Olympians as a trick, was condemned to spend eternity in Tartarus chained to a tree filled with fruit he could not eat and up to his chest or chin in water he could not drink; or **Salmoneus**, who claimed to be Zeus and drove in his chariot to imitate thunder, was subjected to eternal torment in Tartarus.

The story of **Niobe** is a prime example of the danger of arrogance. Niobe had the audacity to compare herself to Leto, the mother of Artemis and Apollo, thus elevating herself and her children to the level of the divine. Insulted, the two gods struck all of Niobe's children dead and turned her into a rock that perpetually wept. Likewise, young **Phaethon**, who pridefully believed he could drive the chariot of his father, the Sun, lost control and burned everything in sight before Zeus knocked him from the sky with a thunderbolt. Similar warnings against hubris are found in the stories of **Bellerophon**, who bridled the winged **Pegasus** and tried to ride up to Olympus and join the deities' revelry, and **Arachne**, who challenged Athena to a weaving contest and was changed into a spider as punishment.

Another whose only sin was tactlessness was the great Theban seer **Tiresias**. When Tiresias was walking in the woods one day, he came upon two great serpents copulating; he struck them with his staff, and was thereupon transformed into a woman. Seven years later, she/he passed by the same place and came upon the same two serpents copulating; she/he struck them again with the staff and was turned back into a man. Some time later, Zeus and Hera were arguing over who had more pleasure in sex, the man or the woman: Zeus said it was the woman, while Hera claimed men got more pleasure from the act. To settle the argument, they consulted Tiresias, since he had experienced life as both sexes, and Tiresias sided with Zeus. In her anger, Hera struck Tiresias blind. Since Zeus could not undo the act of another deity, he gave Tiresias the gift of prophecy in compensation.

Indeed, any type of hubris or arrogance, no matter the circumstance, is an attitude that no god will leave unpunished.

(Excerpts fromhttp://upge.wn.com/?t=ancientgreece/index35.txt, http://www.milica.com.au/greek_myths/olymp/zeus_t.htm, http://www.mythencyclopedia.com/Am-Ar/Apollo.html, http://en.wikipedia.org/wiki/Ages_of_Man, http://www.theoi.com/Ouranios/Psykhe.html, http://www.sparknotes.com/lit/mythology/themes.html, http://www.pantheon.org/articles/t/tiresias.html)

Proper Nouns

1. **Anchises** [æŋˈkaisi:z]:安喀塞斯,特洛伊王子。
2. **Aeneas** [iˈni:əs]:特洛伊战争中的勇士。
3. **Peleus** [ˈpi:ljus]:珀琉斯。
4. **Thetis** [ˈθi:tis]:忒提斯,海的女神。
5. **Aegina** [i:ˈdʒainə]:埃伊娜。
6. **Antiopa**:安提俄珀,底比斯国王之女,以美貌著称。
7. **Danae** [ˈdænəi:]:达那厄,阿哥斯国王之女。
8. **Europa** [juəˈrəupə]:欧罗巴,被化作牡牛的宙斯拐到克里特岛。
9. **Leda** [ˈli:də]:勒达,斯巴达王廷达瑞俄斯之妻。
10. **Alcmena** [ælkˈmi:nə]:阿尔克墨涅,底比斯国王安菲特律翁之妻,被宙斯诱奸后生下大力神赫剌克勒斯。
11. **Ganymede** [ˈgænimi:d]:伽倪墨得斯,因年少貌美,宙斯化作鹰把他掠到天上为众神侍酒。
12. **Io** [ˈaiəu]:艾奥,宙斯的情人。
13. **Isis** [ˈaisis]:伊希斯,古埃及的母性与生育之神,她是一位反复重生的神。
14. **Callisto** [kəˈlistəu]:卡利斯托,宙斯心爱的女神,被赫拉所憎恨并被她变为一只熊。
15. **Artemis** [ˈɑ:timis]:阿耳忒弥斯,月神和狩猎女神,阿波罗的孪生姐妹。
16. **Cassandra** [kəˈsændrə]:卡珊德拉,特洛伊公主,能预卜吉凶。
17. **Daphne** [ˈdæfni]:达佛涅,居于山林水泽的仙女。
18. **Hyacinthus** [ˌhaiəˈsinθəs]:雅辛托斯,阿波罗所钟爱的美少年。
19. **Tithonus** [tiˈθəunəs]:提托诺斯,特洛伊城的创建者拉俄墨冬之子。
20. **Aurora** [ɔːˈrɔːrə]:奥罗拉,黎明女神。
21. **Endymion** [enˈdimiən]:恩底弥翁,希腊神话中月之女神所爱的英俊牧童。
22. **Selene** [siˈli:nə]:塞勒涅,月神。
23. **Syrinx** [ˈsiriŋks]:绪任克斯,阿卡狄亚水泽女神,被潘追求,为保贞洁变为芦苇,潘用此制成潘神箫。
24. **Narcissus** [nɑːˈsisəs]:那耳喀索斯,自恋水中倒影的美少年。
25. **Echo**:厄科,居于山林水泽的仙女。
26. **Eros** [ˈiərɔs]:厄洛斯,爱神。
27. **Psyche** [ˈpsaiki]:普绪刻,罗马神话中以少女形象出现的人类灵魂的化身。
28. **Tantalus** [ˈtæntələs]:坦塔罗斯,吕狄亚王,因犯有罪孽被罚站在冥界齐颈的水中,头上有果树,但他却不能喝到水、吃到果子。
29. **Salmoneus**:萨尔摩纽斯,因假借宙斯之名为宙斯所杀。
30. **Niobe** [ˈnaiəubi]:尼俄柏,因自夸儿女而导致儿女全被杀死。
31. **Phaethon** [feiəθən]:法厄同,太阳神之子。
32. **Bellerophon** [beˈlerəfən]:柏勒罗丰,科林斯英雄。
33. **Pegasus** [ˈpegəsəs]:珀加索斯,生有双翼的神马,被其足蹄踩过的地方有泉水涌出,诗人饮之可获灵感。
34. **Arachne** [əˈrækni]:阿剌克涅,吕狄亚少女,善织绣。
35. **Tiresias** [taiˈri:siæs]:忒瑞西阿斯,古希腊城邦底比斯的盲人占卜者,先知。

After You Read

Knowledge Focus

1. Solo Work: Answer the following questions according to what you have learned from the text.

1) Which beautiful Goddess is queen of Zeus, God of the Sky?
   A. Metis   B. Aphrodite   C. Demeter   D. Hera
2) Who prayed to Gaia for help because Apollo pursued her, and was turned into a laurel?
   A. Hebe   B. Aura   C. Syrinx   D. Daphne
3) Apollo, God of Music, fell for which young Trojan princess who cruelly rejected him?
   A. Clytemnestra   B. Cassandra   C. Leda   D. Laodice
4) Who fell in love with Syrink, but could not fulfill that love because she was turned into a reed-bed?
   A. Apollo   B. Zeus   C. Hades   D. Pan
5) Psyche, the mortal woman turned Goddess of the Soul, fell for which God?
   A. Hades   B. Ares   C. Eros   D. Apollo
6) Who fell in love with Narcissus, but could not express her feelings so wasted away until she merely a voice?
   Answer:_____ (One Word)
   Narcissus had also fallen in love, but with whom?
   Answer:_____ (One Word)
7) This fellow invited all the gods to feast at his palace. The entrée was his own son, Pelops. The gods were not amused, and punished him in the underworld by making it "tantalizingly" impossible to eat or drink anything.
   A. Sisyphus   B. Atreus   C. Ixion   D. Tantalus
8) Niobe incurred the wrath of Leto, by boasting she had more beautiful children than the goddess. How was she punished for her pride?
   A. She was blinded.   B. She was turned into a monster.
   C. All her children were killed. D. She was flayed alive.
9) Who claimed that she was better at weaving than Athena—the patron goddess of weaving herself?
   A. Arachne   B. Andromeda   C. Achene   D. Atalanta
10) Who granted Tiresias the gift of prophecy?
    A. Apollo   B. Zeus   C. Hera   D. two serpents

2. Pair Work: Discuss the following questions with your partner.

1) What is Zeus's love life like?
2) What is Apollo's love life like?
3) Can you tell love stories in Greek mythology that end tragically?
4) Do you know any love story from Greek mythology that has a happy ending?
5) Which is the major reason for humans to be punished by Greek gods? Please speak with examples.

3. Pair Work: What is Gods' relationship with humans? Illustrate it with cases told in Text A.

the relationship	cases

Language Focus

1. Fill in the blanks with the words you have learned in the text.

> consent   advances   bridge   yield   disguise
> shelter   condemn   trait   approach   sting

1) We begin our independent lives only when we emerge from the womb and lose its protective _____.
2) These apple trees _____ plenty of fruit this year.
3) Law is an utterance determined by the common _____ of the commonwealth.
4) It is always best to _____ someone by speaking about something other than work.
5) Sexual harassment can include unwelcome sexual _____, requests for sexual favors, and other verbal, nonverbal, or physical conduct of a sexual nature.
6) When Winston Churchill lost the 1945 election, his wife remarked that the defeat might be a blessing in _____.
7) In "_____ transfer," whatever you say about other people influences how people see you.
8) The _____ of jealousy is even worse than the sting of a bee.
9) It is hard to claim that gays are out to destroy the traditional family when they are trying to join it, or to _____ them for trying to serve their country.
10) Politeness will _____ a lot of difficulties.

2. Fill in the blanks with the proper form of the words in brackets.

1) They often deny this point and _____ (consequence) deny one aspect of the truth.
2) They are different in nature, though some formal _____ (resemble) between two things.
3) In any event, your friendships and the organizations of which you are a member are the arenas in which your growth and _____ (transform) occur.
4) When you analyze something to death you are being extremely _____. (arrogance)
5) The _____ (combine) of interest and skill are very compelling reasons to choose a particular career.
6) Religion is not the only source of _____. (divide)
7) As a human being, we should demonstrate our intellectual and moral superiority by respecting others for who they are—instead of _____ (reject) them for who or what they are not.
8) They have made a solemn statement that their internal affairs are not to be _____ (interference) in.

9) Apparently, it pays for consumers of controversial news to take a moment and consider that the opposite _____ (interpret) may be true.

10) The average person would rather leave their dreams _____ (fulfill) than risk everything in an attempt to achieve the seemingly impossible.

3. **Fill in the blanks with the proper prepositions or adverbs that collocate with the neighboring words.**

1) The jellyfish, _____ the shape of mushrooms and about the size of dogs, changed color depending on their mood or behavior state.

2) Many of us fall _____ love with people because we want to be them.

3) The doctor told me the good news: I was going to have a disease named _____ me.

4) If you cannot get the money you want, then ask _____ other things that do not cost the company anything.

5) Not having a college degree means you are over three times more likely to wind _____ unemployed.

6) There is no failure to those who spring _____ higher like a ball after falling down.

7) The country could end _____ becoming simply a low-cost manufacturing base, not a source of innovation.

8) Children are to be treated with respect for their person and individuality and may not be subjected _____ corporal punishment or any other humiliating treatment.

4. **Proofreading: The following passage contains ten errors. Each indicated line contains a maximum of one error. In each case, only ONE word is involved. Read the passage and correct the errors.**

King Acrisius of Argos was uncertain in battle and unluck in the hunt. "My (1) _____
daughter, Danae, grows tall and ripe," he said to himself one day. "Her eyes fog (2) _____
over when I speak to her. She is ready for the husband, but am I ready for a
son-in-law? I dislike the idea and always have. A son-in-law will be a younger man
wait for me to die so he can take the throne. Perhaps he will even try to hasten that (3) _____
sad event. But she is ready and princesses must not be spinsters...a grave decision...I (4) _____
shall consult on the oracle." He sent to the oracle at Delphi, and a messenger (5) _____
returned with this prophecy: "Your daughter will bear a son who will one day kill
you."

"The Pythoness' auguries are supposed to be accurate," he thought. "And are (6) _____
they? What if I were slay my daughter now while she is still childless; how then can (7) _____
she have a son to kill me? But, must I kill her to keep her childless? ..." (8) _____

Thereupon he shut the beautiful young girl in a brass tower which he had
specially built by no doors and only one tiny window. The tower was surrounded by (9) _____
high walls and guarded by sentries and savage dogs. Here Acrisius locked his
daughter away, and so murderous was his temper in those days that no one dared ask (10) _____
him who had become of the laughing young girl.

Comprehensive Work

1. **Understanding.** If you think about it, it is not difficult to find that all people and gods, even the greatest and the wisest, have to yield to self-interest. Thus, it may be fair for an ancient Greek philosopher to say:

   Men would live exceedingly quiet if these two words, mine and thine, were taken away.

   Now, do not use the words "I", "you", "my" or "yours," see if you can break the philosopher while illustrating the following statement.

   We live, not as we wish to, but as we can.

2. **Dumb Show.** An individual or a small group acts out a scene of a popular Greek myth told in Text A, to see if the rest of the class can guess what the performance represents. The players should rely on their gestures, using words only when necessary.

3. **Writing Practice.** Dictionaries define "myth" as traditional story accepted as history, but as the smartest of all ages, why should we be chained to the many old stories? Pick up your pen and create your own myth, make yours history!

Planner for Writing Your Own Greek Myth

My Title: _____   My Name: _____

Think about this first:
What will this myth explain about the world? (Ex. Why the wind blows)
_____

Introduction (Beginning):
When did your story happen? (Ex.: Long ago ...—Not once upon a time...)
_____

Where will your story take place? (setting)
_____

Who will be in your story? (characters)
(usually a god and a mortal and others)
_____

What happens in the story? (plot)
First thing:
_____

One detail about it:
_____

Second thing:
_____

One detail about it:
_____

Third thing:
_____

One detail about it:
_____

How will this myth end? (Conclusion)
_____

Read More

Text B Atalanta and the Golden Apples

When she was born, Atalanta's father was so disappointed that she was not a son that he ordered she be disposed of immediately. The tiny infant was laid atop a mountain without clothing to warm her or food to sustain her. But Atalanta didn't die as her father so vehemently wished. A mother bear happened upon the infant and took her back to her den, suckling her just as she did her own young.

Atalanta grew to be strong and beautiful. She also became an extraordinary runner. She was proud that she could outrun even the fastest athletes and vowed that she would not marry any man who couldn't outrun her.

Because of the maiden's beauty, many men wanted to claim her for his own. But Atalanta got tired of their constant attentions and decided to make them cease.

She declared that she would hold a foot race. Every man that wished to win her hand in marriage would be allowed to participate. Her terms were somewhat harsh. She retained the right to kill any man who failed to beat her in the race. However, she agreed to marry any man who could outdistance her.

Race after race, men boasted that Atalanta would be his. But no one could beat the swift young girl and many a man died with her name on his lips and her arrow through his heart.

Melanion, Atalanta's cousin also fell for the beautiful maiden but he wasn't about to be another of her victims. So he prayed to Aphrodite, goddess of love, soliciting her assistance in winning his lady fair.

Aphrodite had grown tired of Atalanta's refusal to fall in love and decided that she would help Melanion win the race. She gave him three golden apples, telling him that no one could resist the beautiful fruit, but to use them wisely.

The day of the race, Atalanta caught sight of the golden apples in Melanion's hands. At first she thought to herself, "This man will not make it around the first bend with such extra weight in his hands."

However, the longer she stared at the apples, the more she wanted them for herself. "Once this idiot is dead," she thought, "those apples will be mine."

The race began and Atalanta quickly gained the lead, laughing to herself that Melanion was the lamest contestant she had ever seen. But at that moment, she caught the glimpse of one of the apples rolling just off the road in front of her.

Of course, Atalanta could not help but leave the road to gather the precious fruit. It took it no

time at all for her to catch up with Melanion and, once again, outdistance him. Pleased with herself that she had one of the apples and still retained the lead, Atalanta couldn't help but mock her male competitor.

"Did you really think you could run faster than me?" she laughed. But just as before, her attention was lost when she noticed another golden apple roll past her; this one thrown further off the road than the one before.

She left the track to gather up the second fruit, noticing that Melanion was now further in the lead. This time it took her longer to catch up to her competitor, but she eventually did and slowly pulled ahead once more.

With the finish line in sight, Atalanta was already planning in her head how she would kill the young upstart who thought he could trick her into loosing the race. But low and behold, she saw the third apple roll past her, this time much further away from the track and the finish line.

Atalanta could not resist chasing the fruit, certain that she could still beat Melanion. However, when she looked up as she once again made it back to the track, he was mere feet from the finish line. Atalanta began running faster than she ever had before, but alas, she could not catch him and Melanion crossed the finish line first and won her hand in marriage as promised.

(Excerpted from http://www.associatedcontent.com/article)

Questions for Reflection

1. See these five pictures below and retell the whole story of Atalanta.

2. Discuss: What are the morals this legend tries to tell people?

_____
_____

Text C Orpheus and Eurydice

In ancient times there was a King of Thrace by the name of Oeagrus. Not satisfied with mortal women, he fell in love with the Muse Calliope. She found him to her taste, and of their union was born a boy, whom they named Orpheus. Calliope had the divine gift of song, and she taught her son

well. So beautiful was the boy's singing that the god Apollo himself was charmed, and made him a gift of a lyre that played so sweetly it made even the stones weep.

When he grew older, a herald came to tell him of Jason's quest to bring back the Golden Fleece. Willingly he joined the other braves of Greece on the voyage, using his music to help them overcome many hardships along the way. But he was eager to get back to Thrace, for he was in love with a beautiful maiden called Eurydice. Fate however was not kind to them: right after they were married she stepped on a viper, and was bitten, and died.

Orpheus was inconsolable. His harp in hand, he took the path of the spirits of the dead, and started down to the Lower World. He charmed his way past all the guardians, all the way to the abode of the god Hades, Lord of the Underworld. He begged Hades and Persephone for his Eurydice, and swore that he either would return to earth with her, or else remain in the realm of the dead forever. Their hard hearts softened by his singing, the gods relented. They told

him to go back up to the Upper World, and his wife would follow him, but not to look back or else he would lose her forever. Just as he reached the surface he turned to make sure she had not gotten lost in the thick fog. She was right behind him, but had not yet stepped into the open air. Hermes the messenger, who had been sent to follow them unseen, reached out to pull her back into the realm of the dead. Orpheus had only a moment to lift her veil, to gaze upon her face one last time, and then she was gone.

Heartbroken, Orpheus could not bear to look at another woman, and for the next three years he served as priest in Apollo's temple. Girls still chased after him, but he turned them all away, leaving them furious for being spurned. Not that he became a stranger to the ways of desire, not at all. It is just that now his passion was the love of youths. He taught the men of Thrace the art of loving boys, and revealed to them that this love was the way to feel young again, to touch the innocence of youth, to smell the flowers of spring. Lovers he had many. Of all, he loved young Calais the best, winged Calais, son of Boreas, the North Wind, his friend and companion on the Argos.

But his love for Calais was fated to come to a sudden end. It was in early spring, during the

Dionysian festival. That was the time when Thracian women took on the role of Maenads, the wild and crazy attendants of Dionysus, the god of wine, passion and abandon. They hated Orpheus for turning them away when they desired him, for keeping to himself the boys they lusted after, and for mocking them for being free with their love. That day they came upon him while he was singing so sweetly that even the birds had grown quiet and the trees had bent down to listen. He was singing of the gods who had loved boys, of Zeus and

Ganymede, of Apollo and his lovers, of how even gods can lose their beloveds to the claws of death.

Lost in his music he did not notice the angry Maenads at the edge of the forest. In a fit of rage, they stormed down on him. "No time for us sweet man, pretty man?" cried one. "Have our bodies, our voices, no power to charm you, unnatural man?" cried another. "Know then the fury of what you scorn!" shouted all, and they beat him to the ground with tree branches, and tore him limb from limb and threw his remains in the river. Orpheus, the gentlest of men, died, but his head and his  lyre floated away on the river Hebros, still singing, and drifted all the way to the island of Lesbos. There on the beach a great snake rushed to eat him, but it was turned into a stone by Apollo. The head was placed in a sacred cave where it prophesied for a long time. His lyre, at the request of Apollo and the Muses, was flung by Zeus into the heavens, where it can still be seen today as a constellation.

Orpheus in the mean time found himself back in the underworld, this time for good, and there he strolled through the Elyssian Fields, once again inseparable from his Eurydice.

Plutarch tells us that the Maenads who killed Orpheus were punished for their deed by their husbands, who branded them by covering their legs and arms with tattoos. Other say that the gods were angry with them and were going to kill them for their deed, but Dionysus punished them first by binding them with roots and plunging them feet-first into the ground and turning them into oak trees.

(Excerpted from http://www.gay-art-history.org)

Questions for Reflection

True or False.

1) (   ) Oeagrus fell in love with Muse Calliop, and he got loved back.
2) (   ) Orpheus got his music talent from his mother.
3) (   ) Orpheus lost his lover when they were planning their wedding.
4) (   ) The Lord of the Underworld was deeply moved by Orpheus, thus granted him a chance to be united with his love.
5) (   ) Orpheus turned Thrician girls away because none of them could match his late love's beauty.
6) (   ) As taught by Orpheus, the love for young girls and boys was the way to feel young again.
7) (   ) During the Dionysian festival, Thracian women would became wild and crazy.
8) (   ) Orpheus died tragically, beaten and torn into pieces by angry Thracian women.

Websites to Visit

http://library.thinkquest.org/06aug/01660/Atlanta.html

It may be fair for Melanion, after winning the race, to have a wonderful life together with his

beautiful wife Atalanta, just as told in many fairy tales. But, would they? Visit this website to read another version of this story and see what happened to the couple.

http://www.mainlesson.com/display.php?author=colum&book=fleece&story=jason
Love won't last long, so it says. You may know it as the story of the Golden Fleece, or of the Argonauts, but it is really the story of Jason and Medea, arguably the most haunting couple of all time. Visit this website to find the soured love.

Songs to Enjoy
Both the following songs are telling the Icarus story. Listen to the lyrics and sense if they have different focus.

Flight of Icarus
by Iron Maiden

As The Sun Breaks, Above The Ground,
An Old Man Stands On The Hill,
As The Ground Warms, To The First Rays Of Light
A Birdsong Shatters The Still.
His Eyes Are A Blaze,
See The Madman In His Gaze.
Fly, On Your Way, Like An Eagle,
Fly As High As The Sun,
On Your Way, Like An Eagle,
Fly And Touch The Sun.
Now The Crowd Breaks And A Young Boy Appears
Looks The Old Man In The Eye
As He Spreads His Wings And Shouts At The Crowd
In The Name Of God
My Father I'll Fly.
His Eyes Seem So Glazed
As He Flies On The Wings Of A Dream,
Now He Knows His Father Betrayed
Now His Wings Turn To Ashes To Ashes His Grave.
Fly, On Your Way, Like An Eagle,
Fly As High As The Sun,
On Your Way, Like An Eagle,
Fly, Touch The Sun.

The Melting Point of Wax
by Thrice

I've waited for this moment all my life and more
And now I see so clearly what I could not see before
The time is now or never and this chance won't come again
throw caution and myself into the wind
There's no promise of safety with these secondhand wings
But I'm willing to find out what impossible means
A leap of faith
A parody of an angel
Miles above the sea
I hear the voice of reason screaming up to me
"You've flown far too high boy now you're too close to the sun
Soon your makeshift wings will come undone"
But how will I know limits from lies if I never try?
There's no promise of safety with these second hand wings
But I'm willing to find out what impossible means
Climb through the heavens on feathers and dreams
'cause the melting point of wax means nothing to me
Nothing to me
Nothing to me
I will touch the sun or I will die trying die trying
Die on these second hand wings
Willing to find out what impossible means
Climb through the heavens on feathers and dreams
'cause the melting point of wax means nothing to me
Nothing to me
Nothing to me
Means nothing to me miles above the sea

Unit 8
The Age of Heroes (I)

> The longer I occupy myself with questions of ancient mythology, the more diffident I become of success in dealing with them, and I am apt to think that we who spend our years in searching for solutions to these insoluble problems are like Sisyphus perpetually rolling his stone uphill only to see it revolve again into the valley.
>
> ——Sir James G. Frazer, *The Golden Bough*

Unit Goals

- To understand the concept of "hero" in classical mythology
- To know the myths of Perseus and Hercules
- To be able to tell the stories of the famous Twelve Labors of Hercules
- To learn the useful words and expressions that describe heroes and their heroic myths
- To improve language skills and critical thinking through the content of this unit

Before You Read

1. Do you know the meaning of the following phrases?
   ◇ choice of Heracles
   ◇ hydra-headed
   ◇ cleanse the Augean Stable
   ◇ the Shirt of Nessus
   ◇ pillars of Heracles
   Which figure in classical mythology will you associate these phrases with?

   _____

2. What kind of people will you regard as a hero? What heroic characteristics should he/she possess? Please nominate a hero in your mind. Search for some information about him/her and prepare a 5-minute presentation to the class.

Start to Read

Text A The Age of Heroes (I)

The "age of heroes" in Greek mythology is fairly well defined. It is the generation or two leading up to the Trojan War, during which most of the greatest Greek heroes were active, and from which the Greek tragedians took most of the material for their plays. This section will deal with four major figures from this period (**Hercules**, **Jason**, **Theseus**, **Oedipus**), and one (**Perseus**) from a slightly earlier period.

It will be obvious that these tales share many repeated themes and motifs: the hero's mysterious birth and his quest to regain his inheritance; the father or grandfather who tries to kill the hero out of fear; the impossible quest or set of tasks, imposed by a rival who seeks to dispose of the hero; the love-struck enemy princess who helps him; the descent into the underworld; the fated disaster and the attempt to evade it; most of all, perhaps, the contrast between the heroes' public achievements and their tragic private lives. In the ultimately bleak world of the Greek sagas, it sometimes seems that the most dangerous thing a hero can do—far worse than confronting **Hydras** or **Minotaurs** or **Gorgons**—is to marry to have children.

Perseus

Perseus was the son of Zeus and a mortal woman named **Danae**. Danae's father, **King Acrisius**, learned after consulting an oracle that he would have not sons. Danae was his only daughter. He also learned that Danae's unborn son would kill him. He tried to escape his fate by locking Danae in a tower (or an underground bronze chamber, depending on the version of the story). While locked up, Danae was visited by Zeus and from their union came their son Perseus. When Acrisius became aware of the baby, he had both mother and child placed in a wooden chest and put out to sea.

They were saved by a fisherman named **Dictys**, the brother of King **Polydectes**. Polydectes fell in love with Danae, who did not return the feelings. Polydectes devised a plan to get rid of Perseus so he could have Danae. The king levied a tax of a horse from every man on the island. Perseus, being raised by a poor fisherman, did not have any money for a horse. He offered the king any request and he would fulfill it. Wanting to be rid of Perseus, the king asked for the head of **Medusa**. Medusa was a Gorgon whose look could turn a person to stone. Medusa lived with her two sisters. All of them had golden wings, claws of brass, and serpents for hair.

Perseus received help from two of the gods, Athena and Hermes. They provided him with winged sandals to get in and out of the cave quickly and quietly. They also gave Perseus the cap of darkness, which made the wearer invisible, a sword and a pouch to put Medusa's head in.

Perseus traveled to a cave where three witches lived. They had only one eye and a tooth between them. Perseus needed them to tell him the secret location of Medusa's cave. Perseus waited until one of them took out the eye to hand it to another, and grabbed it. While holding the eye hostage, Perseus forced them to tell him the location of Medusa and her two sisters. After getting the location of Medusa's cave, Perseus threw the eye into a nearby lake.

Using the cap of darkness, he entered Medusa's cave. He used a polished bronze shield to watch the three gorgons so not to look at them directly and turn to stone. He waited for them to fall asleep. Once asleep, he took out his sword and used the shield to guide his swing. He chopped off Medusa's head, stuffing it quickly into his pouch. He used the winged sandals to get out of the cave before Medusa's sisters were able to locate him.

After cutting off Medusa's head, Perseus started his journey back to his home. On the way, he encountered a beautiful woman named **Andromeda** chained to some rocks. He learned from her that her mother, **Cassiopeia**, had offended Poseidon by stating that her own beauty was greater than the **Nereids** who attended Poseidon. To punish her, Poseidon had sent a flood and a sea serpent to harass the people of her country. An oracle had told Andromeda's father Cephus to sacrifice his Andromeda to the serpent to appease Poseidon. Andromeda begged Perseus to save her. Perseus agreed to help her, but first he wanted King Cephus to give him Andromeda's hand in marriage. Cephus agreed.

When the sea serpent came for Andromeda, Perseus jumped on top of it and battled it to the death. Perseus was victorious and he then freed Andromeda. He went to her father to claim her in marriage, but Cephus had failed to mention that Andromeda had already been promised to **Phineus**. Phineus, with a small army, came to interrupt Perseus and Andromeda's wedding. Perseus handled this by pulling Medusa's head out of the bag and turned Phineus and his army all to stone.

Upon returning home, Perseus found his mother hiding from the King in a religious site. King Polydectes had begun pursuing her, which forced her to retreat to the temple for refuge. Perseus crashed a banquet of the king. When Perseus told his tale and how he had cut off Medusa's head, the king doubted his story. To prove the deed was actually done, Perseus pulled the head out of the bag. The king and all his guests were turned to stone.

Perseus, Andromeda, and Danae (his mother) returned to their home at Argos. Acrisius, afraid of the prophecies that his grandson would kill him, fled to **Larissa**. Perseus followed him to Larissa, not for revenge, but to make peace with him. While there, Perseus entered a discus-throwing contest. He accidentally threw the disk into the crowd and killed one of the spectators. He discovered the spectator was his grandfather Acrisius.

So saddened by this accident, Perseus could not return to Argos to claim his throne. Instead, he took the throne of the city of **Tiryns** and there he established the city of **Mycenae**. He and had six children with Andromeda to whom he was faithful the rest of his life.

Hercules

Of all the Greek heroes, Hercules was by far the most famous. He was a mortal man, who through hard work became immortal and joined the gods of Olympus. Hercules was the son of Zeus and **Alcmene**. Alcmene's husband **Amphiteryon** was out avenging her brother's death at the hands of pirates. Zeus, disguised as Amphiteryon, came to her and told her stories of how he killed the

pirates to avenge her brother's death. That night Zeus went to bed with Alcmene and impregnated her. The next day the real Amphiteryon returned with his stories of avenging the pirates, and he could not understand why his wife was irritated with him and seemed disinterested in the stories. It was then that Amphiteryon consulted a blind seer and became aware of what Zeus did.

Zeus talked Athena into tricking Hera into suckling Hercules. As the story goes, Athena and Hera came upon a baby abandoned at the walls of **Thebes**. Athena suggested to Hera to suckle the poor abandoned baby. Hera did so, but the baby sucked so hard that she had to push him away. The force was so strong that the milk from her breast spurted out and became the **Milky Way**.

Hercules had several teachers in his youth who taught him well. Here is a partial list of his teachers and the areas they instructed him in:

◇ **Amphitrton** — chariot driving
◇ **Autolycus** — boxing
◇ **Castor** — art of riding horses in battle
◇ **Cheiron** — (centaur) politics, manners, and wisdom
◇ **Eumolpus** — playing the lyre and singing
◇ **Eurytus** — archery

Not only was he well trained, but Hercules also received lavish gifts from the gods of Olympus. He was well equipped with special swords, shields, bows, and horses.

Hercules, of all of Zeus's illegitimate children seemed to be the focus of Hera's anger. She sent a two-headed serpent to attack him when he was just an infant. He simply strangled the snake with one head in each hand. When Hercules married **Megara** of Thebes, Hera drove Hercules to madness. This madness caused Hercules to kill his wife and all of his children. He did not stop this killing streak until Athena struck him with a rock, knocking him unconscious. When he awoke, he realized what he had one and consulted the Oracle of **Delphi** to see how he could purify himself. The oracle instructed him to complete twelve labors that King **Eurystheus** set before him, and he could be purified and also attain immortality.

1. ***Kill the Nemean Lion:*** The lion had a skin which could not be penetrated by any sword or spear. Hercules had to kill the lion with his bare hands.

2. ***Kill the Hydra of Lerna:*** Hercules attacked the Hydra and began to chop off its many heads. Yet each time he chopped off a head, the Hydra would grow two more in its place. He called on his friend Iolaus to burn each wound which did not allow the heads to grow back. In this way he defeated the Hydra. Eurystheus refused to count this labor because Hercules had help in completing it.

3. ***Capture the Golden Hind:*** The Golden Hind was a deer with golden antlers. Hercules hunted it for a year and finally captured it with a net while it was sleeping. After completing this Labor, Hercules joined Jason and the Argonauts for a period of time.

4. ***Capture the Erymanthian Boar:*** Hercules captured the boar in a snowdrift and brought it

back in chains.

5. **Clean the Stables of Augeas:** The Stables of Augeas held thousands of cattle and had not been cleaned in thirty years. Hercules had to clean all of them in a single day. To accomplish this, Hercules diverted two rivers into the stables to carry away all the dung. He also made a deal with King Augeas to receive one tenth of the cattle as payment for his work. After completing the work, the King refused to pay. In addition, Hercules did not receive credit for the labor because Eurystheus stated he did the labor for profit.

6. **Drive out the Stymphalian Birds:** The Stymphalian Birds were man-eating birds. Hercules used a bronze rattle to confuse and drive out the birds.

7. **Fetch the Cretan Bull:** The bull was a beautiful creature given to King Minos of **Crete** by Poseidon. Hercules had a long struggle wrestling the bull, but he captured it, brought it to **Tiryns**, and released it.

8. **Capture the Horses of Diomedes:** Four horses of the wicked **Thracian** king Diomedes were man eating animals. Hercules drove them down to the sea. Diomedes then to attacked Hercules. Hercules clubbed Diomedes and fed him to his horses. He then harnessed the horses, took them back to Tiryns, and then set them free on Mount Olympus.

9. **Bring back the Amazon Girdle:** Hercules simply asked the queen of the Amazons for the girdle, and she gave it to him. Hera was so angry at the ease in which he got the item that she disguised herself and warned the other Amazon women that Hercules planned to abduct the queen. When Hercules saw the army coming after him, he figured the queen had betrayed him. He then killed her and escaped with the girdle.

10. **Steal Cattle of Geryon:** Hercules had to defeat a son of Ares and several other monsters. In doing so, he was able to complete this task.

11. **Retrieve the Golden Apples of Hesperides:** Hercules convinced the Titan **Atlas** to help him with this task. Hercules agreed to take the weight of the world while Atlas retrieved the apples from his daughters. When Atlas returned, he did not want the weight of the world again. Hercules agreed to keep the world but asked Atlas to take it for just a minute so he could get some cushions for his head. Once Atlas took the weight again, Hercules took the apples and walked away. On the way back from this journey, Hercules came across the Titan **Prometheus**, who was chained to a rock. He killed the bird which came every day to feed on his liver, and freed Prometheus.

12. **Retrieve Cerberus from the Underworld:** Hercules had to fight Hades to get into the underworld. Hercules was able to injure Hades, who left for Mont Olympus to be healed. He then wrestled the three-headed dog Cerberus with his bare hands and took it back to Eurystheus. After seeing the dog, Eurystheus had Hercules return the creature to the underworld. With this last act, Hercules completed his tasks, was purified, and made immortal.

So the Labors were completed.

The other deeds which Hercules carried out, in the course of his Labors or afterwards, are far too many to list. He briefly sailed with the **Argonauts**. He is said to have released Prometheus from his chains on Mount Caucasus, and Theseus from his imprisonment in the underworld. He successfully wrestled with Death for the soul of **Alcestis**, who had willingly agreed to die in the place of her husband **Admetus**. He killed innumerable giants, monsters, and brigands, most notably the giant **Antaeus**, a child of **Gaia** who drew his strength from earth; Hercules hoisted him up in the air and strangled him. He waged a number of wars, some just, some less so, against cities and kings who

offended him: for instance, when king **Laomedon** of Troy refused him the promised reward for rescuing his daughter from a sea-monster, Hercules came back with an army, sacked Troy, killed Laomedon, and put his son on the throne.

After the Labours were over Hercules took a second wife: **Deianira**, a princess of **Calydon**, whom he won by defeating his rival, the river god **Achelous**, in a wrestling contest. Returning home, they came to a river where the centaur **Nessus** offered to carry Deianira across; but on the way he tried to rape her, and Hercules, from the river bank, shot him with a poisoned arrow. The dying Nessus pretended remorse, and told Deianira to take some of the blood from his wound: if she ever lost Hercules' affection, it would act as an infallible love potion.

Later Hercules fell in love with another woman, **Iole,** princess of **Oechalia**. He pursued her with some vigour, in the process murdering her brother, and making war on her city. In an attempt to reclaim his love, Deianira soaked a tunic in the centaur's blood and sent it by a servant to Hercules. When he put it on, the poison began to burn him, and when he tried to tear it off it tore away his flesh. Raging in intolerable pain, he flung the messenger into the sea (while Deianira, hearing the news, hanged herself in remorse); then he built a funeral pyre on **Mount Oeta** and burned himself to death. But, although his mortal body died, his divine part ascended to heavn, where his father Zeus welcomed him as a god and married him to Hebe, the goddess of youth.

(Excerpted from http://historylink102.com/greece2/)

Proper Nouns

1. **Hercules** ['hə:kjuli:z]：赫拉克勒斯，希腊神话中的勇士。
2. **Jason** ['dʒeisən]：伊阿宋，希腊神话中的勇士。
3. **Theseus** ['θi:sju:s; -siəs]：忒修斯，希腊神话中的勇士。
4. **Oedipus** ['i:dipəs; 'e-]：俄狄浦斯，希腊神话中的勇士。
5. **Perseus** ['pə:sju:s; -siəs]：珀耳修斯，希腊神话中的勇士。
6. **Hydra** ['haidrə]：许德拉，希腊神话中的蛇怪。
7. **Minotaur** ['mainətɔ:]：弥诺陶洛斯，希腊神话中的人身牛头怪物。
8. **Gorgon** ['gɔ:gən]：希腊神话中的蛇发女怪。
9. **Danae** ['dænə; 'dænei:]：达那厄，珀耳修斯的母亲。
10. **King Acrisius of Argos**：阿哥斯城邦的国王阿克里西俄斯，是珀耳修斯的外祖父。
11. **Dictys** ['diktis]：狄克堤斯，塞里福思岛国王的弟弟，从海上救回了珀耳修斯和他的母亲。
12. **Polydectes** [pɔuli'dektis]：波吕得克忒斯，塞里福思岛的国王。
13. **Medusa** [mi'dju:zə]：美杜莎，古希腊神话中3位蛇发女怪之一。
14. **Andromeda** [æn'drɔmidə]：安德洛墨达，希腊神话中的埃塞俄比亚公主，珀耳修斯的妻子。
15. **Cassiopeia** [ˌkæsiəu'pi:ə]：卡西俄珀亚，安德洛墨达的母亲。
16. **Nereids** ['niərid]：涅瑞伊得，海中仙女。

17. **Phineus** ['fi:nju:s]:菲纽斯。
18. **Larissa**:拉里萨,希腊地名。
19. **Tiryns** ['ti:rins]:梯林斯,希腊古城。
20. **Mycenae** [mɑi'si:ni:]:迈锡尼,希腊南部古城。
21. **Alcmene** [ælk'mi:nə]:阿尔克墨涅,赫拉克勒斯的母亲。
22. **Amphitryon** [æm'fitriən]:安菲特律翁,底比斯王,阿尔克墨涅的丈夫。
23. **Thebes** [θi:bz]:底比斯古城。
24. **Milky Way**:银河,银河系。
25. **Autolycus** [ɔː'tɔləkəs]:奥托吕科斯,希腊神话中著名的窃贼和骗子,奥德修斯的外祖父。
26. **Castor** ['kɑːstə]:卡斯托耳,和波吕丢刻斯并称为双子星(Castor and Pollux)。
27. **Cheiron** ['kaiərɔn]:喀戎,希腊神话中半人半马的聪明博学的怪物(亦作 Chiron)。
28. **Eumolpus** [ju:'mɔlpəs]:欧摩尔波斯,波塞冬之子。
29. **Eurytus** ['ju:ritəs]:欧律托斯,俄卡利亚王。
30. **Megara** ['megərə]:墨伽拉(人名,希腊神话中底比斯国王克瑞翁的女儿);迈加拉(地名,在古雅典附近)。
31. **Delphi** ['delfai]:德尔斐,希腊古城。
32. **Eurystheus** [juə'risθju:s; -θiəs]:欧律斯透斯,希腊神话中迈锡尼国王,珀耳修斯的孙子。
33. **Nemean** [ni'mi:ən] **Lion** 涅墨亚狮子,赫拉克勒斯勒死的猛狮,这是他完成的12项英雄业绩之一。
34. **Hydra of Lerna**:勒拿九头蛇,即怪物许德拉。
35. **Golden Hind**:克律涅亚山里金角铜蹄的赤牡鹿。
36. **Erymanthian** [ˌeri'mænθiən] **Boar**:厄律曼托斯山上的野猪。
37. **Stables of Augeas** [ɔː'dʒi:æs]:奥吉亚斯王的牛厩。
38. **Stymphalian** [stim'feiliəm] **Birds**:斯廷法罗湖上的怪鸟。
39. **Cretan** ['kri:tən] **Bull**:克里特岛神牛。
40. **Crete** [kri:t]:希腊克里特岛。
41. **Tiryns**:梯林斯,希腊迈锡尼文明的一个重要遗址。
42. **Thracian** ['θreiʃən] **Horses**:色雷斯马。
43. **Diomedes** [ˌdaiə'mi:di:z]:狄俄墨得斯,战神阿瑞斯的儿子。
44. **Amazon Girdle**:阿玛宗女王的腰带。
45. **Cattle of Geryon** ['geriən]:革律翁的牛群。
46. **Apples of Hesperides** [he'speridi:z]:摘取赫斯珀里得斯的金苹果。
47. **Atlas** ['ætləs]:阿特拉斯,希腊神话中的巨神,以肩膀扛顶着天。
48. **Prometheus** [prəu'mi:θju:s; -θiəs]:普罗米修斯,希腊神话中的人物,为人类盗火种而甘愿受罚。
49. **Cerberus** ['sə:bərəs]:刻耳柏洛斯,希腊神话中的冥府守门狗。
50. **Argonaut** ['ɑ:gənɔt]:希腊神话中的阿尔戈英雄。
51. **Alcestis** [æl'sestis]:阿尔刻斯提斯,阿德墨托斯的妻子,主动提出代替其夫赴死。
52. **Admetus** [æd'mi:təs]:阿德墨托斯,阿尔戈英雄之一。
53. **Antaeus** [æn'ti:əs]:安泰俄斯,该亚和波塞冬之子,希腊神话中的大力士,在摔跤比赛中被赫拉克勒斯摔死。
54. **Gaia** [geiə]:该亚,大地女神。
55. **Laomedon** [lei'ɔmidən]:拉俄墨冬,特洛伊的创建人。

56. **Deianira** [ˌdiːəˈnɑiərə; ˌdeiə-]：得伊阿尼拉，赫拉克勒斯之妻。
57. **Calydon** [ˈkælidən]：卡吕冬，古希腊城市。
58. **Achelous** [ˌæki'ləuəs]：阿克洛俄斯，河神。
59. **Nessus** [ˈnesəs]：涅索斯，希腊神话中的马人怪。
60. **Iole** [iˈəulə]：伊俄勒，俄卡利亚古城的公主。
61. **Oechalia**：俄卡利亚，希腊古城。
62. **Mount Oeta**：俄塔山。

After You Read

Knowledge Focus

1. Solo Work: Decide whether the following statements are true or false.

1) (   ) The most dangerous thing for a Greek hero, according to the text, is to marry and have children.
2) (   ) According to an oracle, Perseus would kill Zeus after he was born.
3) (   ) Polydectes was very interested in the beautiful Danae, and therefore was affectionate with Danae and her child.
4) (   ) Medusa was the only one of the Gorgons to have golden wings, claws of brass, and serpents for hair.
5) (   ) Perseus killed Medusa by looking directly into her eyes and turned her into a stone.
6) (   ) After taking the throne from his grandfather, Perseus ended up happily with his wife for the rest of his long life.
7) (   ) Hercules was the son of Alcmena and her husband Amphitryon.
8) (   ) Hercules was born with versatile gifts, including boxing and archery.
9) (   ) Hercules carried out twelve labours because he wanted to be the greatest hero of all times.
10) (   ) Hercules eventually died of the poison given by his wife.

2. Pair Work: Discuss the following questions with your partner.

1) What kind of people were "heroes" in Greek tales? Do these tales share anything in common?
2) What was the story regarding Perseus' birth? Who were his parents?
3) Why was Perseus given the task of killing Medusa, the hideous Gorgon?
4) How did Perseus kill Medusa? What magical tools did he use to complete his task?
5) What happened to Perseus after he killed Medusa?
6) Who was Hercules? How was he born and who were his parents?
7) What suffering did Hercules go through during his birth? Why did he suffer so much?
8) What led to the famous Twelve Labors of Hercules?
9) Please give a brief account of Hercules' twelve labors. What did he do for each of his labors?
10) How did Hercules die? Please comment on the reason of his death.

Ancient Greek and Roman Mythology

Cue Card 1: Perseus vs. Medusa

◇ son of Zeus and Danae
◇ the oracle
◇ Danae gave birth to Perseus
◇ floated out to sea
◇ rescued by a fisherman
◇ the King's unwelcome attentions
◇ be sent off to an impossible quest—Medusa
◇ Medusa—one of the Gorgons
◇ offended Athena
◇ magical tools
◇ cut off Medusa's head

Cue Card 2: Hercules' Death

◇ Deianira, Hercules' second wife
◇ Nessus offered to carry Deianira across the river
◇ Nessus was shot by Hercules
◇ Deianira was persuaded to take some blood from his wound
◇ Hercules fell in love with Iole
◇ Deianira wanted to reclaim his love
◇ soaked a tunic
◇ Hercules was burned with poison
◇ his divine ascended to heaven

Language Focus

1. Fill in the blanks with the words or expressions you have learned from the text.

motif	dispose of	evade	locate(v.)
oracle	make peace with	disguise (n.)	
talk...into...	partial	retrieve	

1) Computers are used to store and _____ information efficiently.
2) The police have assured the public that the escaped prisoners will not _____ recapture for long.
3) I _____ him _____ making concessions on the question.
4) If you are trying to _____ a particular book, you can ask the labrairian for help.
5) The _____ of betrayal and loss is crucial in all these stories.
6) His job is not only to _____ problems but (also) to meet unexpected challenges.
7) The general has ordered a _____ withdrawal of troops from the area.
8) He put on a large hat and glasses as a _____ and hoped no one would recognise him.
9) She wanted to _____ her next-door neighbors, so she called on them on the first day when she moved there.

10) An _____ in Greek mythology was often a priest who gave people wise but often mysterious advice from a god.

2. Fill in the blanks with the proper form of the word in the brackets.
1) The large _____ (inherit) from his aunt meant that he could buy his own boat.
2) He traces his _____ (descend) back to an old Norman family.
3) His vulgarity made him _____ (welcome) in our home.
4) The path was obscured almost to the point of _____ (invisible).
5) Several rioters were _____ (force) removed from the town square.
6) It took hours of negotiations to bring about a _____ (reconcile) between the two sides.
7) She faces the _____ (Hercules) task of bringing up four children single-handedly.
8) Half the people questioned said they were opposed to military _____ (intervene) in the civil war.
9) He gave them his honest opinion, _____ (fear) of the consequences.
10) I felt the soil creep and heave beneath me, like some _____ (monster) serpent.

3. Fill in the blanks with the proper prepositions or adverbs that collocate with the neighboring words.
1) In the loss of enough records, fear becomes the norm, and _____ of fear, one attacks another in order to survive.
2) One part of the ship was flooding but no one was aware _____ the danger.
3) They could not afford to offend him _____ sticking up for Owen.
4) He is believed to have been shot by a rival gang _____ revenge for the shootings last week.
5) I found her letter _____ accident as I was looking _____ my files.
6) Ben began to get increasingly irritated _____ her questions.
7) All the police officers were equipped _____ shields to defend themselves _____ the rioters.
8) The autopsy revealed that his murderer had struck him _____ the head _____ an iron bar.

4. Proofreading: The following passage contains ten errors. Each indicated line contains a maximum of one error. In each case, only ONE word is involved. Read the passage and correct the errors.

After his labors Hercules married Deianeira, the daughter of King Oeneus. The (1) _____
couple did not live happily ever after, although. One day in their travels Hercules (2) _____
and Deianeira had to cross a river swelling by floods. Hercules swam across but left
his wife to be ferried across by a centaur boatman, who attempted to rape Deianeira.
Hercules then shot the centaur by one of the arrows poisoned with the Hydra's (3) _____
blood. (4) _____

The dead centaur extracted his revenge by offering Deianeira his blood, (5) _____
promising that it would act as a love ointment to keep her husband faithful to her.

One day Deianeira began to doubt that Hercules was interested in another
woman. So she gave Hercules a shirt on which she had spread some of the dying (6) _____
centaur's blood. When Hercules put on the shirt the poisoning blood began to do its (7) _____
work, burning Hercules' meat to the bone. Hercules could not die. So he built (8) _____

himself a funeral pyre. He spread his lion-skin cloak on the pyre and laid down (9) _____
on it. The flames burned up the moral part of him, while the immortal part
descended to Mount Olympus, where Zeus set him among the stars. (10) _____

Comprehensive Work

1. Greek Heroes vs. Modern Heroes

The popularity of the heroic tradition seen in Greek and other ancient cultures has continued unbroken to the present day. Legends immortalize cultural heroes, fairy tales echo heroic themes, folk tales show average men, women, and children acting heroically, and even fables sometimes show animals taking the role of the hero.

Compare the characteristics of Greek and modern HEROES, and complete the following forms.

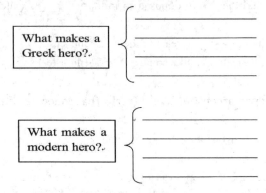

2. A Writing Practice

What is a hero? What does it take to be a hero? Please write a short essay describing the heroic characteristics of Hercules.

Please close your essay by nominating a modern-day hero, someone who exhibits many of those same characteristics.

Text B Hercules: An Ageless Icon

The word Herculean is synonymous with superhuman strength, and can be found in almost any English dictionary. But the man and myth, which is Hercules today, is not the same one as first recorded millennia ago. No man has touched the course of human events, nor captured the imagination of so many generations, as the Greek hero, Heracles. But who was the real man, and how did he transcend mythology itself, to become an ageless icon?

The story of Hercules, or Heracles as he was known in the original Greek texts, is a long and complex one, which grew even longer, and more confusing as the character of Hercules evolved in both literature and theatre. In Greek mythology, he was the mortal son of the great god Zeus, and blessed with extraordinary strength by his demi-god birth. It is interesting to note that Greek mythology singled him out from birth, since it also labeled him as the twin of Iphocles.

Perhaps most famous of all Hercules' exploits were his adventures, or Twelve Labors. While these were far from his only adventures, they were the ones which most captured the imagination of classical storytellers and poets. A further series of adventures take place simultaneously with Twelve Labors, and were known as the Parerga. Then, after he was freed from his service to Eurystheus, King of Argos, Hercules undertook a further series of adventures, including Troy, Ellis, and Pylons. Other adventures appear to have followed these, but many have decayed due to age and poor storage, and it is likely that others were passed on purely through oral traditions, and were never recorded when oration, as a means of storytelling, died out. One mention is made of him as aiding the Olympian gods against a race of giants, but this much-later text is often viewed as a work of complete fiction.

Linguists and historians are quick to point out the fallacies of Hercules' Grecian godhood, since the word "Hercules" most likely means "glorious gift of Hera," and no Greek god was ever given a name which was compounded from another god or goddess' name. Many believe, in fact, that he was probably, at one point, a real man. One man in particular, a chieftain of Tiryns in Mycenaean times and a vassal to Argos, is believed to be the real Hercules. He was, from all surviving accounts, a strong man, highly connected, and it was said of him that he had "the ear of the Gods Themselves." From this description, it is easy to see how a legend could begin of a man who was not only blessed by the gods, but also related to them. For certain, Greek art and literature was enamored with him from the very beginning. He was always depicted as an enormously strong man of moderate height, a huge eater and drinker, very amorous, and generally kind but capable of random outbursts of brutal rage. Many of the surviving representations of Hercules are statues, though Euripides features the hero in several of his plays.

By the age of the Roman Empire, most of the Greek gods and heroes had either been radically altered or completely forgotten. But, as in most matters pertaining to conquest, the conquerors took what they wanted from the conquered, and that included mythologies. Where the Romans borrowed from the Greek myths, they did so with impunity. The legend of Heracles was one such borrowed myth. The Romans changed his name from Heracles to Hercules, and his position from mortal man to immortal god. Under Rome, Hercules became the God of merchants and traders, dispensing luck freely, and was often prayed to for rescue from danger.

Besides becoming a god, Hercules changed in many other ways at the hands of the Imperialistic Romans. Artificial legends, more fiction than fact, told of Hercules' return from raiding Greyon's cattle (one of the Twelve Labors), and how he visited the future site of Rome along the way. Supposedly, by Roman accounts, he also introduced more humane rites in place of human sacrifice, and even taught the people to worship himself after he killed the monster Cacus and earned their respect. This final act is so contrary to the Hercules of Greek myth that the image of Hercules would be forever changed by it.

Of course, by the fall of Rome, the old gods of the Empire had been replaced or regulated to subservient positions by Christianity. Hercules was no exception. Once again divested of his godhood, he returned to his former status as a great and powerful hero. By the time Medieval literature truly began to flourish in the thirteenth century, Hercules had become little more than a romantic figure of chivalrous virtues, far from the dynamic hero of Classical Greece. In the Romance of Alexander, for example, the hero's tent is described as being decorated with images of the Herculean Dodekathlos. And, in the French romance Les Prouesses et Vaillances du Pruex Hercule, published in Paris in 1500, Hercules' labors were claimed in the honor of a Boeotian princess. Many other liberal licenses were taken with the myth of Hercules during the medieval period, when writers and artists interpreted the myths through the eyes of popular ideals of chivalry and intrigue. The legend of Hercules grew more heroic and complex at the hands of medieval writers; so complex, in fact, that it became nearly impossible to distinguish between the original legend and the fictitious additions of the Saxon-influenced Medieval literature.

As the Renaissance began, and scientific and literary study increased, however, scholars began to relearn the ancient Greek, which had been abandoned for the Church's Latin during the Dark Ages. With Greek as their ally, scholars delved into the undiluted mythology of Classical Greece, and efforts were made to recapture the original spirit of the mythological figures. However, the heroic Hercules was beyond such reversals. The romantics of the medieval era had already forever altered him into the flawless hero, and people were loath to see that hero destroyed.

If Hercules is still a familiar name today, however, it is not because of his Roman godhood, nor because of his medieval perfection. Instead, it can be attributed to his Greek roots, in that he was always more than simply a muscular demi-god. Like most Greek heroes, he had great strength and courage, but also terrible weaknesses and faults. He, like the rest of humanity, was subject to the unpredictability of fate and the violably of human nature. However, the war-entrenched world of the early twentieth century needed a Hercules who possessed none of the moral or bloody blemishes, which so reminded them of Hitler and his own Ubermensch. In 1934, two Americans, Jerry Siegel and Joe Shuster, created a hero with Herculean roots who was to be a defender of all humanity and possessed a humanitarianism that went beyond heroic. That creation, the comic hero Superman, would eventually spawn a whole genre of super heroic fiction, which calls up images of the mighty Hercules even today.

In the 1950s and 60s, the silver screen reached out to take up the legend, and a new age of heroes began. By the late 1980s, several more Herculean-based movies propelled themselves into history on the back of modern interpretations of Greek mythology. Then, in the early 1990s, a popular television show, starring Kevin Sorbo as the legendary Hercules, brought the ancient myths into an entirely new light, choosing to overlook the more lurid and brutal sides of the Greek hero for his more humane aspects. And then, in 1997, the myth reached its evolutionary pinnacle with the Walt Disney Organization's release of a full-length animated interpretation of the Herculean legends, in which Hercules was not the illegitimate son of Zeus and a mortal woman, but rather the kidnapped child of Zeus and his wife, the goddess Hera.

In the millennia since Hercules found his origins in Greek mythology as the hero Hercules, he has evolved from a being flawed like any other to an untouchable icon, far outreaching even the ancient gods of Olympus. And yet, through it all, the only thing, which has never changed, is Hercules' basic sense of human compassion, proving once and for all that some things even evolution cannot strip away from humanity.

(Excerpted from http://www.essortment.com/all/herculesgreekh_rmgk.htm)

Questions for Reflection

1. How did Hercules' story evolve in the course of the history? Please fill in the following form with what you have read in the text.

Times Periods	Hercules' Image
Greek time	
Roman Empire	
Medieval time	
Renaissance	
the 20th century	
the 21st century	

2. Through all the evolution of Hercules' story, what remains unchanged all the time?

Text C Perseus and Medusa

PERSEUS was the son of Jupiter and Danaë. His grandfather Acrisius, alarmed by an oracle which had told him that his daughter's child would be the instrument of his death, caused the mother and child to be shut up in a chest and set adrift on the sea. The chest floated towards Seriphus, where it was found by a fisherman who conveyed the mother and infant to Polydectes, the king of the country, by whom they were treated with kindness. When Perseus was grown up Polydectes sent him to attempt the conquest of Medusa, a terrible monster who had laid waste the country. She was once a beautiful maiden whose hair was her chief glory, but as she dared to vie in beauty with Minerva, the goddess deprived her of her charms and changed her beautiful ringlets into hissing serpents. She became a cruel monster of so frightful an aspect that no living thing could behold her without being turned into stone. All around the cavern where she dwelt might be seen the stony figures of men and animals which had chanced to catch a glimpse of her and had been petrified with the sight. Perseus, favored by Minerva and Mercury, the former of whom lent him her shield and the latter his winged shoes, approached Medusa while she slept, and taking care not to look directly at her, but guided by her image reflected in the bright shield which he bore, he cut off her head and gave it to Minerva, who fixed it in the middle of her Aegis.

Milton, in his "Comus," thus alludes to the Aegis:

"What was that snaky-headed Gorgon-shield
That wise Minerva wore, unconquered virgin,
Wherewith she freezed her foes to congealed stone,
But rigid looks of chaste austerity,
And noble grace that dashed brute violence
With sudden adoration and blank awe!"

Armstrong, the poet of the "Art of Preserving Health," thus describes the effect of frost upon the waters:

"Now blows the surly North and chills throughout
The stiffening regions, while by stronger charms

Than Circe e'er or fell Medea brewed,
Each brook that wont to prattle to its banks
Lies all bestilled and wedged betwixt it banks,
Nor moves the withered reeds...
The surges baited by the fierce North-east,
Tossing with fretful spleen their angry heads,
E'en in the foam of all their madness struck
To monumental ice.

...

Such execution,
So stern, so sudden, wrought the grisly aspect
Of terrible Medusa,
When wandering through the woods she turned to stone
Their savage tenants; just as the foaming Lion
Sprang furious on his prey, her speedier power;
Outran his haste,
And fixed in that fierce attitude he stands
Like Rage in marble!"
—Imitations of Shakespeare.

(Excerpted from http://www.bartleby.com/181/152.html)

Questions for Reflection

1. What is told in Milton's poem? Can you explain the meaning of those lines?
2. Which scene of Perseus' story is described in Armstrong's poem? Discuss the meaning of the poem with your classmates.

Websites to Visit

http://www.perseus.tufts.edu/Herakles/labors.html
If you are interested in Hercules' Twelve Labors, visit this website for more detailed information. There are also beautiful illustrations to each of Hercules' labor story.

http://www.abc.net.au/arts/wingedsandals/storytime1.htm
This website provides an interesting animated cartoon film featuring Perseus' life story and his fight with Medusa. Visit the website if you want to know more about Perseus' story.

Unit 9
The Age of Heroes (II)

> Look ye, countrymen and Thebans, this is Oedipus the great,
> He who knew the Sphinx's riddle and was mightiest in our state.
> Who of all our townsmen gazed not on his fame with envious eyes?
> Now, in what a sea of troubles sunk and overwhelmed he lies!
> Therefore wait to see life's ending ere thou count one mortal blest;
> Wait till free from pain and sorrow he has gained his final rest.
> —Sophocles, *Oedipus Rex*

Unit Goals

- To understand the concept of "hero" in classical mythology
- To know the myths of Jason, Theseus and Oedipus
- To be able to tell the stories of Jason, Theseus and Oedipus
- To learn the useful words and expressions that describe heroes and their heroic myths
- To improve language skills and critical thinking through the content of this unit

Before You Read

1. The Riddle of the Sphinx

Have you ever heard of the riddle of the Sphinx? The sphinx, in Greek tradition, is a treacherous and merciless monster. Those who cannot answer her riddle will be gobbled up whole and raw. Do you know her riddle?

1) Please write down the riddle.

_____

2) Compare what you've written down with the riddle in Text A to see whether your memory is correct.
3) Who solved the riddle of the Sphinx?

_____

4) Napoleon, the French Emperor, once made a similar riddle. Can you work out the answer of his riddle?

My empire extends far and wide; I wash my comb in the tide. Whilst I crow, the sun doth rise; And in my breast, all Europe lies.

What is it? _____

5) The Sphinx not only appears in Greek mythology, it is also a cultural icon of Ancient Egypt. Please compare the following two pictures. What similarities and differences can you find between the Greek Sphinx and the Egyptian Sphinx?

2. Oedipus Complex

Do you know Oedipus Complex? Form groups of three or four students. Try to find, on the Internet or in the library, more information about the meaning or the origin of this term. Then prepare a five-minute classroom presentation and report to your classmates.

Start to Read

Text A The Age of Heroes (II)

Jason

Jason is perhaps one of the less heroic of the Greek heroes—fully human, and dependent in most of his adventures on the help of his companions and his wife. His story falls into two distinct parts: the romantic adventure of the Argonauts and the quest for the **Golden Fleece**, and the tragedy of the marriage of Jason and **Medea**.

Jason was the son of **Aeson**, the rightful king of Iolcos (a small kingdom in **Thessaly**), whose throne had been usurped by his half-brother **Pelias**. Jason was brought up in secret in the hills, and tutored by the wise old centaur **Chiron**.

When he reached manhood he set off for Iolcos to claim his father's kingdom. On the way, he helped an old woman across a river, losing one of his sandals in the process. The old woman was in fact the goddess Hera, who had her own reasons for hating Pelias (who had refused to sacrifice to her), and who decided to help Jason. When the youth arrived in Iolcos, Pelias was alarmed: an oracle had warned him to beware of a man with only one sandal. Like Polydectes in the Perseus legend, he

decided that the best way to get rid of this inconvenient young hero was to send him off on a dangerous quest, and so he promised Jason that he would surrender the throne if Jason could bring him back the Golden Fleece.

The Golden Fleece was a treasure famous in Jason's family. A generation or two earlier, a young Thessalian prince and princess had been about to be sacrificed, by the machinations of their wicked stepmother, when a magnificent golden ram with wings flew down and carried them off to the east. The girl, **Helle**, fell off and drowned in what was thereafter known as the

Hellespont, but the boy, **Phrixus**, arrived safely in **Colchis**, a rich and eerily magical barbarian land on the far shore of the Black Sea, where king **Aeetes**, son of the sun god, welcomed him and gave him his daughter in marriage. The ram was sacrificed, and its golden fleece hung up in a sacred grove guarded by a dragon.

Jason had a great ship built, **the Argo** ('swift') — according to some, the first ship, or the first ocean-going ship, ever built. He assembled a crew of fifty Argonauts that included most of the heroes of the age. They had many adventures on the journey: The loss of young **Hylas**, stolen by amorous water-nymphs (and of his lover Hercules, who left the ship to search for him); **Pollux**'s boxing match to the death with the brutal king **Amycus**; a pleasant if slightly nervous interlude with the women of **Lemnos**, who had killed their husbands, and whose queen **Hypsipyle** fell in love with Jason; a battle with the **Harpies** which tormented the blind king **Phineas**; an encounter with the bronze giant **Talus** (whom they killed by shooting out the bronze nail in his ankle and letting the ichor that animated him drain out); the deadly passage between **the Clashing Rocks**, which would crush any ship that passed between them. At last they arrived at Colchis.

King Aeetes did not welcome them. He told Jason that to win the Golden Fleece he must carry out a series of impossible tasks: to yoke a pair of fire breathing bulls and plough a field with them, to sow it with dragon teeth, and then to kill the warriors who would grow from the teeth. However, the king's daughter Medea, herself a powerful sorceress, fell in love with Jason. She helped Jason to carry out the tasks, giving him a magic ointment that made him invulnerable to fire or sword, showing him how to trick the earth-born warriors into killing one another, and charming the dragon guardian to sleep so that Jason could kill it and steal the fleece. And as the Argo escaped from Colchis, with Medea on board, she aided their escape by a ruthless stratagem —killing her little brother and throwing the pieces of his body overboard to distract the pursuing Colchian ships.

After many more adventures — including Jason's marriage to Medea along the way — the Argonauts returned to Iolcos and delivered the Golden Fleece to Pelias. Pelias, however, refused to surrender the throne. Once again, Medea took bold steps to solve the problem. Having already magically restored the youth of Aeson, Jason's father, she persuaded Pelias's daughters that they could do the same for their father, by chopping him up into pieces and boiling him in a cauldron of magical herbs. They did so — but (Medea having left out the vital ingredient) Pelias failed to survive the treatment. However, Jason and Medea did not profit by this murder, for they were banished from Iolcos.

They went into exile in Corinth, where Medea bore Jason two children. However, Jason was clearly beginning to regret his marriage to a barbarian witch, and at last decided to divorce her in order to marry **Glauce**, the king of Corinth's daughter. Euripides' tragedy *Medea* deals with the enraged Medea's revenge for this betrayal: she sent the bride a poisoned robe and crown, which burned both her and her father to death; then murdered her own children by Jason, and flew away in a chariot drawn by dragons towards Athens (where she reappears in the story of Theseus). Jason was left to mourn, until at last he met a sad and ironic end: as he sat brooding under the rotting hulk of the Argo, a piece of its stern fell and killed him.

Theseus

Theseus is the most famous hero of Athens. His mother was **Aethra**, daughter of King **Pittheus** of **Troezen**. His father was either King **Aegeus** or the Poseidon, the god of the Sea.

King Aegeus was unable to have children from his first two wives. He consulted the Oracle at Delphi for an answer to his problem. Aegeus did not understand the oracle's answer which was in the form of a riddle. Aegeus went to the wise King Pittheus to find the understanding. Pittheus understood the riddle but did not reveal it to Aegeus. Instead, he got Aegeus drunk and took him to his daughter Aethra to lay with. That same night, unknown to Aegeus or Pittheus, Poseidon also shared the bed of Aethra.

When Aegeus left, he put a sword and sandals under a rock. He left instructions with Aethra to tell his son about them when he was older. She was to tell him to move the rock and bring the sword and sandals to Athens so Aegeus would recognize his son.

Theseus grew up to be a strong and witty young man. When he was old enough, he attempted to move the stone under which his father had buried the sword. He was unable to move it, so he built a pulley system to lift the rock. With the pulley system, Theseus was able to retrieve the sword and sandals.

He set out for Athens overland. He was advised to take the much safer boat route but refused. Instead, he traveled through the dangerous **Isthmus of Corinth**. On his journey, he encountered many evil men who preyed on travelers. He defeated them all, making them suffer the same fate they would bestow on their victims. By the time he reached Athens, he was famous for his deeds.

King Aegeus did not yet recognize Theseus as his son, and he was worried that this popular young man might try to steal his throne. To prevent this, he sent Theseus on a mission to kill the Marathonia Bull and bring it back to Athens. Theseus caught the bull and returned it to the king. The king's wife Medea, who was a sorceress, recognized Theseus and suggested poisoning the young hero. King Aegeus recognized the sword Theseus was wearing just before the poisoned wine was given to his son. Medea and her son were banished from the kingdom for their part in the plot kill Theseus.

Several years earlier, Crete attacked Athens. To ward off the attack, the Athenians had agreed to pay a yearly tribute of seven boys and girls to feed a **Minotaur**. The Minotaur was a monster with a head of a bull and body of a man. Theseus offered to be one of the men to be given to the Minotaur. When Theseus arrived in Crete, Ariadne, the daughter of the king fell in love with him at first sight. She gave him a sword and spool of string he could use to find his way back out of the labyrinth which the Minotaur lived. Theseus went into the maze and found the Minotaur sleeping near the center. He killed the monster and escaped with the others from Athens.

Theseus, along with his fellow Athenians and **Ariadne**, escaped to their ship and headed back to Athens. On their way, they stopped at the island of **Naxos**. Some stories suggest that Theseus abandoned Ariadne on this island. Others say the god **Dionysus** stole her away. In any case, Theseus headed back to Athens without her.

Theseus had forgotten a promise he had made to his father. The ship carrying the fourteen Athenians always flew a black flag. Theseus had promised his father to change the flag to white on the voyage home if he had survived. Aegeus, seeing the black flag threw himself into the sea, believing that his son had died on his mission. The sea was named the Aegean in his honor.

Due to his father's death, Theseus now became the king of Athens. He was credited with moving the government to a democratic style of governing.

Another story for which Theseus was famous was for his attempt to court one of the daughters of Zeus. Theseus set his sights on Helen, a princess of Sparta. Theseus, along with his friend **Peirithous**, was able to abduct **Helen of Sparta** when she was only ten years old. In return for his help, Theseus agreed to assist Peirithous to try and court another of Zeus's daughters **Persephone**, the queen of the underworld. Theseus and Peirithous entered the underworld on their quest. To their surprise, Hades welcomed them in and asked them to sit down. They found out that Hades had no intention of giving up his queen, whom he had worked so hard to keep. They sat in chairs of forgetfulness and could not escape, being held there by each chair's powers. It was not until Hercules happened upon them that Theseus was released. Hercules was unable to release Peirithous, and he had to remain in the underworld.

On returning to Athens, Theseus found that the Athenians were angry at him for his abduction of Helen. His throne was assumed by **Menestheus** and he was no longer welcomed in the city. He found a refuge with King Lycomedes (even thought the king envied Theseus) on the island of **Scyros**. While walking along a cliff, Lycomedes shoved Theseus off the cliff to his death.

Oedipus

Oedipus was the mythical king of Thebes. He was the son of **Laius** and **Jocasta** and became king of Thebes after killing his father, solving the riddle of **the Sphinx** and unknowingly marrying his mother. After Oedipus is king, his sons fight over the throne and kill each other.

Variations on the Oedipus legend are mentioned in fragments by several ancient Greek poets including **Homer**, **Hesiod** and **Pindar**.

Much of what is known of Oedipus comes from a famous play by **Sophocles**: *Oedipus the King*.

Long before Oedipus was born, Laius, Oedipus' father, had kidnapped a young boy and was then cursed by the boy's father. The weight of this curse bore down onto Oedipus himself. An oracle prophesied that he would kill his father and marry his mother, Jocasta. Seeking to avoid such a fate, Laius was very careful with his wife Jocasta and did not touch her. Since Jocasta did not know of the prophecy, she felt she must have a child, for the only way for her to gain honour was to get pregnant.

When Oedipus was born, Laius had the infant's ankles pierced with a brooch and had him exposed on **Mount Kithairon** (placed in the wilderness to die). His soft-hearted servant, however, could not carry out Laius' order and instead handed the boy to a shepherd who presented the child to King and Queen of Corinth, who raised him as their own son.

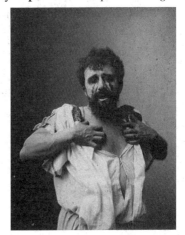

At a party thrown by King of Corinth, a drunk guest called Oedipus a bastard and claimed that the King was not his real father. Seeking to confirm his lineage, not believing the man, Oedipus sought out the Oracle at Delphi. Instead of telling him his lineage, the Oracle related the same prophecy as was told to his father: that he would kill his father and marry his mother. After descending the mountain, on a road where three roads meet, he met an unarmed man with a staff on his own pilgrimage, riding a chariot. The man in the chariot demanded that Oedipus stand aside so he could pass, finally hitting Oedipus with his staff. Oedipus killed the stranger and all but one of his entourage. The man he had killed, unknown to Oedipus, was King Laius, Oedipus' real father.

Oedipus decided that the drunkard at the party was lying, and decided not to return home in order to avoid King of Corinth. As he traveled, Oedipus encountered a mythical creature that was terrorizing Thebes. Oedipus saved the city by answering the riddle of the Sphinx. Q: "What walks on four legs in the morning, two legs in the afternoon, and three legs in the evening?" A: "Man, as a baby man crawls on four legs; as an adult walks on two legs; when old, man uses a cane." Since Oedipus answered the Sphinx's riddle correctly, he was offered the now-vacant throne of Thebes and the now-widowed queen's hand in marriage. Oedipus accepted both offers. Within a short time, divine signs of misfortune and pollution descended on Thebes.

The people of Thebes are begging the king for help; he must discover the cause of the plague. Oedipus swears to find the person responsible for the pestilence and execute him as well as anyone who aids him. He questions everyone in the palace, including his wife, Jocasta. Eventually, when the blind seer **Tiresias** informs Oedipus that he himself is both the source of the pollution and the murderer, the king does not believe him. Oedipus insists that the culprit is **Creon**, Jocasta's brother, whom he believes is plotting to usurp the throne. Oedipus then accuses Tiresias of lying and being a false prophet. It is not until a messenger arrives with news that King of Corinth (his supposed father) has died of natural causes that a horrified Oedipus finally solves the mystery of his birth. In a moment of recognition, he realizes that he has not only killed his own father but has also married his own mother (with whom he has had four children). When Jocasta learns the horrible truth, she hangs herself in the very chamber where she and her son have unknowingly committed incest. Seizing the brooches from her dress, Oedipus blinds himself.

Detective, murderer, judge, and jury, Oedipus condemns himself to wander in darkness throughout the land for the rest of his life.

(Excerpted from http://historylink102.com/greece2/http://upge.wn.com/?t=ancientgreece/index33.txt)

Proper Nouns

1. **Jason** [ˈdʒeisən]：伊阿宋，希腊神话中的英雄，率领阿尔戈英雄们到海外寻找金羊毛，历经艰险，终于在美狄亚的帮助下取得了成功。
2. **Golden Fleece**：金羊毛。
3. **Medea** [miˈdiə]：美狄亚，希腊神话中科尔喀斯国王之女，以巫术著称伊阿宋的妻子。

4. **Aeson** [ˈiːsən]：埃宋，伊阿宋的父亲。
5. **Thessaly** [ˈθesəli]：忒萨利，希腊古城。
6. **Pelias** [ˈpiːliæs, ˈpe-]：珀利阿斯，伊阿宋同母异父的兄弟。
7. **Chiron** [ˈkaiərən]：喀戎，马人。
8. **Helle** [ˈheli]：赫勒，希腊神话中的一位公主。
9. **Hellespont** [ˈhelispɔnt]：赫勒斯蓬特海峡，今天被称为达达尼尔海峡，位于土耳其欧亚两部分之间，连接马尔马拉海与爱琴海。
10. **Phrixus** [ˈfriksəs]：佛里克索斯，阿塔玛斯和涅斐勒之子，为逃脱继母伊诺的迫害，骑上金毛羊飞往科尔基斯。
11. **Colchis**：科尔基斯国，高加索南部古国，在今格鲁吉亚境内。
12. **Aeetes**：埃厄忒斯，科尔基斯国王，金羊毛的拥有者。
13. **The Argo** [ˈɑːgəu]：阿耳戈船，伊阿宋乘坐的寻找金羊毛的船。
14. **Hylas** [ˈhailəs]：许拉斯，赫拉克勒斯的密友。
15. **Pollux** [ˈpɔləks]：波吕丢刻斯，阿耳戈勇士之一，和卡斯托耳并称为双子星（Castor and Pollux）。
16. **Amycus** [ˈæməkəs]：阿密科斯，凶残好斗，最后被波吕丢刻斯打碎头骨而死。
17. **Lemnos** [ˈlemnɔs]：利姆诺斯岛，位于希腊。
18. **Hypsipyle** [hipˈsipələ]：许普西皮勒，拉姆诺斯岛女王。
19. **Harpy** [ˈhɑːpi]：希腊神话中的鸟身女妖，头部及身躯似女人，生有鸟翼与鸟爪。
20. **Phineas** [ˈfiniæs]：菲尼阿斯，菲纽斯国王，也拼作 Phineus。
21. **Talus** [ˈteiləs]：塔罗斯。
22. **the Clashing Rocks**：阿耳戈船在旅途中遇到重重困难，其中以撞岩(Clashing Rocks)最为著名，撞岩又叫叙姆普勒加得斯(Symplegades [simˈplegədiz])，它好像自动门一样开开合合，挡住了黑海的入口。阿耳戈勇士们费尽九牛二虎之力才得以通过。
23. **Glauce** [glaus]：格劳刻，伊阿宋的第二任妻子。
24. **Theseus** [ˈθiːsjuːs; -siəs]：忒修斯，希腊神话中的英雄之一。
25. **Aethra** [ˈeθrə]：埃特拉，忒修斯的母亲。
26. **Pittheus**：皮透斯，或庇透斯。
27. **Troezen** [ˈtrəuzən]：特罗曾，希腊古城。
28. **Aegeus** [ˈiːdʒiəs]：埃勾斯，忒修斯的父亲，希腊神话中的雅典国王。
29. **Isthmus of Corinth**：科林斯地峡。
30. **Minotaur** [ˈmainətɔː]：弥诺陶洛斯，人身牛头怪物。
31. **Minos** [ˈmainɔs]：弥诺斯，克里特岛的国王。
32. **Ariadne** [ˌæriˈædni]：阿里阿德涅，克里特公主，帮助忒修斯杀死弥诺陶洛斯，并走出迷宫。
33. **Naxos** [ˈnæksɔs]：那克索斯岛，希腊岛屿。
34. **Dionysus** [ˌdaiəˈnaisəs]：狄俄倪索斯，希腊神话中的酒神。
35. **Peirithous** [ˈpiriθəus]：庇里托俄斯，忒修斯的好朋友。
36. **Helen of Sparta**：希腊神话中最美丽的女人。
37. **Persephone** [pəˈsefəni; pə-]：珀耳塞福涅，宙斯之女，后成为冥王哈得斯之妻。
38. **Menestheus** [məˈnesθjuːs]：墨涅斯修斯，一说为忒修斯的儿子。
39. **Scyros** [ˈsairɔs]：斯基罗斯岛。
40. **Oedipus** [ˈiːdipəs; ˈe-]：俄狄浦斯，希腊神话最著名的悲剧人物之一。
41. **Laius** [ˈlaiəs]：拉伊俄斯，底比斯国王，后为其子俄狄浦斯所杀。

42. **Jocasta** [dʒəuˈkæstə]：伊俄卡斯忒,俄狄浦斯的母亲。
43. **the Sphinx** [sfiŋks]：斯芬克斯,希腊神话中带翼的狮身女怪,传说常叫过路行人猜谜,猜不出者即遭噬食。
44. **Homer**：希腊诗人荷马。
45. **Hesiod** [ˈhiːsiɔd;ˈhes-]：赫西奥德,公元前8世纪希腊诗人。
46. **Pindar** [ˈpində]：品达,古希腊抒情诗人。
47. **Sophocles** [ˈsɔfəkliːz]：索福克勒斯,古希腊悲剧诗人。
48. **Mount Kithairon**：基瑟隆山。
49. **Tiresia** [təˈrisiə]：提列西亚,希腊神话中的先知。
50. **Creon** [ˈkriːɔn]：克瑞翁,希腊神话里底比斯国王。

Knowledge Focus

1. Solo Work: Decide whether the following statements are true or false.

1) (　) Compared with other heroes, Jason is more human and he is dependent on his companions and his wife in his various adventures.
2) (　) Jason was sent off on a quest to find the Golden Fleece because he wanted to help his half-brother Pelias to get the throne.
3) (　) With the help of Medea, Jason completed many adventures on his journey and arrived at Colchis.
4) (　) Jason divorced with Medea because he fell in love with another beautiful lady.
5) (　) As a national hero of Sparta, Theseus had a life that moves from romantic and heroic youth to a painful and tragic old age.
6) (　) When Theseus learned of the tribute to Crete, he volunteered to be one of the sacrifices and kill the Minotaur.
7) (　) Theseus was noted for his introduction of a democratic style of governing into Athens.
8) (　) The legend of Oedipus was also a combination of heroic adventure and tragic old age.
9) (　) The oracle that Oedipus would kill his father and marry his mother proved right eventually.
10) (　) After Oedipus died, the troubles of the Theban royal family ended accordingly.

2. Match each figure with its description according to what you have learned in the text.

1) Jason　　　a. She helped Jason in many of his adventures but was eventually abandoned by him.
2) Pelias　　　b. the national hero of Athens who killed the Minotaur and married the queen of the Amazons.
3) Medea　　　c. Theseus' father who threw himself into what was now called the Aegean Sea.
4) Theseus　　d. a tragic hero who killed his father and married his mother.
5) Aegeus　　　e. a hero who sailed with a group of men called the Argonauts in the ship Argo to find the Golden Fleece.

6) Oedipus   f. Oedipus' mother who mistakenly married Oedipus and had children with him.
7) Jocasta   g. a creature with the head of a woman and the body of a lion. She lay outside Thebes and killed people who could not answer her riddle.
8) Sphinx   h. He sent Jason to find the Golden Fleece.

3. Pair Work: Discuss the following questions with your partner.
1) What is the Golden Fleece? Why was Jason sent off on a quest to find the Golden Fleece?
2) What adventures did Jason and his Argonauts have on their journey?
3) How did Medea, daughter of King Aeetes, helped Jason to get the Golden Fleece?
4) Who was the parentage of Theseus? What task was left by Theseus' father?
5) Did he reunite with his father after Theseus killed the Minotaur?
6) What was the oracle regarding to Oedipus fate? Was the oracle true?
7) What was the riddle of the Sphinx? Retell Oedipus' encounter with the Sphinx in your own words.
8) What do you think is the central idea of Oedipus' story? Please comment on his life.

Language Focus
1. Fill in the blanks with the words or expressions you have learned from the text.

| machination | interlude | yoke | invulnerable to | banish |
| bestow | ward off | lineage | credit (v.) | pilgrimage |

1) Most Muslims try to make a _____ to Mecca at least once in their life.
2) On the morning of New Years day, we first must set off a string of fire crackers to _____ the evil.
3) Every farmer knows how to _____ the oxen together.
4) The Chancellorship of the University was _____ upon her in 1992.
5) Their attempts to counter the _____ of the rebels finally succeeded.
6) Her time in Paris was a happy _____ in a difficult career.
7) Leonardo is often _____ with being a greater mathematician than he actually was.
8) The command bunker is virtually _____ a nuclear attack.
9) She is very proud of her ancient royal _____.
10) They were _____ from the library for making a noise.

2. Fill in the blanks with the proper form of the word in the brackets.
1) He has a _____ (right) claim to the property.
2) In the heart of the jungle, they felt _____ (vulnerable) to an attack from the air.
3) The novel starts when a child of unknown _____ (parent) is left at the house of the local priest.
4) The new movie looks _____ (comprehend) bad.
5) _____ (exhilarate) is a strong feeling of excitement and happiness.

6) I keep getting _____ (contradict) advice — some people tell me to keep it warm and some tell me to put ice on it.

7) A religious _____ (devote) is one who journeys to a shrine or sacred place.

8) _____ (predict), after the initial media interest, the refugees now seem to have been forgotten.

9) He was an English actor and theater manager, as well as the foremost _____ (tragedy) of his day.

10) We were to realize years later how _____ (prophet) he spoke on that occasion.

3. **Fill in the blanks with the proper prepositions or adverbs that collocate with the neighboring words.**

1) It is very easy to become dependent _____ sleeping pills.

2) Alone in London, without friends, work, or money, Shelley fell _____ despair.

3) You should beware _____ undercooked food when staying in hot countries.

4) The Chinese ship had 25 crew _____ board, taking to 146 the number of seafarers currently held hostage by Somali pirates.

5) China welcomed foreign aid _____ the form of material and cash.

6) When he set out _____ Bath again, there was a general expectation.

7) This relationship is called Boyle's law, _____ honor of the English physicist who discovered it.

8) Latvia is likely _____ be allowed to run a 7% deficit for this year— _____ return for promising, really and truly, to reach 4% in 2014.

9) Once all the bees had warmed up, they lifted off for their new home, which, _____ no one's surprise, turned out to be the best of the five boxes.

10) He was angry _____ having to fork over so much money _____ such simple repairs.

4. **Proofreading: The following passage contains ten errors. Each indicated line contains a maximum of one error. In each case, only ONE word is involved. Read the passage and correct the errors.**

    King Aeetes' most valuable possession was a golden ram's fleece. When Jason and the crew of the Argo arrived Colchis seeking the Golden Fleece, Aeetes was willing to relinquish it and set Jason a series of seemingly impossible tasks with the price of obtaining it. Medea fell in love with Jason and agreed to use her magical to help him, in return with Jason's promise to marry her.

    Jason fled in the Argo after obtaining the golden fleece, taking Medea and her young brother, Absyrtis, with him. King Aeetes pursued them. In order to delay the pursuit, Medea killed her brother and cut his body into pieces, scattered the parts behind the ship. The pursuers had to stop and collect Absyrtis' dismembered body in order to give it properly burial, and so Jason, Medea and the Argonauts escaped.

    After the Argo returned safely to Iolcus, Jason's home, Medea continued using her sorcery. She returned the youth of Jason's aged father, Aeson, by cutting his throat and filling his body with a magical potion. She then offered to do same for Pelias the king of Iolcus who had usurped Aeson's throne. She tricked Pelias' daughters into killing him, but left the corpse without any youth-restoring potion.

1) _____
2) _____
3) _____
4) _____
5) _____
6) _____
7) _____
8) _____
9) _____
10) _____

Comprehensive Work

1. Retell the story of Jason, Theseus and Oedipus according to the Cue Card.

Cue Card 1: Jason and the Golden Fleece

- son of Aeson
- claim his father's kingdom
- Pelias
- the Golden Fleece
- the Argo
- adventures
- King Aeetes
- impossible tasks
- Medea's help
- delivered the Golden Fleece to Pelias

Cue Card 2: Theseus killed the Minotaur

- Theseus
- Tribute to Crete
- Minos and his queen
- A Labyrinth to hide the secrete
- Ariadne's help
- Kill the Minotaur
- returned home with triumph
- Aegeus threw himself into the sea

Cue Card 3: Oedipus

- Oedipus
- prophecy
- abandoned to die
- rescued by a shepherd
- brought up in Corinth
- grew up and returned to Thebes
- killed his father by accident
- the Sphinx
- answered the riddle and became King of Thebes
- married Queen Jocasta
- struck by a plague
- uncovered the truth
- Oedipus blinded himself

2. The Tragedy of Oedipus: Discussion and Writing

Oedipus is one of the most tragic heroes in Greek mythology. His story appealed to many tragedians, of whom the most famous was Sophocles and his play *Oedipus the King*.

The following lines are taken from Sophocles' play. Read them carefully and answer the following questions.

> *Look ye, countrymen and Thebans, this is Oedipus the great,*
> *He who knew the Sphinx's riddle and was mightiest in our state.*
> *Who of all our townsmen gazed not on his fame with envious eyes?*
> *Now, in what a sea of troubles sunk and overwhelmed he lies!*
> *Therefore wait to see life's ending ere thou count one mortal blest;*
> *Wait till free from pain and sorrow he has gained his final rest.*

1) What is the riddle of the Sphinx? How did Oedipus answer the riddle?

2) In the sentence "*He who knew the Sphinx's riddle and was mightiest in our state*", why does the author say that Oedipus is the mightiest in the state?

3) Examine the sentence "*in what a sea of troubles sunk and overwhelmed he lies*". What does the word "trouble" refer to? What troubles did Oedipus go through?

4) Read the last sentence of the excerpt. What is the meaning of this sentence? Explain in your own words.

5) What do you think of Oedipus' fate? What can you learn from his story and his life? Please write a composition commenting on his life.

Read More

Text B Jason and the Argonauts

The Greek myth of Jason and the Golden Fleece is one of the oldest myths of a hero's quest. It is a classic story of betrayal and vengeance and like many Greek myths has a tragic ending. It begins when Jason's Uncle Pelias kills Jason's father, the Greek King of Iolkos, and takes his throne. Jason's mother brings him to Cheiron, a centaur (half man, half horse) who hides him away and raises him on the Mountain of Pelion.

When Jason turns 20, he journeys to see Pelias to reclaim his throne. At a nearby river, Hera the Queen of the Gods approaches him disguised as an old woman. While carrying her across the river he loses a sandal and arrives at court wearing only one. Pelias is nervous when he sees Jason missing a sandal, for an oracle has prophesied that a man wearing only one sandal shall usurp his throne.

Jason demands the return of his rightful throne. Pelias replies that Jason should first accomplish a difficult task to prove his worth. The task is for Jason to retrieve the Golden Fleece, kept beyond the edge of the known world in a land called Colchis (modern-day Georgia in Southwest Asia). The story of the fleece is an interesting tale in itself. Zeus, the King of the Gods, had given a golden ram to Jason's ancestor Phrixus. Phrixus later flew on the golden ram from Greece to Colchis, whose king was Aietes, the son of Helios the Sun God. Aietes sacrificed the ram and hung the fleece in a sacred grove guarded by a dragon, as an  oracle had foretold that Aietes would lose his kingdom if he lost the fleece.

Determined to reclaim his throne, Jason agrees to retrieve the Golden Fleece. Jason assembles a team of great heroes for his crew and they sail aboard the Argo. The first stop of the Argonauts is the Greek Isle of Lemnos, populated only by women. Unknown to Jason and his crew, the women have murdered their husbands. The Argonauts fare much better though; in fact the women use the occasion as an opportunity to repopulate the island.

After many more adventures, the Argo passes Constantinople, heading for the Straits of Bosphorus. The Straits of Bosphorus are a narrow passageway of water between the Sea of Marmara, the Aegean Sea and the Black Sea. To the ancient Greeks, this was the edge of the known world. The Straits are extremely dangerous due to the currents created by the flow of water from the Black Sea. The ancient Greeks believed that clashing rocks guarded the straits and that the rocks would close together and smash any ship sailing through. Jason had been told by a blind prophet he assisted how to fool the rocks. He was to send a bird ahead of him. The rocks would crash in on it and then reopen, at which point he could successfully sail through.

When Jason finally arrives in Colchis he asks King Aietes to return the golden fleece to him as it belonged to his ancestor. Reluctant, the king suggests yet another series of challenges to Jason. He must yoke fire-breathing bulls, plough and sow a field with dragons' teeth and then overcome the warriors who will rise from the furrows. Aietes is confident the tasks are impossible but unbeknownst to the king, his daughter Medea has taken a liking to Jason. She offers to assist Jason if he will marry  her. He agrees. Medea is a powerful sorceress and Jason is successful.

Jason and Medea return to Greece where Jason claims his father's throne, but their success is short-lived. Uncomfortable with Medea's magic, the locals drive Medea and Jason out of Iolkos. They go into exile in Corinth where the king offers Jason his daughter in marriage. He agrees and so violates his vow to the gods to be true only to Medea. Furious, Medea kills the woman, kills Medea and Jason's children and then ascends to Mount Olympus where she eventually marries Achilles. Jason goes back to Iolkos where his boat the Argo is on display. One day, while he sits next to the boat weeping, the decaying beam of his ship the Argo falls off and hits him on the head, killing him outright.

(Excerpted from http://www.pbs.org/mythsandheroes/myths_four_jason.html)

Questions for Reflection

1. The story of Jason is one of _____ and _____ and like many Greek myths has a _____ ending.
2. Why does the text say that the story of Jason is one of betrayal?
3. Why is Jason's story one of vengeance?
4. What tragic ending does Jason's story have? Retell the story in your own words.

Text C Oedipus Complex

Description

In the Oedipus complex, a boy is fixated on his mother and competes with his father for maternal attention. The opposite, the attraction of a girl to her father and rivalry with her mother, is sometimes called the Electra complex.

Sexual awakening

At some point, the child realizes that there is a difference between their mother and their father. Around the same time they realize that they are more alike to one than the other. Thus the child acquires gender.

The child may also form some kind of erotic attachment to the parent of the opposite sex. Whilst their understanding of the full sexual act may be questioned, some kind of primitive physical sensations are felt when they regard and think about the parent in question.

The primitive desire for the one parent may also awaken in the child a jealous motivation to exclude the other parent. Transferring of affections may also occur as the child seeks to become independent and escape a perceived "engulfing mother". A critical point of awakening is where the child realizes that the mother has affections for others besides itself. Primitive jealousies are not necessarily constrained to the child and both parents may join in the game, both in terms of competing with each other for the child's affections and also competing with the child for the affection of the other parent.

Note that opposition to parents may not necessarily be sexually based — this can also be a part of the struggle to assert one's identity and rebellion against parental control.

The process of transitioning

A critical aspect of the Oedipal stage is loosening of the ties to the mother of vulnerability, dependence and intimacy. This is a natural part of the child becoming more independent and is facilitated by the realization that the mother desires more than just the child.

The Oedipal move blocks the routes of sexual and identification love back to the mother. She becomes a separate object, removed from his ideal self. Thus she can be the subject of object love. This separation and externalization of love allows a transition away from narcissism of earlier stages.

The father's role in this is much debated. In a number of accounts, such as Lacan's symbolic register, the child transitions their attentions from mother to father. The father effectively says "You must be like me — you may not be like the mother — you must wait to love her, as I do." The child thus also learns to wait and share attention.

Separation

The boy thus returns to the mother as a separate individual. That separation may be emphasized with scorn and a sense of mastery over women. That can also be seen in the long separation of boys and girls in play and social relationships. This is a source of male denigration of women.

Women become separated reminders of lost and forbidden unity. Their unique attributes, from softness to general femininity are, in consequence, also lost and must be given up as a part of the distancing process. Women become thus both desired and feared. The symbolic phallus becomes a means of protection for the boy and the rituals of mastery used to cover up feelings of loss.

Separation leads to unavailability and hence the scarcity principle takes effect, increasing desire. Women thus create a tension in boys between a lost paradise and dangerous sirens. Excessive separation leads to a sense of helplessness that can in turn lead to patterns of idealized control and self-sufficiency.

Whilst the boy becomes separated from the mother, it is a long time before he can be independent of her and hence must develop a working relationship that may reflect the tension of love and difference he feels.

The relationship thus may return to a closer mother-son tie, where the point of healthy distance is a dynamically negotiated position, such that comforting is available but is required only upon occasion.

What about the girls?

Most writings about the Oedipal stage focus largely or exclusively on boys, who are seen to have a particular problem as they start with an attachment to the Mother that they have to relinquish both from the point of view of individual independence and especially as a result of the social incest taboo which forbids excessively-close in-family relationships.

The Electra complex, identified by Carl Jung, occurs where a triangle of mother-father-daughter plays out is not a part of traditional psychoanalysis. It is neither a direct mirror image of Oedipus, as the start position is female-female connection. Jung suggested that when the girl discovers she lacks penis that her father possesses, she imagines she will gain one if he makes her pregnant, and so moves emotionally closer to him. She thus resents her mother who she believe castrated her.

The father symbolizes attractive power and a potentially hazardous male-female relationship is formed, with predictable jealousies and envy as the mother completes the triangle. The dangers of incestuous abuse add, and perhaps develop, the female position of siren temptation.

Girls, as well as boys, need to find independence and their separation from the mother is a matter of creating a separate femininity. This is not as strong a separation as boys and girls can sustain a closer female-female relationships with the mothers. This perhaps explains something of why relationships with others is a more important part of a female life than it is for a male.

The father does provide a haven from female-female jealousies, and so a healthy father-daughter relationship may be built, that also includes appropriate distance. As with mother-son, once the incest taboos are established, a uniquely satisfying opposite-sex relationship can be built, although secret desires for the father can result in the girl feeling some guilt about the relationship.

(Excerpted from http://changingminds.org/disciplines/psychoanalysis/concepts/oedipus_complex.htm)

Questions for Reflection

1. What is Oedipus Complex? What do we call the attraction of a girl to her father and rivalry with her mother?
2. What feeling develops during the Oedipal stage? Is it natural?
3. Why does the author say that the Oedipus stage is a natural process in the boy's transitioning?
4. What about girls' feeling towards the father? Is there any difference between girls' feelings and that of the boys?

Movies to Watch
Jason and the Argonauts (2000)

Jason and the Argonauts is a 2000 TV movie based on the classic myth of Jason and the Golden Fleece.

At a young age, Jason witnesses the brutal deposement and murder of his father at the hands of his uncle Pelias. Twenty years later, Jason returns home to claim his rightful place as king, but Pelias orders him to be executed, and in order to save himself Jason is forced to go on a dangerous quest to find the legendary Golden Fleece. So Jason gathers a motley crew of men and sets sail on the Argos.

Unit 10

The Trojan War

> Was this the face that launch'd a thousand ships
> And burnt the topless towers of Ilium?
> Sweet Helen, make me immortal with a kiss.
> —Christopher Marlowe, British playwright, poet

Unit Goals

- To have a general understanding of the origins and the process of the Trojan War
- To learn about the city Troy and the life of Helen
- To learn the useful words and expressions that describe the Greek mythology
- To improve language skills and critical thinking through the content of this unit

Before You Read

1. The following pictures are all related to the Trojan War. Can you identify them?

2. Form groups of three or four students. Try to find, on the Internet or in the library, more information about the pictures above. Choose one as your topic and prepare a five-minute classroom presentation.

3. See if you know the right answers to the following questions. Check your answers after reading Text A.
   1) Do you know the origins of the Trojan War?
   2) Can you tell us the two parties involved in the Trojan War?
   3) Do you still remember Eris? Why did she throw on to the table a golden apple labeled "For the Most Beautiful." at the wedding of King Peleus and the sea-nymph Thetis?

Start to Read

Text A The Trojan War

The Trojan War was a great military adventure of ancient times, undertaken by the kings of ancient Greece against the city of **Troy**. It lasted for ten years and cost many lives, but also produced many heroes.

How it all started

All started at the celebrated wedding of **Peleus** and **Thetis**, who would later become the parents of hero **Achilles**. The goddess **Eris**, enraged for not being invited to the wedding, decided to toss a Golden Apple, inscribed "For the Fairest", among the goddesses. Immediately, **Hera**, **Athena** and **Aphrodite** started to fight over the apple.

To put an end to the incident, god **Zeus** appointed **Paris**, a Trojan prince and reputedly the handsomest of all men, to be the judge who would decide which of the three competitors was to win the controversial trophy.

Rather than trust the prince's impartial judgement, all three goddesses attempted to win by bribery: Hera promised him dominion over the whole world; Athena offered certain victory in every battle; Aphrodite merely offered the most beautiful woman in the world: **Helen**, a daughter of Zeus. Paris did not hesitate for a moment, quickly accepting the offer made by the goddess of love.

The abduction of Helen

Claiming his "prize", was not an easy task for Paris. Helen at the time was married to **Menelaus**, king of **Sparta** and brother of the wealthy **Agamemnon**, king of **Mycenae**. Despite this

fact and ignoring the warnings he received from his brother and sister **Helenus** and **Cassandra** who were seers (they had the capacity to foretell the future), Paris left for Sparta.

Menelaus and Helen's brothers all welcomed him at their palace and entertained him for nine days. When the king left the palace to attend his grandfather's funeral, Paris seized the opportunity and left off for Troy, taking Helen with him.

The Greek army sets off for Troy

Menelaus, being furious at Paris for what he had done, called on all the Greek kings to help him punish the Trojan. His campaign was successful: In a few months, a great army was gathered in **Aulis**, ready to set sail. Being the most powerful of all kings, Agamemnon, king of Mycenae and brother of Menelaus, took the position of Chief Commander. **Odysseus** was reluctant to go. When **Palamedes** visited, it is said, Odysseus pretended to be mad : he yoked an ass and an ox to a plough, and began to sow salt. Palamedes, to try him, placed the infant

Telemachus before the plough, whereupon the father could not continue to play his part. He stopped the plough, and was obliged to undertake the fulfilment of the promise he had made when he was one of the suitors of Helen.

But, unfortunately, unfavorable winds kept the fleet from setting out for Troy. **Calchas**, the most renowned seer at the time, blamed the ill winds on Agamemnon, whose boastful claim that he could hunt better than goddess **Artemis** had offended her and thus punished the Greeks. In order to appease the angry goddess, the seer contended that Agamemnon should sacrifice on an altar, his beloved daughter **Iphigenia**. Despite the king's reservations, the girl was finally brought to Aulis by Odysseus and **Diomedes**, under the pretext of her marrying Achilles. At the time, however, that Iphigenia was placed on the altar ready to be sacrificed, a cloud descended and the girl was taken away by Artemis. In her place, the goddess left a deer to be sacrificed.

All the events taking place in Aulis are vividly described in **Euripides**'s tragedy named *Iphigenia in Tauris*, in which it is claimed that the girl was rescued by Artemis and taken away to serve as her priestess in **Tauris**.

Once the winds changed, the fleet set out. However, **Philoctetes** was bitten by a snake during a stopover at Lemnos (one of the Aegean islands). The stench of his wound and the sound of his agony were so unbearable, that his shipmates—urged by Odysseus—abandoned him there.

The long siege begins

Before the Greek army disembarked from the ships, Menelaus and Odysseus went to meet king **Priam** to seek a diplomatic settlement of the issue, in order to avoid military conflict. While the elderly king saw favorably the return of Helen and the spartan gold in order to avoid confrontation with the mighty Greeks on the battlefield, his 50 sons would not succumb to the threat of war, opting to stand by the side of their brother Paris.

Having no other option, the Greeks decided to land and start the Trojan War. Rather than mount a direct attack on the formidable fortress of Troy, the Greeks chose instead to destroy the surrounding towns and cities. Troy depended on these settlements for its supply of provisions and aid.

Despite Zeus's strict directions to the immortals not to actively engage in the Trojan War, almost all of the Olympians lined up on either the Greek or the Trojan side. Aphrodite, chosen by Paris as the fairest of all goddesses, naturally sided with the Trojans. So did Artemis and her brother **Apollo**. Hera and Athena, being the ones who lost the beauty contest to Aphrodite, took the part of the Greeks. The same decision was taken by **Poseidon**, **Hermes** and **Hephaestus**.

The final year of the war

After nine long years, despite their victories in the surrounding area of Troy, the Greeks never came close to penetrating the colossal walls of Troy, which were built by gods Apollo and Poseidon.

At the tenth year, the balance of the outcome of the Trojan War was apparently tipping in favor of the Trojans, thanks to the reinforcements they received from foreign lands. Two of the most well known army leaders who came to Troy's rescue, were the **Amazon** queen **Penthesileia** and **Memnon**, the king of **Ethiopia**. Both of them, managed to inflict great damages on the Greek army.

A dispute between Achilles and Agamemnon was dramatic. Agamemnon took **Chryseis**, a daughter of Apollo's priest. Her father heard of this and begged for her return but Agamemnon

refused to release her. Upon hearing about this, Apollo shot fiery arrows at the Greek Army, killing many Greeks.

Achilles wanted to appease Apollo. Then the prophet Calchas said that the only solution was to return Chryseis. At this point, Agamemnon complied, but not before taking Achilles' maiden, **Briseis**. When this happened, Achilles refused to fight anymore.

Patroclus, a great friend of Achilles, had a plan to relieve the pressure off the Greeks. He wanted to use Achilles' armor to scare the Trojans off. The plan worked until Patroclus ran into **Hector**. Despite having Achilles' armor, the Trojan hero was able to kill him. When Achilles found out about the death of his great friend, he wanted to avenge his death. He went to Hephaestus to get new armor, then he rejoined the battle to avenge the death of Patroclus by killing Hector.

After killing Hector, Achilles knew that his death was near. Achilles was vulnerable only in one place: his heel. Paris killed Achilles with an arrow guided by Apollo. After the death of Achilles, both Odysseus and **Ajax** wanted the armor of Achilles. The Greeks decided that Odysseus would receive the armor, causing Ajax to go mad and kill a flock of sheep. As he regained his sanity, he realized what he had done and he killed himself.

The Greeks come up with a strategic plan

After Achilles' death, Odysseus captured the Trojan seer Helenus, brother of Paris. After a lot of persuasion, the seer revealed to the Greeks that, in order, to win the Trojan War, they should pursue the following: **Neoptolemus**, Achilles' son, should join the fighting; They should recover Philoctetes from the island of **Lemnos**, where he was left deserted. He should later use the bow and arrows of **Hercules** on the battlefield; One of the bones of Agamemnon's grandfather, **Pelops**, should be brought to Troy; Eventually, the **Palladium**, an ancient wooden statue of goddess Athena, should be captured from the Trojan citadel called the Pergamum. The mission to fulfill all those prerequisites to win the Trojan War, was undertaken by none others than Odysseus and Diomedes, and they achieved them all.

Beware of Greeks bearing gifts!

As soon as Philoctetes was cured from his wound, he managed to kill Paris, using the bow and arrows of Hercules. Despite, however, of some victories on the battlefield that quickly ensued as soon as the prerequisites stipulated by Helenus were fulfilled, the walls of Troy seemed impregnable, driving the Greeks into despair.

As a last resort, Odysseus came up with an ingenious plan to get inside the city: With Athena's help, **Epeius**, an artisan, constructed an enormous wooden horse, which was hollow inside. Led by Odysseus, a small army of Greek soldiers hid inside the horse while the rest of the Greek fleet sailed away.

When the Trojans found the horse, which bore an inscription which said that it was a gift dedicated to Athena, they had a big debate about what to do with it. While some argued that it was a part of a Greek ploy and therefore they should push it over a cliff or burn it, others contended that they should bring it inside the city to replace their stolen Palladium, convinced that it would bring them luck.

When the two prophets Cassandra and **Laocoon** explicitly tried to warn their fellow Trojans that Greeks were actually hidden inside the horse, no one believed them! When Laocoon, in an effort to prove his claim, hurled his spear against the horse, two enormous serpents rose out of the sea and attacked the seer's sons. After a tremendous struggle, the beasts finally killed the two boys and Laocoon, who rushed to their defence.

The Trojans interpreted this horrible tragedy as a punishment that goddess Athena sent to their priest, because he tried to desecrate her divine gift to the city. Even those who doubted the good intentions of the Greeks were finally convinced to take the horse inside the city, when somewhere outside the walls they met **Sinon**, a Greek soldier who was tied and his clothes were torn to shreds.

According to his story, which apparently was ingeniously devised by cunning Odysseus, he had escaped from the Greeks when they wanted to sacrifice him to appease Athena, who was enraged when her palladium was stolen. Furthemore, Sinon claimed that the wooden horse was constructed as an additional gesture to appease the goddess. As a matter of fact, it was designed to be so enormous, so that it would not fit to get inside the walls: The Greeks knew that placing the horse inside the city, would certainly bring victory to the Trojans! Harming the horse, Sinon warned, would turn the wrath of Athena against the Trojans.

After the final shred of doubt was lifted, the Trojans breached their mighty walls and took the wooden horse inside, overjoyed by their victory over the Greeks. When all of them fell drunken asleep following a wild celebration, Sinon quickly released the Greek soldiers from the inside of the horse and using a beacon, signaled to the Greek fleet to approach Troy. Those inside opened the wall gates and the Greeks, without facing hardly any resistance, overtook the city in a single bloody night. This signaled the end of the Trojan War.

The Greeks ravage Troy

During the night that they sacked Troy, the Greeks committed a lot of horrible atrocities that offended both men and gods. As for Helen, the culprit for the outbreak of the Trojan War, Menelaus could not bring himself to kill her as he had vowed to do, unable to resist her beauty and her pleas to be saved.

(Excerpted from http://historylink102.com/greece2/http://upge.wn.com/?t=ancientgreece/index33.txt)

Proper Nouns

1. **Troy** [trɔi]：特洛伊(小亚细亚西北部古城)。
2. **Peleus** [ˈpiːljus]：珀琉斯, 阿耳戈英雄之一。

3. **Thetis** [ˈθetis; ˈθiː-]：忒提斯，海的女神。
4. **Achilles** [əˈkiliːz]：阿喀琉斯，荷马史诗《伊利亚特》中最伟大的英雄。
5. **Eris** [ˈeris]：厄里斯，不和女神。
6. **Hera** [ˈhiərə]：赫拉，天后，主神宙斯之妻。
7. **Athena** [əˈθiːnə]：雅典娜，智慧、技艺、勤俭和战争女神。
8. **Aphrodite** [ˌæfrəuˈdaiti]：阿佛洛狄忒，爱与美的女神，相当于罗马神话中的维纳斯。
9. **Zeus** [zjuːs]：宙斯，奥林山神中最为强大的天神，雷电之神，天、地、神、人的统治者。
10. **Paris** [ˈpæris]：帕里斯，特洛伊王子，诱拐了海伦而引发特洛伊战争。
11. **Helen** [ˈhelən]：海伦，世界上最美的女人，斯巴达国王之妻。被特洛伊王子劫持或同其私奔，从而引发了十年的特洛伊战争。
12. **Menelaus** [ˌmeniˈleiəs]：墨涅拉俄斯，阿伽门农的弟弟；海伦的丈夫。
13. **Sparta** [ˈspɑːtə]：斯巴达，伯罗奔尼撒半岛东南部古希腊的一个城邦，以其军事主义著名，于公元前6世纪达到全盛。
14. **Agamemnon** [ˌægəˈmemnən]：阿伽门农，特洛伊战争中希腊军队的统帅。
15. **Mycenae** [maiˈsiːniː]：迈锡尼，伯罗奔尼撒半岛东北部的古希腊城市，在青铜器时期作为一个早期文化中心繁荣一时。
16. **Helenus**：赫勒诺斯，著名的特洛伊先知，曾警告他的兄弟帕里斯不要劫持海伦，后来又告诉希腊人他们能取得特洛伊战争的胜利。
17. **Cassandra** [kəˈsændrə]：卡珊德拉，特洛伊公主，能预卜吉凶。
18. **Aulis**：奥利斯，希腊中东部维奥蒂亚洲的一个古老港口，据传说，在特洛伊战争期间它是古希腊船队的出发点。
19. **Odysseus** [əuˈdisjuːs]：俄底修斯，伊塔卡国王；特洛伊战争英雄，长达十年的特洛伊战争结束后又流浪了十年，最后返回故土伊塔卡。
20. **Palamedes**：帕拉米迪斯，被阿伽门农派去请俄底修斯出征，使用狡诈的手段逼迫他承认是在装疯，从而迫使他加入希腊军队攻打特洛伊。
21. **Telemachus** [tiˈleməkəs; tə-]：忒勒玛科斯，俄底修斯和佩内洛普之子。
22. **Calchas** [ˈkælkəs]：卡尔卡斯，预言者。
23. **Artemis** [ˈɑːtimis]：阿耳忒弥斯，月亮和狩猎女神。
24. **Iphigenia** [iˌfidʒiˈnaiə]：伊菲革涅亚，阿伽门农的女儿。
25. **Diomedes** [ˌdaiəˈmiːdiːz]：狄俄墨得斯，瑟雷斯之王，用人肉喂马，被赫拉克勒斯用棍棒打死，将肉喂给马吃。
26. **Euripides** [juəˈripidiːz]：欧里庇得斯，古希腊戏剧家。
27. ***Iphigenia in Tauris***：《陶里斯岛上的伊菲革涅亚》，古希腊戏剧家欧里庇得斯的作品。
28. **Tauris**：陶里斯，黑海的一个克里米亚半岛。
29. **Philoctetes** [ˌfilɔkˈtiːtiːz]：菲罗克忒忒斯，赫拉克勒斯将自己的弓箭留传给他，因此而成为希腊最伟大的射手。
30. **Priam** [ˈpraiəm]：普里阿摩斯，特洛伊战争时的特洛伊王。
31. **Apollo** [əˈpɔləu]：阿波罗，司艺术、医药、音乐、诗歌和修辞之神，有时被称为太阳神。
32. **Poseidon** [pɔˈsaidən]：波塞冬，海神。
33. **Hermes** [ˈhəːmiːz]：赫耳墨斯，商业、发明、灵巧之神；盗贼的保护神；众神的信使、书吏及报信者。
34. **Hephaestus** [hiˈfiːstəs]：赫淮斯托斯，跛脚的打铁和金属冶炼业和手工艺之神；众神的工匠。
35. **Amazon** [ˈæməzɔn]：阿玛宗人，相传曾居住在黑海边的一族女战士。

36. **Penthesileia** [ˌpenθəsiˈleiə; -ˈliːə]：彭忒西勒亚，战神阿瑞斯之女，阿玛宗女王，帮助特洛伊人作战，后被阿喀琉斯所杀。
37. **Memnon** [ˈmemnɔn]：门农，埃塞俄比亚之王，为阿喀琉斯所杀，被宙斯赐予永生。
38. **Ethiopia** [ˌiːθiˈəupiə]：埃塞俄比亚，位于非洲东北部的一个国家。
39. **Chryseis** [kraiˈsiːis]：克律塞伊斯，阿波罗的祭司之女。
40. **Briseis** [brɑiˈsiːis]：布里塞伊斯，美女，阿喀琉斯将其诱拐走，并称她为妾；后来被阿伽门农偷走，这一耻辱迫使阿喀琉斯暂时放弃了战争。
41. **Patroclus** [pəˈtrɔukləs]：帕特洛克罗斯，希腊勇士，阿喀琉斯的仆从和朋友。
42. **Hector** [ˈhektə]：赫克托耳，特洛伊军的统帅，特洛伊最英勇的战士。
43. **Ajax** [ˈeidʒæks]：本文指 Great Ajax 埃阿斯（大），特洛伊战争中的希腊勇士，与俄底修斯争夺阿喀琉斯的盔甲时因败于俄底修斯而发了疯并自杀。
44. **Neoptolemus** [ˌniːɔpˈtɔləməs]：涅俄普托勒摩斯，阿喀琉斯的儿子。
45. **Lemnos** [ˈlemnɔs]：莱姆诺斯岛，希腊东北部一岛屿，位于爱琴海中，远离土耳其海岸，莱斯博斯岛的西北方向。
46. **Hercules** [ˈhəːkjuliːz]：赫剌克勒斯，希腊神话中著名的大力神。
47. **Pelops** [ˈpiːlɔps]：珀罗普斯，坦塔罗斯(Tantalus)之子，被他父亲所杀并用他的肉宴请众神。
48. **Palladium** [pəˈleidiəm]：雅典娜的古代的木雕像。
49. **Epeius**：厄珀俄斯，特洛伊战争中使希腊人取胜的木马的制造者。
50. **Laocoon** [leiˈɔkəuɔn]：拉奥孔，特洛伊的太阳神祭师，因警告特洛伊人不要中木马计而连同其二个儿子一起被两条海蟒杀死。
51. **Sinon** [sinɔ̃]：西农，希腊士兵。

After You Read

Knowledge Focus

1. Fill in the blanks according to what you have learned in the text above.

1) The goddess _____, enraged for not being invited to the wedding, decided to toss a Golden Apple, inscribed "For the Fairest", among the goddesses.

2) The three goddesses paraded before Paris and they each offered him a bribe: Hera promised him _____, Athena _____, and Aphrodite merely offered _____.

3) _____ visited Menelaus and Helen at Sparta, seduced Helen, and carried her off with him to Troy.

4) Achilles was vulnerable only in one place: _____. Paris killed Achilles with an arrow guided by Apollo.

5) The Greek army and fleet assembled at Aulis, but were delayed for a long time by _____.

6) At the tenth year, the balance of the outcome of the Trojan War was apparently tipping in favor of _____, thanks to the reinforcements they received from foreign lands.

7) After Achilles' funeral, Odysseus and _____ contested to inherit his divinely made armour.

8) A prophet declared that Troy would fall if the Palladium, the sacred image of _____, should be captured from the Trojan citadel called the Pergamum.

9) Led by _____, a small army of Greek soldiers hid inside the horse while the rest of the Greek fleet sailed away.

10) When Laocoon, in an effort to prove his claim, hurled his spear against the horse, two enormous _____ rose out of the sea and attacked the seer's sons.

2. Read the text again and put the following sentences into the correct order.

1) Convinced by the lies of the Greek agent Sinon that the Greeks had left the enormous wooden horse to Athena when they sailed for home, and ignoring the warnings of Cassandra and the priest Laocoon, the Trojans dragged it inside the city.
2) The Greek army and fleet assembled at Aulis, but were delayed for a long time by contrary winds.
3) Instead of trusting the prince's impartial judgement, all three goddesses attempted to win by bribery.
4) When the Greeks landed they sent a delegation to demand the return of Helen, but the Trojans refused.
5) Paris visited Menelaus and Helen at Sparta, seduced Helen, and carried her off with him to Troy.
6) Philoctetes managed to kill Paris, using the bow and arrows of Hercules.
7) Menelaus found Helen, but could not bring himself to kill her; he forgave her and took her back as the victorious Greeks sailed for home.
8) The gods were at a banquet to celebrate the wedding of Peleus and Thetis, when Eris, who had not been invited, turned up and threw a Golden Apple, inscribed "For the Fairest", among the goddesses.
9) Achilles avenged the death of Patroclus by killing Hector.
10) Menelaus appealed to his fellow Greek kings to help him recover his wife.

3. Pair Work: Discuss the following questions with your partner.

1) Do you think that the abduction of Helen is the cause of the Trojan War in history?
2) Would you take the bribery offered by the three goddesses if you were Paris? Why or why not?
3) If you were Agamemnon, would you sacrifice your beloved daughter Iphigenia?
4) Do you think it is right for Odysseus to abandon Philoctetes when he was wounded?
5) The elderly king of Troy saw favorably the return of Helen to avoid confrontation with the mighty Greeks on the battlefield. Is that a wise decision?
6) Every one is vulnerable in one place or another. Do you agree?
7) What should the Trojans do if they discovered the secret in the wooden horse?
8) Is Helen innocent? Can she decide her own fate?
9) Who is the real victim of war?
10) What lesson can we learn from the Trojan War?

Language Focus

1. Fill in the blanks with the proper forms of words or expressions you have learned in the text.

| impartial | capacity | stench | opt | succumb to |
| appease | formidable | cunning | ploy | ensue from |

1) The city _____ after only a short siege.
2) She has an enormous _____ for hard work.
3) Bitter argument _____ this misunderstanding.
4) The design team met many _____ obstacles.
5) He is a _____ old fox.
6) It was all a _____ to distract attention from his real aims.
7) Workers have to tolerate the _____ of burning rubber.
8) The customer service manager is trying her best to _____ the angry lady who bought a fake.
9) Jack Henderson is a well-known _____ judge. His judgements are always fair and neutral.
10) He _____ to go to Paris rather than London.

2. Fill in the blanks with the proper form of the word in the brackets.

1) Tom Jackson is _____ (reputed) a master in this field.
2) Rose _____ (entertainment) friends at dinner.
3) I was _____ (fury) when he crashed my car.
4) I support this measure without _____ (reserve).
5) After _____ (embark) from the ship, we went through passport control.
6) Our troops have _____ (penetration) into enemy territory.
7) Young birds are very _____ (vulnerably) to predators.
8) Moscow is a _____ (impregnability) city during the Second World War.
9) So you fitted that wire through that little hole there: that's very _____ (ingeniously)!
10) I am shocked by the _____ (atrocious) of this man's crimes.

3. Fill in the blanks with the proper prepositions or adverbs that collocate with the neighboring words.

1) The motoring company lost 3 million dollars due to Strong's wrong decision and CEO was enraged _____ his stupidity.
2) He will be furious _____ being kept waiting.
3) The managing director of HP speaks favorably _____ the plan because he finds it feasible and sound.
4) The British Royal Air Force (RAF) inflicted heavy losses _____ the Germany during the Second World War.
5) Yesterday I run _____ an old friend in the street.
6) The imaginative ideas participants came up _____ were extraordinary.
7) All the students are _____ a loss to understand those texts because their teacher cannot explain them explicitly.

Ancient Greek and Roman Mythology

4. **Proofreading:** The following passage contains ten errors. Each indicated line contains a maximum of one error. In each case, only ONE word is involved. Read the passage and correct the errors.

As the rise of modern critical history, Troy and the Trojan War were consigned 1) _____
to the realms of legend. In 1870s, however, the German archaeologist Heinrich 2) _____
Schliemann excavated a hill, called Hisarlik by the Turks, near town of Chanak 3) _____
(Çanakkale) in north-western Anatolia.
There he discovered the ruin of a series of ancient city, dated from the Bronze 4) _____
Age to the Roman period. Schliemann declared one of these cities—at first Troy I, 5) _____
later Troy II—be the city of Troy, and this identification was widely accepted at that 6) _____
time. After Schliemann, the site was further excavated with the direction of Wilhelm 7) _____
Dörpfeld (1893—1894) and later Carl Blegen (1932—1938). In 1988 excavations
were resumed by a team of University of Tübingen under the direction of Professor 8) _____
Manfred Korfmann. The question of Troy's status in the Bronze Age world has been
the subject of a sometime acerbic debate between Korfmann and the Tübingen 9) _____
historian Frank Kolb in 2001—2002. Remainings found in the ditch were dated to 10) _____
the late Bronze Age, the alleged time of Homeric Troy.

Comprehensive Work

1. **Questions for Discussion:**

   1) In history, some people attribute wars, failures, and the fall of a country to beauty like Helen of Troy. Do you think it is fair?

   2) Do you think war is an effective solution to disputes between countries? If not, can you give some solutions?

2. **Translate the following paragraph into Chinese.**

   At the nuptials of Peleus and Thetis (mother and father to Achilles) all the gods were invited with the exception of Eris, or Discord. Enraged at her exclusion, the goddess threw a golden apple among the guests, with the inscription, "For the fairest." Thereupon Hera, Aphrodite, and Athena each claimed the apple. Zeus, not willing to decide in so delicate a matter, sent the goddesses to Mount Ida, where the beautiful shepherd Paris(a prince of Troy) was tending his flocks, and to him was committed the decision. The goddesses accordingly appeared before him. Hera promised him power and riches, Athena glory and renown in war, and Aphrodite the fairest of women for his wife, each attempting to influence his decision in her own favor. Paris decided in favor of Aphrodite and gave her the golden apple, thus making the two other goddesses his enemies.

3. **Writing**

   The archaeological site at Hisarlik in Turkey, identified by Heinrich Schliemann as historical Troy, was added to the UNESCO World Heritage list in 1998. Hisarlik local government decides to promote the site. Please write an article describing the site, its history, and the Trojan War.

Read More

Text B Troy

Troy (Greek: Τροία, *Troia*, also Ἴλιον, *Ilion*; Turkish *Truva*, *Troya*; Latin: *Troia* is preferred, but *Ilium* is a more poetic term) is a legendary city and center of the Trojan War, as described in the *Iliad*, one of the two epic poems attributed to Homer. The archaeological site at Hisarlik in Turkey, identified by Heinrich Schliemann as historical Troy, was added to the UNESCO World Heritage list in 1998.

This site, which represents much of the cultural history of the Western world, is an inspiration to those who yearn to believe that the legendary accounts in Greek mythology have a basis in reality. Even if every detail is not true, the ideals and morals expressed in these tales are foundational to western culture, and the artifacts and remains that have been unearthed at the site provide an illuminating experience of life in ancient times. Thus the finding and preservation of this site is of great value to humankind.

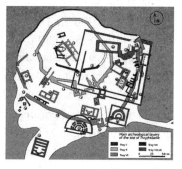

Legendary Troy

According to mythology, the Trojans were the ancient citizens of the city of Troy in the Troad region of Anatolia (now Turkey). Although part of Asia, Troy is presented in the legend as part of the Greek culture of City states. Troy was known for its riches gained from port trade with east and west, fancy clothes, iron production, and massive defensive walls.

The Trojan royal family was started by the Pleiad Electra and Zeus, the parents of Dardanus. Dardanus, who according to Greek myth was originally from Arcadia but according to Roman myth was originally from Italy, crossed over to Asia Minor from the

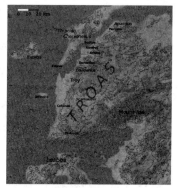

island of Samothrace, where he met King Teucer. Teucer was himself also a colonizer from Attica, and treated Dardanus with respect. Eventually, Dardanus married Teucer's daughters, and founded Dardania (later ruled by Aeneas). Upon Dardanus' death, the Kingdom was passed to his grandson Tros, who called the people Trojans and the land Troad, after himself. Ilus, son of Tros, founded the city of Ilium (Troy) that he called after himself. Zeus gave Ilus the Palladium. Poseidon and Apollo built the walls and fortifications around Troy for Laomedon, son of Ilus the younger. When Laomedon refused to pay, Poseidon flooded the land and demanded the sacrifice of Hesione to a sea monster. Pestilence came and the sea monster snatched away the people of the plain.

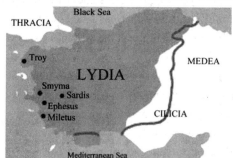

One generation before the Trojan War, Heracles captured Troy and killed Laomedon and his sons, except for young Priam. Priam later became king. During his reign, the Mycenaean Greeks invaded and captured

Troy in the Trojan War (traditionally dated from 1193—1183 B.C.E.). The Maxyans were a west Libyan tribe who said that they were descended from the men of Troy, according to Herodotus. The Trojan ships transformed into naiads, who rejoiced to see the wreckage of Odysseus' ship.

Trojan rule in Asia Minor was replaced by the Herakleid dynasty in Sardis, which ruled for 505 years until the time of Candaules. The Ionians, Cimmerians, Phrygians, Milesians of Sinope, and Lydians moved into Asia Minor. The Persians invaded in 546 B.C.E.

Some famous Trojans are: Dardanus (founder of Troy), Laomedon, Ganymede, Priam and his children Paris, Hector, Teucer, Aesacus, Oenone, Tithonus, Antigone, Memnon, Corythus, Aeneas, Brutus, and Elymus. Kapys, Boukolion, and Aisakos were Trojan princes who had naiad wives. Some of the Trojan allies were the Lycians and the Amazons. The Aisepid nymphs were the naiads of the Trojan River Aisepos. Pegsis was the naiad of the River Granicus near Troy. "Helen of Troy" was born not in Troy but Sparta.

Mount Ida in Asia Minor is where Ganymede was abducted by Zeus, where Anchises was seduced by Aphrodite, where Aphrodite gave birth to Aeneas, where Paris lived as a shepherd, where the nymphs lived, where the "Judgement of Paris" took place, where the Greek gods watched the Trojan War, where Hera distracted Zeus with her seductions long enough to permit the Achaeans, aided by Poseidon, to hold the Trojans off their ships, and where Aeneas and his followers rested and waited until the Greeks set out for Greece. The altar of Panomphaean (source of all oracles) was dedicated to Jupiter the Thunderer (*Tonatus*) near Troy. Buthrotos (or Buthrotum) was a city in Epirus where Helenus, the Trojan seer, built a replica of Troy. Aeneas landed there and Helenus foretold his future.

Such was the fame of the Trojan story in Roman and medieval times that it was built upon to provide a starting point for various legends of national origin. The most famous is undoubtedly that promulgated by Virgil in the *Aeneid*, tracing the ancestry of the founders of Rome, more specifically the Julio-Claudian dynasty, to the Trojan prince Aeneas. Similarly Geoffrey of Monmouth traces the legendary Kings of the Britons to a supposed descendant of Aeneas named Brutus.

Homeric Troy

In the *Iliad*, the Achaeans set up their camp near the mouth of the river Scamander (presumably modern Karamenderes), where they had beached their ships. The city of Troy itself stood on a hill, across the plain of Scamander, where the battles of the Trojan War took place. The site of the ancient city today is some 15 kilometers from the coast, but the ancient mouths of alleged Scamander, some 3,000 years ago, were some 5 kilometers further inland, pouring into a bay that has since been filled with alluvial material. Geological findings have revealed what the Trojan coastline would look like, indicating that Homeric geography of Troy is accurate.

Besides the *Iliad*, there are references to Troy in the other major work attributed to Homer, the *Odyssey*, as well as in other ancient Greek literature. The Homeric legend of Troy was elaborated by the Roman poet Virgil in his work the *Aeneid*. The Greeks and Romans took for a fact the historicity of the Trojan War, and in the identity of Homeric Troy with the site in Anatolia. Alexander the Great, for example, visited the site in 334 B.C.E. and made sacrifices at the alleged tombs of the Homeric heroes Achilles and Patroclus.

Ancient Greek historians placed the Trojan War variously in the twelfth, thirteenth, or fourteenth century B.C.E.: Eratosthenes to 1184 B.C.E., Herodotus to 1250 B.C.E., Douris to 1334 B.C.E..

(Excerpted from http://www.newworldencyclopedia.org/entry/Troy)

Questions for Reflection

1. Fill in the blanks about Mount Ida in Asia Minor according to what you read in the text above.

Mount Ida in Asia Minor is where	1) Ganymede was abducted by ( ),
	2) where Anchises was seduced by ( ),
	3) where Aphrodite gave birth to ( ),
	4) where Paris lived as a ( ),
	5) where the ( ) lived,
	6) where the "Judgement of ( )" took place,
	7) where the Greek gods watched ( ),
	8) where Hera distracted Zeus with her seductions long enough to permit the Achaeans, aided by ( ), to hold the Trojans off their ships,
	9) and where Aeneas and his followers rested and waited until ( ) set out for Greece.

2. Multiple choice

Please decide on the best choice from the four choices marked A, B, C, and D.
1) According to mythology, the Trojans were the ancient citizens of the city of Troy in the Troad region of _____ (now Turkey).
   A. Anatolia   B. Ephesus   C. Miletus   D. Smyma
2) The Trojan royal family was started by the _____ and Zeus, the parents of Dardanus.
   A. Teucer   B. Ilus   C. Pleiad Electra D. Samothrace
3) Upon Dardanus' death, the Kingdom was passed to his grandson Tros, who called the people Trojans and the land _____, after himself.
   A. Ilium   B. Tros   C. Troy   D. Troad
4) _____ and Apollo built the walls and fortifications around Troy for Laomedon, son of Ilus the younger.
   A. Daphne   B. Poseidon   C. Agamemnon   D. Orestes
5) Trojan rule in Asia Minor was replaced by the Herakleid dynasty in Sardis, which ruled for _____ years until the time of Candaules.
   A. 505   B. 546   C. 1193   D. 1183
6) The site of the ancient city today is some _____ kilometers from the coast.
   A. 5   B. 15   C. 30   D. 25

Text C Helen of Troy

In Greek mythology, Helen (in Greek, Ἑλένη — Helénē), better known as Helen of Sparta or Helen of Troy, was daughter of Zeus and Leda, wife of king Menelaus of Sparta and sister of Castor, Polydeuces and Clytemnestra. Her abduction by Paris brought about the Trojan War. Helen was described by Christopher Marlowe as having "the face that launched a thousand ships."

Life of Helen
Birth

In most sources, including the *Iliad* and the *Odyssey*, Helen is the daughter of Zeus and Leda. Euripides' play *Helen*, written in the late fifth century B.C.E., is the earliest source to report the most familiar account of Helen's birth: that Zeus, in the form of a swan, was chased by an eagle, and sought refuge with Leda. The swan gained her affection, and the two mated. Leda then produced an egg, from which Helen was born.

The *Cypria*, one of the Cyclic Epics, has another variant. Helen was the daughter of Zeus and the goddess Nemesis. The date of the *Cypria* is uncertain, but it is generally thought to preserve traditions that date back to at least the seventh century B.C.E. In the *Cypria*, Nemesis did not wish to mate with Zeus. She therefore changed shape into various animals as she attempted to flee Zeus, finally becoming a goose. Zeus also transformed himself into a goose and mated with Nemesis, who produced an egg from which Helen was born. Presumably in the *Cypria* this egg was given to Leda; in the fifth-century comedy *Nemesis* by Cratinus, Leda was told to sit on an egg so that it would hatch, and this is no doubt the egg produced by Nemesis. Asclepiades and Pseudo-Eratosthenes related a similar story, except that Zeus and Nemesis became swans instead of geese. Timothy Gantz has suggested that the tradition that Zeus came to Leda in the form of a swan derives from the version in which Zeus and Nemesis transformed into birds.

Abduction by Theseus

Two Athenians, Theseus and Pirithous, pledged to wed daughters of Zeus. Theseus chose Helen, and Pirithous vowed to marry Persephone, the wife of Hades. Theseus and Pirithous kidnapped Helen and left her with Theseus' mother, Aethra, while they traveled to the underworld, the domain of Hades, to kidnap Persephone. Hades pretended to offer them hospitality and set a feast. As soon as the pair sat down, snakes coiled around their feet and held them there. Helen was subsequently rescued by her brothers, Castor and Pollux, who returned her to Sparta.

In most accounts of this event, Helen was quite young; Hellanicus of Lesbos said she was seven years old and Diodorus makes her ten years old. On the other hand, Stesichorus said that Iphigeneia was the daughter of Theseus and Helen, which obviously implies that Helen was of childbearing age. In most sources, of course, Iphigeneia is the daughter of Agamemnon and Clytemnestra, but Duris of Samos and other writers followed Stesichorus' account.

Marriage to Menelaus

When it was time for Helen to marry, many kings and princes from around the world came to seek her hand or sent emissaries to do so on their behalf. Among the contenders were Odysseus, Menestheus, Ajax the Great, Patroclus, Idomeneus, Menelaus and Agamemnon, the latter two of whom were in exile, having fled Thyestes. All but Odysseus brought many rich gifts with them.

Her father, Tyndareus, would not choose a suitor, or send any of the suitors away, for fear of offending them and giving grounds for a quarrel. Odysseus promised to solve the problem if Tyndareus would support him in his courting of Penelope, the daughter of Icarius. Tyndareus readily agreed and Odysseus proposed that, before the decision was made, all the suitors should swear a most solemn oath to defend the chosen husband against whoever should quarrel with him. This stratagem succeeded and Helen and Menelaus were married. Following Tyndareus' death, Menelaus became king of Sparta because the only male heirs, Castor and Pollux, had died and ascended to Olympus.

Seduction by Paris

Some years later, Paris, a Trojan prince, came to Sparta to marry Helen, whom he had been promised by Aphrodite after he had chosen her as the most beautiful of the goddesses, earning the wrath of Athena and Hera. Some sources say that Helen willingly left behind her husband Menelaus and Hermione, their nine-year-old daughter, to be with Paris, but, since Aphrodite promised Helen to Paris, there is some ambiguity about whether or not Helen went willingly. Some scholars have argued that Helen's abduction by Paris was in fact a rape (termed abduction as per the ancient understanding of raptus). Sources from Herodotus to material culture support this view. Ancient vases depict both the shameless Helen who went willingly to Troy and abduction stories in which Helen is taken by force.

Helen's relationship with Paris varies depending on the source of the story. In some, she loved him dearly (perhaps caused by Aphrodite, who had promised her to Paris). In others, she was portrayed as his unwilling captive in Troy, or as a cruel, selfish woman who brought disaster to everyone around her, and she hated him. In the version used by Euripides in his play *Helen*, Hermes fashioned a likeness of her out of clouds at Zeus's request, and Helen never even went to Troy, having spent the entire war in Egypt.

Fall of Troy

When he discovered that his wife was missing, Menelaus called upon all the other suitors to fulfill their oaths, thus beginning the Trojan War. Almost all of Greece took part, either attacking Troy with Menelaus or defending it from them.

Menelaus had demanded that only he should slay his unfaithful wife; but, when he raised his sword to do so, she dropped her robe from her shoulders, and the sight of her beauty caused him to let the sword drop from his hand.

Herodotus

Herodotus offers a differing account in which Helen never arrived in Troy. In that account Paris was forced to stop in Egypt on his way home. While there, his servants told the Egyptians that Paris had kidnapped the wife of Menelaus, who had offered Paris hospitality. The Egyptians scolded Paris and informed him that they were confiscating all the treasure he had stolen (including Helen) until Menelaus came to claim them and that Paris had three days to leave their shores.

Fate

Helen returned to Sparta and lived for a time with Menelaus, where she was encountered by Telemachus in *The Odyssey*. According to another version, used by Euripides in his play *Orestes*, Helen had long ago left the mortal world by then, having been taken up to Olympus almost immediately after Menelaus' return.

(Excerpted from http://www.newworldencyclopedia.org/entry/Helen_of_Troy)

Questions for Reflection

1. Why was Helen described by Christopher Marlowe as having "the face that launched a thousand ships"?
2. After Helen was rescued by her brothers, Castor and Pollux, where did they return her to?
3. What caused Menelaus to let the sword drop from his hand?

Websites to Visit

http://www.xtec.cat/cirel/pla_le/nottingham/norma_jorba/activities/3_6.pdf
This website provides detailed information on the Trojan War.

Works to Read

Tales of Troy and Greece was written by Andrew Lang and Published by Wordsworth Editions Ltd. The author recounts the Homeric legend of the wars between the Greeks and the Trojans. Paris, Helen of Troy, Achilles, Hector, Ulysses, the Amazons and the wooden horse all figure in this introduction to one of the great legends. Other great legends of the same period are also retold.

Movies to Watch

Troy (2004)

Troy is a 2004 epic war film written by David Benioff and directed by Wolfgang Petersen. It received an Oscar nomination for its costume design. When the film was completed, total production costs were approximately $175,000,000. This makes *Troy* one of the most expensive films made in modern cinema. *Troy* made over US$497 million dollars worldwide, placing it in the 60 of top box office hits of all time.

In the year 1193 before Christ, the prince Paris of Troy stole the beatiful Helen away from her husband Menelaus, the king of Sparta, setting the two nations at war with each other. All the Greek entire armada come to the city of Troy and begun a bloody siege that lasted over ten years, with the Greek forces led by Achilles and the Trojan forces, led by the prince Hector.

Unit 11
After the Trojan War

> Is the upcoming war good to find the solution for humanity or is it just another folly of a stupid species?
> —Stephen Evans

Unit Goals

- To be able to tell the myth of Agamemnon
- To know the story of Odysseus' legendary travels and adventures
- To know the story of Aeneas and the origin of Rome
- To learn about Rome
- To learn the words and phrases that describe Greek mythology
- To improve language skills and critical thinking through the content of this unit

Before You Read

1. See if you know the right answers to the following questions. Check your answers after reading Text A.
   1) Agamemnoon decided to sacrifice his daughter Iphigenia in the Trojan War. What would his wife Clytemnestra do after his return?
   2) Do you think Odysseus would encounter further adventures and disasters on his return from the Trojan War?
   3) Odysseus was absent from home for twenty years. Do you think his wife Penelope was still waiting for him?

2. All the following pictures describe the stories that happened after the Trojan War. Can you identify them?

3. Form groups of three or four students. Try to find, on the Internet or in the library, more information about the pictures above. Choose one as your topic and prepare a five-minute classroom presentation.

Start to Read

Text A After the Trojan War

After the war: Agamemnon

After the capture of Troy, Cassandra, doomed prophetess and daughter of Priam, fell to Agamemnon's lot in the distribution of the prizes of war.

After a stormy voyage, Agamemnon and Cassandra either landed in **Argolis**, or were blown off course and landed in **Aegisthus**' country. **Clytemnestra**, Agamemnon's wife, had taken Aegisthus, son of **Thyestes**, as a lover. When Agamemnon came home he was slain by either Aegisthus (in the oldest versions of the story) or Clytemnestra. According to the accounts given by **Pindar** and the tragedians, Agamemnon was slain in a bath by his wife alone, a blanket of cloth or a net having first been thrown over him to prevent resistance. Clytemnestra also killed Cassandra. Her jealousy of Cassandra, and her wrath at the sacrifice of Iphigenia and at Agamemnon's having gone to war over Helen of Troy, are said to have been the motives for her crime. Aegisthus and Clytemnestra then ruled Agamemnon's kingdom for a time.

Agamemnon's son **Orestes** later avenged his father's murder, with the help or encouragement of his sister **Electra**, by murdering Aegisthus and Clytemnestra (his own mother), thereby inciting the wrath of the **Erinyes** (English: the Furies), winged goddesses who tracked down egregiously impious wrongdoers with their hounds' noses and drove them to insanity. But in the end, Orestes was vindicated because Athena judged that killing his mother was less heinous than killing his father.

(Excerpted from http://en.wikipedia.org/wiki/Agamemnon)

After the war: Odysseus

Leaving Troy, Odysseus and his men sailed off for Ithaca, but were carried away by a storm, which took them to the country of the **Lotus-Eaters**. This people ate the lotus plant, which was sweet but dangerous, since it made you forget everything. Odyseeus managed to get his crew back on the ships, and off they went again.

Next, they landed on the island of the **Cyclop Polyphemus**, allegedly the island of Youra in the Nort Sporades. The giant shut the men inside his cave, ate a few of them and talked with Odysseus, who told the Cyclop his name was "Noone". When Polyphemus had fallen asleep he convinced the men to prepare a treetrunk, making it into a sharp weapon, which they put in the fireplace, and then thrust it into the Cyclops only eye. Crying with pain and anger, Polyphemus opened the cave and tried fumbling to catch the escaping men. They had tied themselves under the giants sheep, though, so the only thing he felt was the backs of the animals. His screams woke the other Cyclops up, and they shouted to him what was wrong. Polyphemus then answered "Noone has blinded me", which made the other Cyclops go back to bed, thinking Polyphemus had finally gone out of his wits.

The next adventure brought the ships to the island of the winds, where the god of the winds **Aeolus** lived. He welcomed Odysseus, and when it was time for him to leave, the god gave him a sack which contained all the winds except the western one, telling the hero not to open it until he had  reached home. For ten days and night the ships sailed at full speed. Odysseus stayed awake for fear that the men would open his sack, but when **Ithaca** was in sight, the exhausted hero slept. The curious crew then opened the sack, unleashing all the winds, taking the ships further away than before. They sailed back to Aeolus island, but were chased away since Aeolus had understood Odysseus was hated by the gods, especially **Poseidon** who hated him for defeating his son the Cyclop.

The ship now reached the island Aiae, where Helios' daughter **Circe** lived. It was full of wild, but friendly animals, which were really transformed humans. The beautiful Circe invited some of Odysseus men, and turned them into swines with a magic potion. When Odysseus went to find them, **Hermes** appeared, presenting him with an antidote. The hero drank it, and took Circe by surprise when he did not transform. He threatened her life, and she turned the swines back to men, and offered Odysseus her love. They all lived together in her palace for a year.

Circe told Odysseus about the sirens. They were terrible creatures with birds bodies and ugly womens' heads, who sang so beautifully that all the sailors would jump in the sea. On Circes advice Odysseus had his men tie him to the mast while filling their own ears with wax, so that he may hear the sirens song without being able to jump. Crazed with the **Sirens** song Odysseus tried to sign to the crew to let him go, but they could not hear anything, and had promised the hero that they would not let him go no matter what.

The ship now came to **Charybdis**, a stream that sucked in and spat out the sea three times a day. After this they met **Scylla**, who lived in a cave on a cliff. She had six heads on snakenecks, three tows of teeth and barked like a puppy. The monster caught six of the men.

He drifted around for nine days, until he reached the island **Ogygia**, where the nymph **Calypso**

lived. Calypso took care of him, caressed him, and promised to make him immortal if he married her. The hero did not respond to this, and sat crying by the shore. When Poseidon was away, Athena took the opportunity to beg Zeus to help Odysseus. The god then sent Hermes to Calypso with a message to let Odysseus go. Odysseus built a raft and sailed for seventeen days, until he reached **Scheria**.

Athena then appeared before him in the shape of a young man, and told him where he was and about the suitors in his palace. They were on the verge of forcing **Penelope** to a decision, since they had discovered she tricked them. She had promised to make a decision whom she would marry when she had finished the death shroud of her father-in-law. At night she tore it up again, but a treacherous maid revealed this to the suitors.

Odysseus now went to the swineherd **Eumaeus**, and revealed his identity to him and **Telemachus**. Together, they went to the palace. Odysseus was disguised as a beggar, and was beaten and ridiculed by the suitors. Only his old dog **Argus** recognized him, wagged its tail and died.

When Penelope looked after the beggar she asked him if he had heard anything of her husband. Odysseus told her he would be back very soon, but Penelope did not dare to belive him. Cleaning him, Odysseus old nurse recognized a scar on his body, but he told her to be silent.

Penelope now put the suitors through a final test. She showed them Odysseus bow and said she would marry whoever could shoot an arrow through the holes of twelve axes in a row. One after one they tried, but they couldn't even pull the string.

The beggar Odysseus asked to have a go, and under ridicule and laughter he shot a perfect arrow through the twelve axes, then turned the bow against the suitors and started killing them with the help of Telemachus. After this the treacherous maids were punished, and finally, the palace was clear.

By killing the suitors, Odysseus had blood on his hands and he cleaned the house with sulfur. Penelope still doubted, but when Odysseus told her that their bed was made of olive tree, a secret only he would know, she finally believed. Odysseus then went to his old father and they all lived happily ever after.

After a meeting with his people, the suitors families and friends wanted revenge, but they fled after fighting Odysseus. Athena then intervened, and peace was made.

(Excerpted from http://www.in2greece.com/english/historymyth/mythology/names/odysseus.htm)

After the war: Aeneas and Rome

Following the fall of Troy Aeneas, son of **Priam**, a Trojan hero second only to **Hector**, fled the fortress; he lost his wife in the escape, himself carrying his aged father on his back and leading his young son by the hand.

Aeneas went through a series of adventures trying to find a place to settle with his fellow Trojans. They encountered **Harpies** and bleeding bogs. At the urging of **Juno**, Aeneas and his companions were attacked by the god of the winds Aeolus. There were then protected by **Neptune**. who keep them from being shipwrecked and from other perils. Finally Aeneas arrived in **Carthage** where **Cupid** disguised himself as the son of Aeneas and influenced the Queen **Dido** to fall in love with Aeneas. Aeneas did fall in love with Dido. **Mercury**, the messenger of the gods, was sent to visit Aeneas twice to remind him of his destiny and to get him to break away from Dido, after which Aeneas resumed his journey to his new land. Upon his departure, Dido took her own life.

After landing in Italy, Aeneas was tried to determine where to settle. Aeneas visited Cumaean **Sibyl**, a prophetess who had access to the underworld through a cave with a hundred openings. Sibyl agreed to be the guide and directed Aeneas to take an item from a nearby magical bough which was sacred to **Proserpine**, wife of **Pluto**. **Charon**, the ferryman of the river **Styx**, allowed Aeneas to pass because of the item from the magical bough. In the underworld, Aeneas spoke to his father **Anchises** and was told where to settle. He returned from the underworld and sailed again to the **Tiber** River in a land called **Latium**.

Aeneas, after beating a rival tribe who had been pitted against him by Juno, began to rule the area where he settled. For twelve generations the throne was passed peacefully down until the thirteenth king, **Numitor**. Numitor was removed from the throne by his own brother **Amulius**. Amulius tried to make sure that none of Numitor's descendents could challenge him for the throne. Amulius killed both of his nephews and appointed his niece **Rhea Silvia** a **Vestal Virgin**. This position forced Rhea to stay a virgin, which would eliminate any prospect of Numitor's children to challenge Amulius.

Mars, the god of war and farming, became enamored with Rhea, and depending on the account, seduced or raped her. She became pregnant and gave birth to two sons, **Romulus** and **Remus**. Amulius had Rhea imprisoned. He put the two boys in a basket and tossed it into the Tiber River. The boys were saved by their father Mars, who sent two animals to feed them. A she wolf fed the boys until they were discovered by a shepherd named Fausulaus. The boys were sheltered by the sheppherd and his wife until they had grown. The boys were united with their grandfather Numitor, and they then planned revenge on Amulius. The three, along with a band of shepherds, stormed the palace and killed Amulius and restored Numitor to the throne.

After restoring Numitor to the throne, Romulus and Remus set out to establish their own city with some of their shepherd followers. They planned to establish the city on the banks of the Tiber where they were discovered. The brothers began to argue over the city's design and name. They decided to settle their dispute by seeking a sign from the gods. They decided that who ever saw a flight of vultures first would be the winner. Remus was positioned on Aventine Hill, while Romulus was on Palentine Hill. Remus was the first to see six vultures, while

shortly after Romulus saw twelve vultures. Remus claimed that he had won since he saw the birds first. Romulus claimed that he had won the contest since he saw a dozen of the birds. A fight broke out between their followers. Remus was killed, and Romulus set himself up as ruler. He named the city Rome.

(Excerpted from http://www.varchive.org/dag/aeneas.htm http://historylink102.com/Rome/roman-founding.htm)

Proper Nouns

1. **Agamemnon** [ˌægəˈmemnən]: 阿伽门农，特洛伊战争中希腊的总统帅。
2. **Argolis** [ˈɑːgəlis]: 阿尔戈利斯，希腊东南部的州。
3. **Aegisthus** [iːˈdʒisθəs]: 埃癸斯托斯，克吕泰涅斯特拉的情夫，后被阿伽门农之子所杀。
4. **Clytemnestra** [ˌklaitəmˈnestrə]: 克吕泰涅斯特拉，阿伽门农之妻。
5. **Thyestes** [θaiˈestiːz]: 梯厄斯忒斯，迈锡尼国王阿特柔斯的弟弟。
6. **Pindar** [ˈpində]: 品达 (约公元前522—约前438)，古希腊抒情诗人 [亦作 Pindaros]。
7. **Orestes** [ɔˈrestiːz; ɔː-]: 俄瑞斯忒斯，斯巴达王，阿伽门农之子。
8. **Electra** [iˈlektrə]: 厄勒克特拉，阿伽门农之女。
9. **Erinyes** [iˈriniiːz]: 复仇三女神；专门报复那些背信弃义以及背叛家人的人。
10. **Odysseus** [əuˈdisjuːs]: 俄底修斯，伊塔卡国王；特洛伊战争英雄。
11. **Lotus-Eater** [ˈləutəsi, iːtə]: 食忘忧果的民族，又写作 Lotophagi。相传俄底修斯发现，食用忘忧果的人终日处于一种懒散、无忧无虑的状态。
12. **Cyclops Polyphemus** [saiˈkləupiːz ˌpɔləˈfiːməs]: 库克罗普斯·波吕斐摩斯，独目巨人。
13. **Aeolus** [ˈiːələs]: 埃俄罗斯，希腊神话中的风神。
14. **Ithaca** [ˈiθəkə]: 伊塔卡岛，希腊西部爱奥尼亚海中群岛之一。
15. **Poseidon** [pɔˈsaidən]: 波塞冬，海神、马神和地震之神。
16. **Circe** [ˈsəːsi]: 喀耳刻，著名女巫，将俄底修斯船上的水手的一半变成了猪。
17. **Hermes** [ˈhəːmiːz]: 赫耳墨斯，商业、发明、灵巧之神；盗贼的保护神；众神的信使、书吏及报信者。
18. **Sirens** [ˈsaiərənz]: 塞壬，长有翅膀的女海妖，用她们甜美的歌声来引诱水手们走向死亡。
19. **Charybdis** [kəˈribdis]: 卡律布狄斯，希腊神话中该亚与波塞冬的女儿，荷马史诗中的女妖。
20. **Scylla** [ˈsilə]: 斯库拉，吞吃水手的六头女海妖。
21. **Ogygia** [əuˈdʒidʒiə]: 奥杰吉厄岛。
22. **Calypso** [kəˈlipsəu]: 卡吕普索，荷马史诗《奥德赛》中的海上仙女。
23. **Scheria**: 斯刻里亚岛，俄底修斯归途中的最后一处落脚点。
24. **Penelope** [piˈneləpi]: 佩内洛普，俄底修斯忠实的妻子。
25. **Eumaeus** [juːˈmiːəs]: 欧迈俄斯，养猪的人。
26. **Telemachus** [tiˈleməkəs; tə-]: 忒勒玛科斯，俄底修斯之子。
27. **Argus** [ˈɑːgəs]: 阿耳戈斯，百眼巨人。
28. **Aeneas** [iˈniːəs]: 埃涅阿斯，特洛伊王子，后来到了意大利，建立了罗马民族。
29. **Priam** [ˈpraiəm]: 普里阿摩斯，特洛伊战争时的特洛伊王。
30. **Hector** [ˈhektə]: 赫克托耳，特洛伊军的统帅，特洛伊最英勇的战士。
31. **Harpy** [ˈhɑːpi]: 鹰身女妖。
32. **Juno** [ˈdʒuːnəu]: 天后，朱庇特之妻，司生育、婚姻等，相当于希腊神话中的赫拉。
33. **Neptune** [ˈneptjuːn]: 海神，即波塞冬。
34. **Carthage** [ˈkɑːθidʒ]: 迦太基，古城名，坐落于非洲北海岸 (今突尼斯)，与罗马隔海相望。最后因为在三次布匿战争 (Punic Wars) 中均被罗马打败而灭亡。
35. **Cupid** [ˈkjuːpid]: 丘比特，爱的化身。
36. **Dido** [ˈdaidəu] (Queen Dido of Carthage): 迦太基女王黛朵，迦太基的创建者和王后。
37. **Mercury** [ˈməːkjuri]: 众神的信使，商业、手工技艺、智巧、辩才、旅行以至欺诈和盗窃的神。

38. **Sibyl** [ˈsibil]：西比尔，年迈的女先知。
39. **Proserpine** [ˈprɔsəpain]：普洛塞尔皮娜（女阎罗）。
40. **Pluto** [ˈpluːtəu]：冥王（相当于希腊神话中的哈得斯）。
41. **Charon** [ˈkɛərən]：卡戎，冥河的船夫，在冥河上摆渡亡魂去阴间的神。
42. **Styx** [stiks]：冥河（环绕地狱的河）。
43. **Anchises** [æŋˈkaisiːz]：安喀塞斯，特洛伊王子。
44. **Tiber** [ˈtaibə]：台伯河（位于意大利中部，流经罗马）。
45. **Latium** [ˈleiʃiəm]：拉丁姆（古意大利罗马东南地区）。
46. **Numitor**：努米托，特洛伊王子埃涅阿斯的后裔。
47. **Amulius**：阿穆利乌斯，特洛伊王子埃涅阿斯的后裔。
48. **Rhea Silvia** [ˈriːəˈsilviə]：瑞亚·西尔维亚，努米托之女。
49. **Vestal Virgin** [ˈvestəl ˈvəːdʒin]：维斯太贞女，献身给维斯太女灶神并在维斯太神庙中守望圣火的处女。
50. **Mars** [mɑːz]：玛尔斯，战神。
51. **Romulus** [ˈrɔmjuləs]：罗穆卢斯，罗马的创建者，瑞摩斯的孪生兄弟。
52. **Remus** [ˈriːməs]：瑞摩斯，瑞亚·西尔维亚和战神之子，被其孪生兄弟罗穆卢斯杀害。

After You Read

Knowledge Focus

1. Fill in the blanks according to what you have learned from the text above.

1) Agamemnoon's wife Clytemnestra had never forgiven him for the sacrifice of their daughter _____.

2) According to the accounts given by Pindar and the tragedians, Agamemnon was slain in a bath by _____.

3) Orestes killed Clytemnestra, which is a terrible blood-guilt. But in the end, Orestes was vindicated because _____ judged that killing his mother was less heinous that killing his father.

4) Odysseus escaped the cave of the _____, a one-eyed ogre tried to eat his men, by blinding him.

5) Odysseus passed the Sirens, seductively musical bird-women whose _____ enticed sailors on to their murderous rocks.

6) Penelope had held suitors off for several years by promising to marry when she had finished weaving her father-in-law's _____, which she wove by day and unraveled by night.

7) Penelope showed suitors Odysseus bow and said she would marry whoever could shoot an arrow through the holes of _____ in a row.

8) Aeneas visited _____, a prophetess who had access to the underworld through a cave with a hundred openings.

9) A _____ fed Romulus and Remus until they were discovered by a shepherd.

10) The virgin priestess _____ was seduced by the god Mars, and gave birth to twin sons, Romulus and Remus, who were cast out by Amulius.

2. **Solo Work: Decide whether the following statements are true or false.**

   1) (　) During Agamemnon's absence his wife Clytemnestra had become the lover of Orion.
   2) (　) When Agamemnon returned home he entangled his wife in a net as she bathed and hacked her to death with an axe.
   3) (　) Agamemnon's son Orestes, when he has grown to manhood, avenged his father's death with the help or encouragement of his sister Electra.
   4) (　) When Polyphemus had fallen asleep Odysseus and his fellow men thrust a steel spear into the Cyclops only eye.
   5) (　) When it was time for Odysseus to leave, the god of the winds Aeolus gave him a sack which contained all the winds.
   6) (　) Odysseus resisted the spells of the witch Circe, who had turned his men (temporarily) into cows, and became her lover for a year.
   7) (　) Calypso looked after Odysseus, caressed him, and promised to make him immortal if they got married.
   8) (　) Odysseus was the only one who could string his great bow, and, having won the contest, he turned his arrows on the suitors and hurted them all.
   9) (　) Carrying his crippled father and his little daughter out of the burning city, Aeneas set sail with a few followers in search of the promised land.
   10) (　) Romulus killed Remus, becoming the first king of the city he called "Rome" after himself.

3. **Pair Work: Discuss the following questions with your partner.**

   1) Do you think the results of jealousy are disastrous?
   2) Clytemnestra's wrath at the sacrifice of Iphigenia and at Agamemnon's having gone to war over Helen of Troy, are said to have been the motives for her crime. What shall we do when we are furious?
   3) Agamemnon's son Orestes was vindicated in the end even though he killed his own mother. Should Orestes be vindicated?
   4) What lesson can we learn from Agamemnon's tragedy?
   5) According the author, how did Odysseus and his men escape from Cyclop Polyphemus?
   6) The curious crew opened the sack given by Aeolus, taking the ships further away than before. How do you think about curiosity?
   7) How can Odysseus resist so many temptations on his way home?
   8) Why did not Odysseus reveal his identity upon coming home?
   9) If you were Odysseus, would you kill suitors when defeating them?
   10) Would you leave your sweetheart for enterprises like Aeneas did?

Unit 11 After the Trojan War

Language Focus

1. Fill in the blanks with the proper forms of words or expressions you have learned in the text.

| impious | fumble | egregious | enamored | avenge |
| convince | thrust | antidote | caress | on the verge of |

1) Tom is very much _____ toward his parents, which hurts his mother deeply.
2) The mugger _____ at his victim with a knife.
3) He _____ in his pocket for some coins.
4) Doctor Johnson gives Susan an _____ against snake-bites.
5) Thailand and Cambodia were _____ war due to territory dispute in 2010.
6) Copperfield _____ his girlfriend Jessica's hand.
7) I am not too _____ with the idea of spending a whole day with him.
8) The prince was determined to _____ his father, the King who was murdered by Claudius.
9) How can I _____ you of her honesty.
10) We are shocked at his _____ incompetence. He made such a stupid mistake in calculating the cost of marketing.

2. Fill in the blanks with the proper form of the word in the brackets.

1) He must be _____ (insanity) to drive his car so fast.
2) The janitor _____ (leash) guard dogs when he found thief in the courtyard.
3) The heroes of the people are _____ (mortal).
4) They hid out in a remote cabin until a _____ (treachery) soldier led the enemy there.
5) Young ladies are attracted by his sad and fastidious but ever _____ (seduce) Irish voice.
6) The dog _____ (wag) its tail excitedly just now.
7) The captain was accused of _____ (incitement) other officers to mutiny.
8) When rioting broke out, the police were obliged to _____ (intervene).
9) The police have _____ (elimination) two suspects from their enquiry.
10) Subsequent events _____ (vindication) his suspicions.

3. Fill in the blanks with the proper prepositions or adverbs that collocate with the neighboring words.

1) His wrath _____ the cruety of Nazi led him to side with the British people.
2) I finally track _____ the reference in a dictionary of quotations.
3) Captain Keats and his crew landed _____ the isand Kakaya safely after 30 days of dangerous voyage.
4) Peace was finally _____ sight after 7 years of bloody war.
5) The explorers built a cottage _____ the cliff of Mount Toller.
6) Apollo apperaed _____ the shape of dolphin.
7) Territory disputes put the two countries _____ the verge of war.
8) He was glad it was _____ him she had revealed her secret.

4. **Proofreading: The following passage contains ten errors. Each indicated line contains a maximum of one error. In each case, only ONE word is involved. Read the passage and correct the errors.**

    At Ithaca, Penelope is having difficulties. Her husband has been gone for 20   1) _____
years, and she does not know for sure whether he is living or dead. Odysseus   2) _____
arrives, at last, complete alone. Upon landing, he is disguising as an old man in rags   3) _____
by Athena. Odysseus is welcomed by his old swineherd, Eumaeus, who does not   4) _____
recognize him, but still treats him well.

    His faithful dog, Argos, is the first recognize him. Aging and decrepit, the dog   5) _____
does its best to wag its tail, and Odysseus, not wanting to be found out, pays him no   6) _____
attention. The disconsolate dog died. The first human to recognize him is his old   7) _____
wet nurse, Euryclea, who knows him well enough to see through the rags,   8) _____
recognizing with him by an old scar on his leg received when hunting boar. His son,   9) _____
Telemachus, does not see through the disguise, and Odysseus reveals his identity to   10) _____
him.

Comprehensive Work

1. Debating.

    Agamemnon's son Orestes, with a command from Apollo to avenge his father's death, killed Aegisthus and Clytemnestra. But to kill one's mother incurred a terrible blood-guilt, At last an Athenian court heard his case argued by Apollo (for the defence) and Athena (for the prosecution), and pronounced the murder justified; Orestes was purified of guilt.

    Now divide the whole class into 2 groups and debate around whether Orestes is guilty. The teacher will be the arbitrator. Take down the remarkable arguments on both sides that impressed you.

The Supporting Party: Orestes is guilty!	The Opposing Party: The murder is justifiable!

2. Translate the following paragraph into Chinese.

    From Troy the vessels first made land at Ismarus, city of the Ciconians, where, in a skirmish with the inhabitants, Odysseus lost six men from each ship. Sailing from there, they were

overtaken by a storm which drove them for nine days along the sea till they reached the country of the Lotus-eaters. Here, after quenching their thirst, Odysseus sent three of his men to discover who the inhabitants were. These men on coming among the Lotus-eaters were kindly entertained by them, and were given some of their own food, the lotus-plant, to eat. The effect of this food was such that those who ate it lost all thoughts of home and wished to remain in that country. It was by main force that Ulysses dragged these men away, and he was even obliged to tie them under the benches of the ships.

Read More

Text B Odysseus

Odysseus or Ulysses (Greek Ὀδυσσεύς Odysseus; Latin: Ulixes), was the mythical Greek king of Ithaca and the main hero in Homer's epic poem, the *Odyssey*. Odysseus also plays a key role in Homer's *Iliad*. King of Ithaca, husband of Penelope, father of Telemachus, and son of Laërtes and Anticlea, Odysseus is renowned for his guile and resourcefulness (known by the epithet Odysseus the Cunning, and said to be third to only Zeus and Athena in wisdom; and is most famous for the ten eventful years it took him to return home after the Trojan War.

Relatively little is known of Odysseus' background except that his paternal grandfather (or step-grandfather) is Arcesius, son of Cephalus and grandson of Aeolus, while his maternal grandfather is Autolycus, son of Hermes and Chione. According to some late sources, most of them were purely genealogical. Odysseus had many children, including, with Penelope, Telemachus and Poliporthes (born after Odysseus' return from Troy). With Circe, he fathered Telegonus, Ardeas, and Latinus. With Calypso, there was Nausinous and with Callidice, came Polypoetes.

Most such genealogies aim to link Odysseus with the foundation of many Italic cities of remote antiquity. Ithaca, an island along the Ionian coastline of Greece, is one of several islands that would have comprised the realm of Odysseus' family, but the true extent of the Cephallenian realm and the actual identities of the islands named in Homer's works are unknown.

Odysseus' legendary travels and adventures are among the best known in world literature. They have been told and retold by the great Greek and Roman writers, Medieval and Renaissance poets of the caliber of Dante and Shakespeare, and modern writers such as James Joyce and Nikos Kazantzakis.

Back to Ithaca

The *Odyssey* contains the epic and mythic story of Odysseus' ten-year voyage to reach Ithaca. After Odysseus and his men depart from Troy, their ships near land. Eurylochus convinces Odysseus to go ashore and loot the nearby city. The city is not at all protected, and all of the inhabitants flee without a fight into the nearby mountains. Odysseus and his men loot the city, and Odysseus  wisely orders the men to board the ships quickly. They refuse, eat dinner, and fall asleep on the beach. The next morning, the Ciconians, allies of Troy and great warriors, return with their fierce kinsmen from the mountains. Odysseus and his men flee to the ships as fast as they can, but many men are left behind: "six benches were left empty in every ship" (The *Odyssey*, Book IX, line 64).

Odysseus and his men then land upon the island of the Lotus-Eaters. Odysseus sends out a small scouting party who eat the lotus with the natives. This causes them to fall asleep, awakening somewhat later, euphoric and intoxicated. Odysseus pursues the scouting party, drags them back to their ships against their will where they set sail again; the drugged men are tied to the benches to prevent them from swimming back to the island.

Land of the Cyclops

Later, a scouting party led by Odysseus and his friend Misenus, lands in the territory of the Cyclops, venturing upon a large cave. They proceed to feast on the livestock they find there. Unknown to them, the cave is the dwelling of Polyphemus, a giant Cyclops who soon returns. Polyphemus refuses hospitality to his uninvited guests and traps them in his cave, blocking the entrance with a boulder immovable by mortal men. He then proceeds to eat a pair of the men each day. Odysseus devises a cunning plan for escape.

To make Polyphemus unwary, Odysseus gives him a bowl of strong, unwatered wine that was given to them by Maron, the priest of Apollo. When Polyphemus asks for his name, Odysseus tells him that it is Οὖτις (Outis, "Nobody," which is also a short form of his own name). In appreciation for the wine, Polyphemus offers to return the favor by eating him last. Once the giant falls asleep, Odysseus and his men use a pine tree—which they have fashioned into a giant spear—to blind Polyphemus. Hearing Polyphemus' cries, other Cyclops come to his cave, instinctively. Polyphemus replies "Οὖτίς με κτείνει δόλῳ οὐδὲ βίηφιν." ("Nobody is killing me either by treachery or brute violence!") The other Cyclops leave him alone, thinking that his outbursts must be madness or the gods' doing.

In the morning, Polyphemus rolls back the boulder to let the sheep out to graze. Polyphemus cannot see the men, but he feels the tops of his sheep to make sure that the men are not riding them, and spreads his arm at the entrance of the cave. Odysseus and his men escape, having tied themselves to the undersides of the sheep. Once Odysseus and his men are out, they load the sheep on board their ships and set sail.

As Odysseus and his men are sailing away, he reveals his true identity to Polyphemus. Enraged, Polyphemus tries to hit the ship with boulders, but because he is blind, he misses. When the ship appears to be getting away at last, Polyphemus raises his arms to his father, Poseidon, god of the sea. He asks him not to allow Odysseus to get back home to Ithaca, adding that if Odysseus does arrive home, he should do so alone, his crew either dead or aboard a stranger's ship.

A troubled crew

Odysseus next stops at Aeolia, home of Aeolus, the favored mortal who received from the gods the power of controlling the winds. Aeolus gives Odysseus and his crew hospitality for a month. Aeolus also provides a bag filled with all the winds except for the one that will lead him home.

Odysseus' crew members suspect that there is treasure in the bag, and two of the men decide to open it as soon as Odysseus falls asleep—just before their home is reached. Subsequently, they are blown away by a violent storm back to Aeolia by Poseidon, where Aeolus refuses to provide any more help, fearing that Odysseus is cursed by the gods. Once again, Odysseus has to start his journey from Aeolia to Ithaca.

When they arrive at Telepylos, the stronghold of the Laestrygonians, they find a gigantic woman, the wife of an equally large Antiphates, king of the Laestrygonians, who promptly calls her husband. He immediately snatches up one of the men and starts to eat him. Two other men run away, but Antiphates raises such a commotion that they are pursued by thousands of Laestrygonians, all of whom are giants. They throw vast rocks from the cliffs, smashing the ships, and spear the men like fish. Odysseus makes his escape with his single ship not trapped in the harbor. The rest of his company is lost.

(Excerpted from http://www.newworldencyclopedia.org/entry/ Odysseus)

Questions for Reflection

1. Please decide on the best choice from the four choices marked A, B, C, and D.

   1) Odysseus' paternal grandfather (or step-grandfather) is _____.

      A. Arcesius   B. Cephalus   C. Aeolus   D. Autolycus

   2) Polyphemus traps Odysseus and his men in his cave, blocking the entrance with a _____.

      A. pine tree   B. boulder   C. giant spear   D. shield

   3) Odysseus gives Polyphemus some strong, unwatered wine that was given to them by Maron, the priest of _____.

      A. Zeus   B. Poseidon   C. Apollo   D. Hera

   4) In appreciation for the wine offered by Odysseus, Polyphemus offers to return the favor by _____.

      A. releasing him   B. making friends with him
      C. releasing all   D. eating him last

   5) _____ gives Odysseus a bag filled with all the winds except for the one that can bring him home.

      A. Aeolia   B. Telepylos   C. Aeolus   D. Laestrygonians

Text C Rome

Rome is the capital city of Italy and of the Lazio region, and is Italy's largest and most populous city.

Rome's history spans more than 2,500 years. It is renowned as one of the founding cities of Western Civilization. Along with its central place in the history of the Roman Empire, Rome has a significant place in the history of Christianity. The name could derive from the names of legendary founders of Rome, the twins Romulus and Remus.

Today, Rome is a modern, cosmopolitan city, and the third most-visited tourist destination in the European Union. Due to its influence in politics, media, the arts, and culture, Rome has been described as a global city and is known worldwide as the "Eternal City."

As one of the few major European cities that escaped World War II relatively unscathed, central Rome remains essentially Renaissance and Baroque in character. The historic center, including numerous religious and public buildings, is listed by UNESCO as a World Heritage Site. That organization has noted it for its "unique artistic achievements," "remarkable examples of great early Christian basilicas," because it "exerted considerable influence on the development of architecture and monumental arts," and is "directly and tangibly associated with the history of the origins of the Christian religion."

History
Foundation

According to Roman tradition, the city was founded by the twins Romulus and Remus on April 21, 753 B.C.E. Archaeological evidence supports the view that Rome grew from pastoral settlements on the Palatine Hill built in the area of what became the Roman Forum, possibly in the middle of the eighth century B.C.E. The original settlement developed into the capital of the Roman Kingdom (ruled by a succession of seven kings, according to tradition), and then the Roman Republic (from 510 B.C.E., governed by the Senate), and finally the Roman Empire (from 27 B.C.E., ruled by an Emperor). Military conquest, commercial predominance, as well as selective assimilation of neighboring civilizations, most notably the Etruscans and Greeks, were part of the city's early growth. Rome had been undefeated in war until 386 B.C.E., when it was briefly occupied by the Gauls.

Roman dominance expanded over the shores of the Mediterranean Sea, reaching a population of one million people, and for almost 1,000 years, Rome was the most politically important, richest and largest city in the Western world, until it was surpassed by the Eastern capital Constantinople.

Fall and Middle Ages

With the reign of Constantine I (306—337), the Bishop of Rome gained political as well as religious importance, eventually becoming known as the Pope and establishing Rome as the center of the Catholic Church. After the sack of Rome in 410 C.E. by Alaric I and the fall of the Western Roman Empire in 476 C.E., Rome alternated between Byzantine and plundering by Germanic barbarians. Its population declined to a mere 20,000 during the Early Middle Ages, reducing the sprawling city to groups of inhabited buildings interspersed among large areas of ruins and vegetation. Rome remained nominally part of the Byzantine Empire until 751, when the Lombards finally abolished the Exarchate of Ravenna. In 756, Pepin the Short (714—768) gave the pope temporal jurisdiction over Rome and surrounding areas, thus creating the Papal States.

Rome remained the capital of the Papal States until its annexation into the Kingdom of Italy in 1870; the city became a major pilgrimage site during the Middle Ages and the focus of struggles between the Papacy and the Holy Roman Empire starting with Charlemagne (747—814), who was crowned its first emperor in Rome in 800 by Pope Leo III. Apart from brief periods as an independent city during the Middle Ages, Rome kept its status of Papal capital and "holy city" for centuries, even when the Pope briefly relocated to Avignon (1309—1377).

Renaissance

The latter half of the fifteenth century saw the seat of the Italian Renaissance move to Rome from Florence. The popes wanted to surpass the grandeur of other Italian cities and created ever more extravagant churches, bridges, and public spaces, including a new Saint Peter's Basilica, the Sistine Chapel, Ponte Sisto, and Piazza Navona. The Popes were also patrons of the arts engaging such artists as Michelangelo, Perugino, Raphael, Ghirlandaio, Luca Signorelli, Botticelli, and Cosimo Rosselli.

The period was also infamous for papal corruption with many popes fathering children, and engaging in nepotism and simony. The corruption of the Popes and the extravagance of their building projects led, in part, to the Protestant Reformation (1517—1648) and, in turn, the Counter-reformation (1560—1648).

Reunification

Italy became caught up in the nationalistic turmoils of the nineteenth century and twice gained and lost a short-lived independence. Rome became the focus of hopes of Italian reunification when the rest of Italy was reunited under the Kingdom of Italy with a temporary capital at Florence. In 1861, Rome was declared the capital of Italy even though it was still under the control of the Pope. During the 1860s the last vestiges of the Papal states were under French protection. And it was only when this was lifted in 1870, owing to the outbreak of the Franco-Prussian War, that Italian troops were able to capture Rome.

Twentieth century

After a victorious World War I (1914—1918), Rome witnessed the rise to power of Italian fascism guided by Benito Mussolini (1883—1945), who marched on the city in 1922, eventually declared a new Empire, and allied Italy with Nazi Germany. This was a period of rapid growth in population, from the 212,000 people at the time of unification to more than one million people, but this trend was halted by World War II (1939—1945), during which Rome was damaged by

both Allied forces bombing and Nazi occupation. After the execution of Mussolini and the end of the war, a 1946 referendum abolished the monarchy in favor of the Italian Republic.

Rome grew momentously after the war, as one of the driving forces behind the "Italian economic miracle" of post-war reconstruction and modernization. It became a fashionable city in the 1950s and early 1960s, the years of la dolce vita ("the sweet life"), and a new rising trend in population continued till the mid-1980s, when the commune had more than 2,800,000 residents; after that, population started to slowly decline as more residents moved to nearby suburbs.

(Excerpted from http://www.newworldencyclopedia.org/entry/Rome)

Questions for Reflection

1. Decide whether the following statements are True or False.
   1) (   ) Rome's history spans more than 2,600 years.
   2) (   ) Today, Rome is a modern, cosmopolitan city, and the second most-visited tourist destination in the European Union.
   3) (   ) Roman dominance expanded over the shores of the Mediterranean Sea, reaching a population of one million people, and for almost 1,000 years.
   4) (   ) Its population declined to a mere 20,000 during the Early Middle Ages, reducing the sprawling city to groups of inhabited buildings interspersed among large areas of ruins and vegetation.
   5) (   ) The latter half of the fifteenth century saw the seat of the Italian Renaissance move to Rome from Florence.

6) (   ) After the execution of Mussolini and the end of the war, a 1945 referendum abolished the monarchy in favor of the Italian Republic.

For Fun

Movies to Watch
Odysseus and the Isle of the Mists (2007)

Odysseus and the Isle of the Mists is a 2007 feature film directed by Terry Ingram and produced by Plinyminor in association with the Sci Fi Channel in Vancouver, B.C.

King Odysseus has been away from Ithaca for twenty years. The first ten he spent fighting the Trojan War; the last ten he spent fighting to get home. Among his adventures is the tale Homer felt was too horrible to tell, the missing book of the Odyssey known as "The Isle of the Mists". Here the Warrior King and his men face the Goddess of the Underworld and her winged horrific creatures, intent on bringing death and destruction to humanity.

Unit 12
Apollo and Daphne

> No one ever kills himself for the love of a woman, but because love—any love—reveals us in our nakedness, our misery, our vulnerability, our nothingness."
>
> —Cesare Pavese

Unit Goals

- To be able to tell the myth of Apollo and Daphne
- To know the life of Apollo
- To learn about Apollo at Delphi
- To learn the words and phrases that describe Greek Gods
- To improve language skills and critical thinking through the content of this unit

Before You Read

1. **Which one of the following do you think is the most miserable? Why?**
   1) loving someone who does not love you at all
   2) having to say goodby to your sweetheart
   3) being chased by someone whom you do not love at all

2. **All the following pictures are related to Apollo. Can you identify each of them?**

3. Form groups of three or four students. Try to find, on the Internet or in the library, more information about the pictures above. Choose one as your topic and prepare a five-minute classroom presentation.

Start to Read

Text A Apollo and Daphne

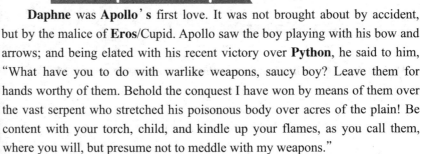

Daphne was **Apollo**'s first love. It was not brought about by accident, but by the malice of **Eros**/Cupid. Apollo saw the boy playing with his bow and arrows; and being elated with his recent victory over **Python**, he said to him, "What have you to do with warlike weapons, saucy boy? Leave them for hands worthy of them. Behold the conquest I have won by means of them over the vast serpent who stretched his poisonous body over acres of the plain! Be content with your torch, child, and kindle up your flames, as you call them, where you will, but presume not to meddle with my weapons."

Aphrodite/Venus' boy heard these words, and rejoined, "Your arrows may strike all things else, Apollo, but mine shall strike you." So saying, he took his stand on a rock of **Parnassus**, and drew from his quiver two arrows of different workmanship, one to excite love, the other to repel it. The former was of gold and sharp-pointed, the latter blunt and tipped with lead. With the leaden shaft, he struck the nymph Daphne, the daughter of the river god **Peneus**, and with the golden one Apollo, through the heart. The god was immediately seized with love for the maiden, and she abhorred the thought of loving. Her delight was in woodland sports and in the spoils of the chase. Many lovers sought her, but she spurned them all, ranging the woods, and taking thought neither of Eros/Cupid nor of **Hymen**. Her father often said to her, "Daughter, you owe me a son-in-law; you owe me grandchildren." She, hating the thought of marriage as a crime, with her beautiful face tinged all over with blushes, threw her arms around her father's neck, and said, "Dearest father, grant me this favor, that I may always remain unmarried, like Artemis/Diana." He consented, but at the same time said, "Your own face will forbid it."

Apollo loved her, and longed to obtain her; and he who gives oracles to all in the world was not wise enough to look into his own fortunes. He saw her hair flung loose over her shoulders, and said, "If so charming in disorder, what would it be if arranged?" He saw her eyes bright as stars; he saw her lips, and was not satisfied with only seeing them. He admired her hands and arms bared to the shoulder, and whatever was hidden from view he imagined more beautiful still. He followed her;  she fled, swifter than the wind, and didn't delay a moment at his entreaties. "Stay," said he, "daughter of Peneus; I am not a foe. Do not fly me as a lamb flies the wolf, or a dove the hawk. It is for love I pursue you. You make me miserable, for fear you should fall and hurt yourself on these stones, and I should be the cause. Pray run slower, and I will follow slower. I am no clown, no rude peasant. **Zeus**/Jupiter/Jove is my father, and I am lord of **Delphos** and **Tenedos**, and know all things, present and future. I am the god of song and the lyre. My arrows fly true to the mark; but alas! An arrow more fatal than mine has pierced my heart! I am the god of medicine, and know the virtues of all healing plants. Alas! I suffer a malady that no balm can cure!"

The nymph continued her flight, and left his plea half uttered. And even as she fled she charmed him. The wind blew her garments, and her unbound hair streamed loose behind her. The god grew impatient to find his wooing thrown away, and, sped by Eros/Cupid, gained upon her in the race. It was like a hound pursuing a hare, with open jaws ready to seize, while the feebler animal darts forward, slipping from the very grasp. So flew the god and the virgin he on the wings of love, and she on those of fear. The pursuer was the more rapid, however, and gained upon her, and his panting breath was blowing upon her hair. Now her strength began to fail, and, ready to sink, she called upon her father, the river god: "Help me, Peneus! Open the earth to enclose me, or change my form, which has brought me into this danger!"

Scarcely had she spoken, when a stiffness seized all her limbs; her bosom began to be enclosed in a tender bark; her hair became leaves; her arms became branches; her feet stuck fast in the ground, as roots; her face became a tree-top, retaining nothing of its former self but its beauty. Apollo stood amazed. He touched the stem, and felt the flesh tremble under the new bark. He embraced the branches, and lavished kisses on the wood. The branches shrank from his lips. "Since you cannot be  my wife," said he, "you shall assuredly be my tree. I will wear you for my crown. With you I will decorate my harp and my quiver; and when the great Roman conquerors lead up the triumphal pomp to the **Capitol**, you shall be woven into wreaths for their brows. And, as eternal youth is mine, you also shall be always green, and your leaf know no decay." The nymph, now changed into a laurel tree, bowed its head in grateful acknowledgment.

Apollo was god of music and of poetry and also of medicine. For, as the poet **Armstrong** says, himself a physician:

> *Music exalts each joy, allays each grief,*
> *Expels disease, softens every pain;*
> *And hence the wise of ancient days adored*
> *One power of physic, melody, and song.*

The story of Apollo and Daphne is often alluded to by the poets. **Waller** applies it to the case of one of his amatory verses, though they did not soften the heart of his mistress, yet won for the poet wide-spread fame.

> *Yet what he sung in his immortal strain,*
> *Though unsuccessful, was not sung in vain.*
> *All but the nymph that should redress his wrong,*
> *Attend his passion and approve his song.*
> *Like Phoebus thus, acquiring unsought praise,*
> *He caught at love and filled his arms with bays.*

The following stanza from **Shelley**'s *Adonais* alludes to **Byron**'s early quarrel with the reviewers:

> *The herded wolves, bold only to pursue;*
> *The obscene ravens, clamorous o'er the dead;*
> *The vultures, to the conqueror's banner true,*
> *Who feed where Desolation first has fed.*
> *And whose wings rain contagion; how they fled,*
> *When like Apollo, from his golden bow,*
> *The **Pythian** of the age one arrow sped*
> *And smiled! The spoilers tempt no second blow;*
> *They fawn on the proud feet that spurn them as they go.*

(Excerpted from: http://www.bartleby.com/181/031.html)

Proper Nouns

1. **Apollo** [əˈpɔləu]: 阿波罗，司艺术、医药、音乐、诗歌和修辞之神，有时被称为太阳神。
2. **Daphne** [ˈdæfni]: 达佛涅，阿波罗所追求的女山神，为了躲避Apollo的拥抱而化为月桂树。
3. **Eros** [ˈiərɔs] /**Cupid** [ˈkjuːpid]: 厄洛斯/丘比特，爱之神；维纳斯的儿子。
4. **Python** [ˈpaiθən, -θɔn]: 皮同，一条巨蛇，后被阿波罗杀死。
5. **Aphrodite** [ˌæfrəuˈdaiti] / **Venus** [ˈviːnəs]: 阿佛洛狄忒/维纳斯，爱与美的女神。
6. **Parnassus** [pɑːˈnæsəs]: 巴那塞斯山，希腊中部一座海拔约2458米（8060英尺）的山，位于科林斯海湾的北边。
7. **Peneus** [piˈniːəs]: 佩纽斯，河神。

8. **Hymen** [ˈhaimen; -mən]：海门，婚姻之神。
9. **Zeus** [zju:s] /**Jupiter** [ˈdʒu:pitə] /**Jove** [dʒəuv]：奥林山神中最为强大的天神，雷电之神，天、地、神、人的统治者。
10. **Delphos**：特尔缶，爱琴海中的一个小岛，阿波罗的出生地。
11. **Tenedos** [ˈtenədɔs]：泰纳多斯，爱琴海中的一个小岛。
12. **Capitol** [ˈkæpitəl]：丘比特神庙，位于卡匹托尔山丘。
13. **Armstrong** [ˈɑːmstrɔŋ]：阿姆斯特朗(1709—1779)，英国诗人。
14. **Waller** [ˈwɔlə]：沃勒(1606—1687)英国诗人，以其爱情诗而闻名，著有《去吧，可爱的玫瑰花》等。
15. **Shelley** [ˈʃeli]：雪莱(1792—1822)，英国浪漫主义诗人，主要作品有长诗《伊斯兰的反叛》、诗剧《解放了的普罗米修斯》及抒情诗《西风颂》《致云雀》等。
16. **Adonais**：《阿多尼斯》，英国诗人雪莱的作品。
17. **Byron** [ˈbairən]：拜伦(1788—1824)，英国诗人，被公认为是浪漫主义运动的先驱。他的著作有《查尔德·哈洛尔德游记》以及讽刺长诗《唐璜》等。
18. **Pythian** [ˈpiθiən]：皮提亚的，属于或有关特尔斐神庙(特尔斐城阿波罗神庙)的或有关其神谕的。

After You Read

Knowledge Focus

1. Fill in the blanks according to what you have learned from the text above.

1) Daphne was Apollo's first love. It was brought about by the malice of _____.
2) Aphrodite/Venus' boy took his stand on a rock of Parnassus, and drew from his quiver two arrows of different workmanship, one to excite _____, the other to repel it.
3) With the _____, Aphrodite/Venus' boy struck Daphne, and with the golden one Apollo, through the heart.
4) Daphne hated the thought of marriage as a _____.
5) Daphne said to her father, "Dearest father, grant me this favor, that I may always remain unmarried, like _____."
6) Apollo is lord of _____ and Tenedos, and know all things, present and future.
7) Daphene called upon her father when Apollo gained upon her: "Help me, Peneus! Open the earth to enclose me, or change my _____, which has brought me into this danger!".
8) Apollo told the laurel tree that when the great Roman conquerors lead up the triumphal pomp to the Capitol, the tree shall be woven into _____ for their brows.
9) The poet _____, a physician, says in his poem "Music exalts each joy, allays each grief, Expels disease, softens every pain;".
10) The following stanza from Shelley's _____ alludes to Byron's early quarrel with the reviewers: "When like Apollo, from his golden bow, The Pythian of the age one arrow sped".

2. Solo Work: Decide whether the following statements are true or false.

1) (   ) Cupid was playing with his knife and arrows when Apollo encountered him.

2) (   ) Cupid drew from his quiver two arrows of different workmanship, one was of gold and sharp-pointed, the latter blunt and tipped with bronze.
3) (   ) With the golden shaft, Cupid struck the nymph Daphne, the daughter of the river god Peneus.
4) (   ) Dephane was delight in woodland sports and in the spoils of the chase.
5) (   ) Apollo gives oracles to all in the world and was wise enough to look into his own fortunes.
6) (   ) Apollo's father is Zeus/Jupiter/Jove.
7) (   ) After calling upon her father, Daphne's feet stuck fast in the ground; her hair became leaves; her arms became branches.
8) (   ) Daphne's face became a tree-top, retaining nothing of its former self.
9) (   ) Apollo believed that as eternal youth is his, the laurel tree shall not be always green, and its leaf will decay sooner or later.
10) (   ) Apollo was god of music and of poetry and also of weather.

3. **Pair Work: discuss the following questions with your partner.**
   1) Do you think that Cupid is evil in striking Apollo and Daphne with two different arrows?
   2) What would you do if someone laughs at you? Why?
   3) Apollo who gives oracles to all in the world was not wise enough to look into his own fortunes. Can man look into his own fortunes?
   4) What can we learn from Apollo's tragedy?
   5) Should Apollo be blamed for his tragedy?
   6) Is interpersonal relationship important for us?
   7) Can we get true love by force?
   8) Would you change yourself into a laurel tree if you cannot escape from your wooer?
   9) What would you do when Daphne asked for help if you were the river god Peneus?
   10) Do you think Apollo love Daphne?

Language Focus
1. Fill in the blanks with the proper forms of words or expressions you have learned in the text.

| elate | kindle | rejoin | lavish | meddle (with) |
| tempt | redress | bold | fawn | allude to |

1) Don't _____ the electrical wiring: you're not an electrician.
2) He _____ money on his friends in the past.
3) "You're wrong!" she _____.
4) She did not say Mr Smith's name, but it was clear she was _____ him.
5) He was greatly _____ by success.
6) She _____ on her superior.
7) Jordan proposed a _____ scheme to rebuild the city center.

8) I am _____ to take the day off.
9) He is the leader who _____ the injustice in 1996.
10) Her cruelty _____ hatred in my heart.

2. Fill in the blanks with the proper form of the word in the brackets.
  1) There was no intended _____ (malicious) in what he said.
  2) He is _____ (repeller) by the very thought of having to work with these evil men.
  3) He is rather _____ (bluntly) in speech, which makes his boss very angry.
  4) "The problem with Establishment Republicans is they _____ (abhoring) the unseemliness of a political brawl", said Patrick J. Buchanan.
  5) Her sweetness of temper has _____ (charming) her aged and youthful companions.
  6) The poor mother _____ (entreaty) the teacher to forgive her son.
  7) Among her many _____ (virtuous) are loyalty, courage and truthfulness.
  8) His pulse was very _____ (feebly) when he was wounded in a traffic accident.
  9) The dog _____ (darting) across the street just now.
  10) She _____ (embracing) her son tenderly when he came home after ten years' absence.

3. Fill in the blanks with the proper prepositions or adverbs that collocate with the neighboring words.
  1) The new employment law brings _____ many improvements in the employment of women.
  2) Mary was elated _____ her success in the recent competition.
  3) I am very content _____ my life at present.
  4) They kindled _____ the gasoline in the petrol tank and destroyed that strong blockhouse.
  5) The sunset tinged the lake _____ pink.
  6) The police are looking _____ the company's accounts.
  7) We are gaining _____ one of mankind's most dreaded diseases.
  8) Do not ask him about his failure; do not evern allude _____ it.

4. Proofreading: The following passage contains ten errors. Each indicated line contains a maximum of one error. In each case, only ONE word is involved. Read the passage and correct the errors.

As the most Hellenic of all gods, Apollo apparently was foreign origin, coming   1) _____
either from somewhere north of Greece or from Asia. Traditionally, Apollo and his   2) _____
twin, Artemis, are born in the isle of Delos. From there Apollo went to Pytho   3) _____
(Delphi), he slew Python, the dragon that guarded the area. He established his   4) _____
oracle by taking in the guise of a dolphin, leaping aboard a Cretan ship, and forced
the crew to serve him. Thus Pytho was named Delphi after the dolphin (delphis),   5) _____
and the Cretan cult of Apollo Delphinius superseded that previously established   6) _____
there by Earth (Gaea). During the Archaic period (8th to 6th century BC), the fame 7) _____
of the Delphic oracle spread as far as Lydia in Anatolia and achieving pan-Hellenic 8) _____
status. The god's medium was the Pythia, the local woman over fifty years old,   9) _____
who, under his inspiration, delivered oracles in the main temple of Apollo.   10) _____

Ancient Greek and Roman Mythology

Comprehensive Work

1. Presentation.

Read Text A again and retell the story of Apollo and Daphne, using the following words or expressions.

Daphne	Apollo	Cupid	arrows	strick	seek	spurn
follow	flee	grow	impatient to	gain upon	call upon	laurel tree
wreaths						

2. Writing

Daphne repeatedly rejected every lover, including Apollo. Suppose you are a good friend of Apollo's. He asks you for advice on whether he should go on chasing her or not. Write a letter to him. You must give at least three reasons why he should (or should not) go on chasing her.

3. Translate the following paragraph into Chinese.

Daphne was Apollo's first love. It was not brought about by accident, but by the cruelty of Eros/Cupid. Apollo saw the boy playing with his bow and arrows; and being himself delighted with a recent victory over a sea monster, he said to him, "What have you to do with warlike weapons, little boy? Leave them for hands worthy of them such as I". The boy was actually the son of Aphrodite. He heard these words and rejoined "Your arrows may strike all things else, Apollo, but mine shall strike you." So saying, he drew two arrows of different workmanship, one to excite love, the other to repel it. With the first, he struck Apollo through the heart, and with the latter he struck the nymph Daphne. Forthwith the god was seized with love for the maiden, and she abhorred the thought of loving. Her delight was in woodland sports. Lovers sought her, but she refused them all, ranging the woods, and taking no thought of love or marriage.

Text B Apollo

Apollo, The son of Zeus and Leto, and the twin brother of Artemis, was the god of music (principally the lyre, and he directed the choir of the Muses) and also of prophecy, colonization, medicine, archery (but not for war or hunting), poetry, dance, intellectual inquiry and the carer of herds and flocks. He was also a god of light, known as "Phoebus" (radiant or beaming, and he was sometimes identified with Helios the sun god). He was also the god of plague and was worshiped as Smintheus (from sminthos, rat) and as Parnopius (from parnops, grasshopper) and was known as the destroyer of rats and locust, and according to Homer's *Iliad*, Apollo shot arrows of plague into the Greek camp. Apollo being the god of religious healing would give those guilty of murder and other immoral deeds a ritual purification. Sacred to Apollo are the swan (one legend says

that Apollo flew on the back of a swan to the land of the Hyperboreans, he would spend the winter months among them), the wolf and the dolphin. His attributes are the bow and arrows, on his head a laurel crown, and the cithara (or lyre) and plectrum. But his most famous attribute is the tripod, the symbol of his prophetic powers.

When the goddesss Hera, the wife of Zeus (it was he who had coupled with Leto) found out about Leto's pregnancy, she was outraged with jealousy. Seeking revenge Hera forced Leto to roam the earth in search of a place to give birth. Sicne Hera had forbidden Leto to stay anywhere on earth, either on terra-ferma or an island at sea, the only place to seek shelter was Delos, being in the center of the Aegean, and also difficult to reach, as there were strong under-currents, because it was said to be a  floating island. Because it was a floating island, it was not considered either of Hera's prohibitions, and so Leto was able to give birth to the divine twins Apollo and Artemis (before Leto gave birth to Apollo, the island was encircled by a flock of swans, this is why the swan was sacred to him). As a gesture of thanks Delos was secured to the sea-bed by four columns to give it stability, and from then on it became one of the most important sanctuaries to Apollo. (A variation of Apollo's birth was that the jealous Hera had incarcerated Ilithyia, the goddess of childbirth, but the other gods intervened forcing Hera to release Ilithyia, which allowed Leto to give birth).

Apollo's first achievement was to rid Pytho (Delphi) of the serpent (or dragon) Python. This monstrous beast protected the sanctuary of Pytho from its lair beside the Castalian Spring. There it stood guard while the "Sibyl" gave out her prophecies as she inhaled the trance inducing vapors from an open chasm. Apollo killed Python with his bow and arrows (Homer wrote "he killed the fearsome dragon Python, piercing it with his darts"). Apollo not only took charge of the oracle but rid the neighboring countryside of widespread destruction, as Python had destroyed crops, sacked villages and polluted streams and springs. However, to make amends for killing Python, as the fearsome beast was the son of Gaia, Apollo had to serve king Admetus for nine years (in some versions eight) as a cowherd. This he did, and when he returned to Pytho he came in the guise of a dolphin bringing with him priests from Crete (Apollo's cult title "Delphinios" meaning dolphin or porpoise, is probably how Delphi was so named). After killing Python and taking possession   of the oracle, the god of light (Phobus) became known as "Pythian Apollo". He dedicated a bronze tripod to the sanctuary and bestowed divine powers on one of the priestesses, and she became known as the "Pythia". It was she who inhaled the hallucinating vapors from the fissure in the temple floor, while she sat on a tripod chewing laurel leaves. After she mumbled her answer, a male priest would translate it for the supplicant. Delphi became the most important oracle center of Apollo, there were several including Clarus and Branchidae.

The most famous mortal loves of Apollo was Hecuba, she was the wife of Priam, the king of Troy. She bore him Troilius. Foretold by an oracle, as long as Troilius reached the age of twenty, Troy could not be defeated. But the hero Achilles ambushed and killed him, when the young prince and his sister Polyxena secretly visited a spring. Apollo also fell in love with Cassandra, the sister of Troilius, and daughter of Hecuba and Priam. He seduced Cassandra on the promise that he would teach her the art of prophecy, but having learnt the prophetic art she rejected him. Apollo, being angry of her rejection punished her, by declaring her prophecies never to be accepted or believed.

Apollo could also be ruthless when he was angered. The mortal Niobe, boasted to Apollo's mother Leto, that she had fourteen children (in some versions six or seven), which must make her more superior than Leto, who had only bore two. Apollo greatly angered by this slew her sons, and Artemis killed Niobe's daughters. Niobe wept so much that she turned into a pillar of stone. Apollo was infuriated when the satyr Marsyas challenged Apollo to music contest. After winning the competition, Apollo had Marsyas flayed alive, for being so presumptuous, as to challenge a god.

Apollo was worshiped throughout the Greek world, at Delphi every four years they held the Pythian Games in his honor. He had many epithets, including "Pythian Apollo" (his name at Delphi), "Apollo Apotropaeus" (Apollo who averts evil), and "Apollo Nymphegetes" (Apollo who looks after the Nymphs). As the god of shepherds he also had the cult titles "Lukeios" (from lykos; wolf), protecting the flocks from wolfs, and "Nomius" (of pastures, belonging to shepherds). Being the god of colonists, Apollo influenced his priests at Delphi to give divine guidance, as to where the expedition should proceed. This was during the height of the colonizing era circa 750-550 BCE. Apollo's title was "Archigetes" (leader of colonists). According to one legend, it was Apollo who helped either Cretan or Arcadian colonists found the city of Troy.

In art Apollo is at most times depicted as a handsome young man, clean shaven and carrying either a lyre, or his bow and arrows. There are many sculptures of Apollo and one of the most famous is the central figure from the west pediment of the Temple of Zeus, at Olympia, showing Apollo declaring victory in favor of the Lapiths in their struggle against the Centaurs.

(Excerpted from http://www.pantheon.org/articles/a/apollo.html)

Questions for Reflection

Please decide on the best choice from the four choices marked A, B, C, and D.

1) Apollo was a god of light, known as "_____" (radiant or beaming, and he was sometimes identified with Helios the sun god).

    A. Muses   B. Smintheus   C. Parnopius   D. Phoebus

2) Which of the following is NOT sacred to Apollo?
   A. Swan.   B. Wolf.   C. Bear.   D. Dolphin.
3) Where did Leto give birth to the divine twins Apollo and Artemis?
   A. Delos.   B. Olympia.   C. terra-ferma.   D. Aegean.
4) Apollo's first achievement was to get rid of the serpent (or dragon) _____.
   A. Sibyl.   B. Python.   C. Gaia.   D. Admetus.
5) Which was the most famous mortal loves of Apollo?
   A. Hecuba.   B. Priam.   C. Troilius.   D. Polyxena.

Text C Apollo and Delphi

Geographically, Delphi is situated 2,000 feet above sea level, set in a semicircular spur of Mount Parnassus which rises to 8069 feet, this natural barrier is known as the Phaedriades (shining ones), and overlooks the Pleistos Valley, 15km southwest from the site is the central Corinthian Gulf where the ancient harbor of Kirrha was situated, it was here the supplicants landed.

Delphi, is the site of the sanctuary to Phoebus Apollo, the Pythian Games and the legendary Oracle "Pythia". The name of the site may commemorate Apollo's cult title which is "Delphinios" meaning dolphin or porpoise. As one legend says, Apollo first came to Delphi in the guise of a dolphin swimming into the Corinthian Gulf bringing with him priests from Crete, but in another version Apollo journeyed from the north pausing at Tempe, in Thessaly, and  gathered laurel. Every fourth year laurel was taken from Tempe to Delphi, which became the prize in the form of a crown worn by the victors of the Pythian Games.

In ancient times Delphi was known as Pytho. Homer tells of a rocky place called Pytho in his Iliad. The mythology attached to Delphi dates back to prehistoric times. It is thought that there was a shrine to the earth-mother "Gaia" and was later shared with Poseidon, who originally was the god of earthquakes and water. The oracle at that period in time was translated from the lapping of the waters, and the rustling of the trees, (the oracle of Dodona, in Epirus, northwestern Greece, translated the rustling from a sacred beech tree). A mythical figure called Herophile, who was more commonly known as "Sibyl" sang the oracle in Gaia's shrine, and from that time on all prophetesses where known by that name. The "Sibylline Rock" can still be seen, and it was here the Sibyl sat and gave out her prophecies speaking in riddles. According to Pausanias, the Sibyl was the daughter of a mortal and a nymph "born between man and goddess, daughter of sea monsters and immortal nymph". Other versions believed she was sister to Apollo, and others his daughter. According to one legend, Gaia gave the oracle to her daughter, the goddess of justice Themis, who in turn passed it on to her sister the moon goddess Phoebe.

Apollo became the main deity when, according to Homer, "he killed the fearsome dragon Python, piercing it with his darts". This is how, in mythology Apollo was introduced to Delphi, by killing the serpent or dragon Python in its lair beside the Castalian Spring. Python was the protector

of Gaia and the sanctuary of Pytho, the young god was given the name "Pythian Apollo" (part of Apollo's cult was a sacred serpent), but only after serving nine years to king Admetus as a cowherd, to make amends for his deadly deed. When Apollo returned to Delphi he took over as its ruler, and to celebrate his deeds they held a festival in his honor every nine years, some versions say eight. It was known as the "Septeria".

Delphi was also known as the center of the world, the Omphalos, a carved symbol of prophetic arts and also represented the "navel of the world". To find out exactly where the center of the world was located, Zeus released two eagles from opposite ends of the earth, one from the east and one from the west, and the precise spot where they met, was in Delphi. Apollo allowed Dionysus to stay in Delphi, but only for three winter months, while he visited the country of the Hyperboreans.

The legend of Heracles is also present at Delphi, when the great hero stole the "Tripod of the Oracle". This legend is depicted in various art forms. In Delphi the east pediment of the Siphnian Treasure House, which is now in the Delphi Museum, shows the struggle between Heracles and Apollo, and Athena acting as go between. There are also fine examples of pottery showing this image.

The Delphic Oracle, is known as the "Pythia". This priestess would be seated on a tripod (Apollo's symbol of prophecy) in a state of trance, the position of the tripod was situated above a fissure in the floor of the temple, from which arose strange hallucinating vapors. She would also be chewing laurel leaves, while in this trance she only mumbled her answer, which a high priest would translate into Apollo's prophecy. Before this took place the supplicants (male only), which were known as Theopropes, had to be purified in a ritual washing ceremony which took place in the Castalian Spring. The Pythia also had to purify herself in the same manner before she performed her duties. The consultation would begin with a ritual sacrifice of an animal, but if the offering was not in a favorable condition and if cold water sprinkled onto the animal made it tremble the supplicant and the animal were turned away. From here the petitioners would enter the sanctum of the temple. Here the question, which had been previously written, was handed to the priest, who in turn asked the Pythia for Apollo's answer. From her sometimes garbled muttering, the priest would translate into hexameter verse. The Pythia never gave a straight answer, Heraclitus the philosopher (circa 500 BCE) said. The oracle neither conceals nor reveals the truth, but only hints at it. The historian Herodotus gave an account of this when he reported of king Croesus of Lydia (circa 546 BCE) who asked if he should invade Persian territory. His reply from the oracle was, if he did invade a mighty empire would be destroyed. Croesus thinking he would be victorious invaded, but it was his own empire that fell and subsequently destroyed.

Every four years Delphi held the Pythian Games, originally they were held every eight but in 582 BCE. The games were reorganized, which took place in the third year of each Olympiad. This festival comprised of musical and athletic events. The music events were in honor of Apollo and

Dionysus and took place in the theatre which held 5,000 spectators. The highest place on the slopes of the sanctuary is the stadium, here 7,000 spectators could watch the games. All types of event took place from running to chariot racing, the museum houses the famous statue found in Delphi called the "Charioteer".

The archaeological finds from Delphi has given archaeologists and historians much information, especially from the inscriptions found in abundance around the site. There are hymns to Apollo, lists of officials and even statements regarding temple money written either on walls or stone slabs. The ancient site of Delphi has a lot to offer in regard to giving an insight of ancient Greece but also the mythology attached to it.

(Excerpted from http://www.pantheon.org/articles/d/delphi.html)

Questions for Reflection
Decide whether the following statements are true or false.
1) (　) The name of Delphi may commemorate Apollo's cult title which is "Delphinios" meaning dolphin or porpoise.
2) (　) According to Virgil, Apollo became the main deity when he killed the fearsome dragon Python.
3) (　) To find out exactly where the center of the world was located, Apollo released two eagles from opposite ends of the earth, one from the east and one from the west, and the precise spot where they met, was in Delphi.
4) (　) The Pythia never gave a straight answer.
5) (　) Every three years Delphi held the Pythian Games.
6) (　) The highest place on the slopes of the sanctuary is the stadium, which can seat 7,000 spectators.

For Fun

Poem to enjoy
　　The following poem on Apollo was written by John Keats (1795—1821), a great British poet of the Romantic Period.

Hymn To Apollo
By John Keats

God of the golden bow,
And of the golden lyre,
And of the golden hair,
And of the golden fire,
Charioteer
Of the patient year,
Where—where slept thine ire,

When like a blank idiot I put on thy wreath,
Thy laurel, thy glory,
The light of thy story,
Or was I a worm—too low crawling for death?
O Delphic Apollo!

The Thunderer grasp'd and grasp'd,
The Thunderer frown'd and frown'd;
The eagle's feathery mane
For wrath became stiffen'd—the sound

Of breeding thunder
Went drowsily under,
Muttering to be unbound.
O why didst thou pity, and beg for a worm?
Why touch thy soft lute
Till the thunder was mute,
Why was I not crush'd—such a pitiful germ?
O Delphic Apollo!

The Pleiades were up,
Watching the silent air;
The seeds and roots in Earth
Were swelling for summer fare;
The Ocean, its neighbour,
Was at his old labour,
When, who—who did dare
To tie for a moment, thy plant round his brow,
And grin and look proudly,
And blaspheme so loudly,
And live for that honour, to stoop to thee now?
O Delphic Apollo!

Works to read

Apollo (Gods and Heroes of the Ancient World) written by Fritz Graf published by Routledge.

Introduction to the book

Fritz Graf here presents a survey of a god once thought of as the most powerful of gods, and capable of great wrath should he be crossed: Apollo the sun god. From his first attestations in Homer, through the complex question of pre-Homeric Apollo, to the opposition between Apollo and Dionysos in nineteenth and twentieth-century thinking, Graf examines Greek religion and myth to provide a full account of Apollo in the ancient world. For students of Greek religion and culture, of myth and legend, and in the fields of art and literature, *Apollo* will provide an informative and enlightening introduction to this powerful figure from the past.

Introduction to the author

Fritz Graf is currently Professor of Greek and Latin and Director of the Center for Epigraphical Studies at The Ohio State University. His main research interests are the religions of the Greek and Roman world, and his numerous publications include *Greek Mythology: An Introduction* (1993), *Magic in the Ancient World* (1997), and with Sarah Iles Johnston, *Ritual Texts for the Afterlife: The Bacchic Gold Tablets* (2006)

Unit 13
Echo and Narcissus

> Narcissus does not fall in love with his reflection because it is beautiful, but because it is his. If it were his beauty that enthralled him, he would be set free in a few years by its fading.
> ——W. H. Auden, American poet

Unit Goals

- To be familiarized with the story of Echo and Narcissus
- To understand the cultural heritage and influences of the story reflected from literary works
- To learn the useful words and expressions that describe the story of Echo and Narcissus
- To improve language skills and critical thinking through the content of this unit

Before You Read

1. Do you have any friends who are distinctively talkative? Do you find their talkativeness adorable or annoying?

   A: I find my friends' talkativeness _____, because:
   1) _____
   2) _____
   3) _____
   4) _____

2. Please find the meaning of the word "narcissism" in the dictionary. Think about the following questions and share your opinions with your classmates.
   1) What is your understanding of the concept of narcissism?
   2) Have you found some typical behaviors indicating the narcissistic tendencies according to your personal experiences?
   3) Are you narcissistic sometimes? What are your narcissistic moments?

3. Please describe and comment on the following carton picture.

Start to Read

Text A Echo and Narcissus

In Greek mythology Echo was a wood nymph who loved a youth by the name of Narcissus. He was a beautiful creature loved by many but Narcissus loved no one. He enjoyed attention, praise and envy. In Narcissus' eyes nobody matched him and as such he considered none were worthy of him.

Echo's passion for Narcissus was equaled only by her passion for talking.

Zeus, the King of the Olympians, was known for his many love affairs. Sometimes the young and beautiful Nymph Echo would distract and amuse his wife **Hera** with long and entertaining stories, while Zeus took advantage of the moment to ravish the other mountain nymphs. When Hera discovered the trickery she punished the talkative Echo by taking away her voice, except in foolish repetition of another's shouted words. Thus, all Echo could do was repeat the voice of another—"That tongue of yours, by which I have been tricked, shall have its power curtailed and enjoy the briefest use of speech."

Narcissus was a vain youth, who was the son of the blue Nymph Leiriope of Thespia. He was beautiful as a child and grew even more so as he matured. By the age of sixteen he had left a trail of broken hearts, from rejected lovers of both sexes. Narcissus wanted nothing to do with falling in love with anyone and rebuffed all attempts at romance.

Echo often waited in the woods to see Narcissus hoping for a chance to be noticed. One day when Narcissus was out hunting stags, Echo stealthily followed the handsome youth through the woods, longing to address him but unable to speak first. When Narcissus finally heard footsteps and shouted "Who is there?" Echo replied "There!" Narcissus called again "Come", Echo replied "Come!" Narcissus called once more "Why do you shun me? Let us join one another." Echo was overjoyed that Narcissus had asked her to join him. She longed to tell him who she was and of all the love she had for him in her heart but she could not speak. She ran towards him and threw herself upon him. Narcissus became angry "Hands off! I would rather die than you should have me!" and threw Echo to the ground. Echo left the woods a ruin, her heart broken. Ashamed she ran away to live in the mountains yearning for a love that would never be returned. The grief killed her. Her body became one with the mountain stone. All that remained was her voice which replied in kind when others spoke.

Narcissus continued to attract many nymphs all of whom he briefly entertained before scorning and refusing them. The gods grew tired of his behavior and cursed Narcissus. They wanted him to know what it felt like to love and never be loved. They made it so there was only one whom he would love, someone who was not real and could never love him back.

A man named **Ameinius** was one of Narcissus' most ardent admirers, and repeatedly vied for his attention. The conceited youth responded by sending his suitor a sword, telling him to prove his adoration. Ameinius proceeded to plunge the sword into his heart, committing suicide to demonstrate his love, but not before he beseeched the gods to punish the vain Narcissus.

The goddess of the hunt, **Artemis**, heard the plea and made Narcissus fall in love, but a kind a love that couldn't be fulfilled.

One day whilst out enjoying the sunshine, Narcissus came upon a clear spring at Donacon in Thespia. As he bent low to take a drink he caught a glimpse of what he thought was a beautiful water spirit. He did not recognize his own reflection and was immediately enamored. Narcissus bent down his head to kiss the vision. As he did so the reflection mimicked his actions. Taking this as a sign of reciprocation Narcissus reached into the pool to draw the water spirit to him. The water displaced and the vision was gone. He panicked, where had his love gone? When the water became calm the water spirit returned. "Why, beautiful being, do you shun me? Surely my face is not one to repel you. The nymphs love me, and you yourself look not indifferent upon me. When I stretch forth my arms you do the same; and you smile upon me and answer my beckoning with the like." Again he reached out and again his love disappeared. Frightened to touch the water Narcissus lay still by the pool gazing in to the eyes of his vision. For hours he sat enraptured by the spring, at last recognizing himself but tortured by the realization that he could never possess the object of his infatuation. Narcissus was tormented, much as he had tormented all those

who in the past had been unlucky enough to fall in love with him.

He cried in frustration. As he did so Echo also cried. He did not move, he did not eat or drink, he only suffered. As he pined he became gaunt loosing his beauty. The nymphs that loved him pleaded with him to come away from the pool. As they did so, Echo also pleaded with him. He was transfixed; he wanted to stay there forever. Narcissus like

Echo died with grief. His body disappeared and where his body once lay a flower grew in its place. The nymphs mourned his death and as they mourned Echo also mourned.

(Excerpted from http://www.echo.me.uk/legend.htm and http://thanasis.com/echo.htm)

Proper Nouns

1. **Zeus** [zju:s]: 宙斯, 奥林匹亚众神之首。
2. **Hera/Juno** [ˈhiərə]: 赫拉/朱诺, 神后, 宙斯之妻。
3. **Liriope** [ləˈraiəpi]: 李瑞奥普, 水中仙女, 那尔西所思之母。
4. **Ameinius** [əˈmeiniəs]: 阿梅伊涅斯, 眷恋那尔西索斯迷人容貌的凡人。
5. **Artemis/Diana** [ˈɑ:timis]: 阿耳特弥斯/狄安娜, 月亮和狩猎女神。

After You Read

Knowledge Focus

1. Fill in the blanks according to what you have learned from the text above.
   1) Echo was a _____ who loved a youth by the name of Narcissus.
   2) Zeus, the King of the Olympians, was known for his _____.
   3) When Hera discovered the trickery she punished the talkative Echo by _____.
   4) Narcissus was a vain youth, who was the son of the blue Nymph _____.
   5) Echo often waited in _____ to see Narcissus hoping for a chance to be noticed.
   6) Echo was _____ that Narcissus had asked her to join him.
   7) The gods grew tired of his behavior and _____.
   8) A man named _____ was one of Narcissus' most ardent admirers, and repeatedly vied for his attention.
   9) The goddess of the hunt, _____, heard the plea and made Narcissus fall in love, but a kind a love that couldn't be fulfilled.
   10) Narcissus's body disappeared and where his body once lay _____ grew in its place.

2. Discuss the following questions with your partner.
   1) What kind of goddess is Artemis? Do you know her story?
   2) What is the biggest shortcoming of Echo?
   3) Why was Hera angry with Echo? What kind of curse did she pass upon the nymph?
   4) What kind of curse did she pass upon the nymph?
   5) Why did Narcissus refuse the love of Echo?
   6) What is the cause of Narcissus's tragedy?

7) How did Narcissus pine away beside the lake?

8) What are the reflections of the nymphs when Narcissus died?

Language Focus

1. Fill in the blanks with the words or expressions you have learned from the text.

be worthy of	passion for	shun	amuse	in repetition of
vain	rebuff	be out doing something		
fall in love with	in frustration			

1) He wanted to show his mastery of vocabulary _____ the same sense in different words and expressions.

2) The real maturity means that when you are in some serious trouble, you can still _____ yourself by mocking at your miseries.

3) It is hard to say that those soap opera stars with pretty faces and attractive figures _____ adoration.

4) Traditional Chinese husbands always regarded themselves as the tough guys who _____ money for the family.

5) He ground his teeth together _____.

6) He should _____ one-sidedness.

7) He has turned all his _____ music into crazy practices of piano playing skills.

8) It is said that you will never _____ someone if you have not read about love.

9) Facts are the most powerful weapons to _____ the rumors.

10) _____ girls are more likely to indulge themselves in shopping.

2. Fill in the blanks with the proper form of the word in the brackets.

1) As a very popular professor he does not need to check the _____ (attend) every time.

2) He has never given up the _____ (pursue) of being a musician since he fell in love with piano when he was a child.

3) You should cherish the _____ (companion) from your loyal friends through all these difficulties.

4) It took some time for her to face the _____ (startle) fact that she is not the biological daughter of her parents.

5) Every _____ (hasten) decision could lead us to failures.

6) Knowing he was an old customer, the waitress directly provided him with his _____ (habit) order.

7) _____ (hunt) is an extremely luxurious recreational activity for modern people.

8) For many people, _____ (spirit) tranquility is far more precious than material enjoyment.

9) His cruel _____ (indifferent) hurt her badly like a sharp dagger.

10) Public _____ (consume) is one of the crucial indexes for national economy.

3. Fill in the blanks with the proper prepositions or adverbs that collocate with the neighboring words.

1) In the story, the princess fell in love with a young shepherd _____ the name of John.
2) She is the most attractive one in the world _____ her lover's eyes.
3) According to the spoiling father, no one is worthy _____ his daughter's love.
4) Edison was known _____ his notorious love affairs with many girls.
5) As an idler, he wanted nothing to do _____ hard working and fulfilling his responsibilities.
6) The girl is surly in danger, because the bad guy has stealthily followed her _____ several dark lanes and backstreets.
7) Ann's husband has been working abroad for three years, so when she met him at the airport, she ran to him and threw herself _____ him immediately.
8) After years of patient education, the father grew tired _____ this good-for-nothing kid.

4. Proofreading: The following passage contains ten errors. Each indicated line contains a maximum of one error. In each case, only ONE word is involved. Read the passage and correct the errors.

Narcissus is a genus of mainly hardy, mostly spring-flowering, natively to   1) _____
Europe, North Africa, and Asia. There are also several Narcissus specie that   2) _____
bloom in the autumn. Though Hortus Thira city 26 wild species, Daffodils for   3) _____
North American Gardens cites between 50 or 100 including species varying and   4) _____
wild hybrids. Through taxonomic and genetic research, it speculated that over   5) _____
time this number will probably continue to be refining. Daffodil is a common   6) _____
English name, sometimes used now for all variations, and is the chief common   7) _____
name of horticultural prevalence used by the American Daffodil Society. The   8) _____
range for forms in cultivation has been heavy modified and extended, with new   9) _____
variations available from specialists almost every year.   10) _____

Comprehensive Work

1. Sharing Ideas: *"Normal" narcissism and "Destructive" narcissism*

According to researchers, distinction must be made between "normal" or "healthy" narcissism on the one hand and "pathological" narcissism on the other. We all have some degree and variety of narcissistic delusion which, if it is not too great, is normal and healthy. But the pathological narcissist has a level of delusion that is divorced from reality.

Characteristic	Healthy Narcissism	Destructive Narcissism
Self-confident	High outward self-confidence in line with reality	Grandiose
Desire for power, wealth and admiration	May enjoy power	Pursues power at all costs, lacks normal inhibitions in its pursuit

Relationships	Real concern for others and their ideas; does not exploit or devalue others	Concerns limited to expressing socially appropriate response when convenient; devalues and exploits others without remorse
Ability to follow a consistent path	Has values; follows through on plans	Lacks values; easily bored; often changes course
Foundation	Healthy childhood with support for self-esteem and appropriate limits on behavior towards others	Traumatic childhood undercutting true sense of self-esteem and/or learning that he/she doesn't need to be considerate of others

Question:

  Could you give some examples about the characteristics given in the upper chart? Personal experiences are preferred, while you can also resort to literary works or mass media materials you've come across before.

_____

2. Differences between male and female narcissists

Some of the possible differences that have been identified between male and female narcissists are described in the following table.

Characteristic	Description
Self-handicapping	Only male, but not female narcissists, employ heightened self-handicapping.
Interpersonal competition	Only male, but not female narcissists, show a preference for a task framed in terms of interpersonal competition.
Self-enhancement	Only male, but not female narcissists, self-enhance when modesty is called for. Females are more likely to enhance their social power through means such as seeking affiliations with "glamorous" others.
Exploitativeness and entitlement	Feelings of exploitativeness and entitlement are less integrated into the construct of narcissism for females relative to males.

Questions for Discussion:

1) Do you agree with the analysis of the differences? Why or why not?
_____

2) Which of the differences are most impressive to you? Why?
_____

3. Orally compose a story about the love between a naive girl and a narcissistic boy. The setting, the characters, and the plot of the story should be original, but the following words and expressions are required to be used.

stretch forth	contrive to
narcissistic (narcissism)	shun
self-esteem	fascination
passion	smite
repel	
grief	

Read More

Text B Echo and Narcissus' Story in *Metamorphoses*

The following story is part of the third book of *Metamorphoses*, a long narrative poem by Ovid about mythological, legendary, and historical characters and circumstances that undergo a transformation.

One day the river god Cephisus impregnates the water nymph Liriope after forcing himself upon her. After she gives birth to a boy, called Narcissus, she asks the prophet Tiresias whether her child will have a long life. The prophet told her that the boy will be the most beautiful man in Greece, however, "If ever he knows himself," Tiresias answers, "he surely dies."

Liriope does not completely understand this perplexing reply. Only the passage of time will reveal it to her.

Narcissus was made by his mother grow up avoiding any contact with rivers and lakes and among a group of masculine companions hunting in the mountains all day. When Narcissus turns sixteen, he is so extraordinarily handsome that young maidens burn with desire for him. While hunting in the woods, he attracts the attention of the mountain nymph Echo, who was robbed of the ability to voice her thoughts after incurring the wrath of the queen of the gods, Juno. Here is what happened.

The king of the gods, Jupiter, had once persuaded Echo to distract Juno with idle conversation so that he could sneak away and meet with a paramour. At the appointed time, Echo jabbers on, depriving Juno of the opportunity to spy on Jupiter. Later, when Juno discovers what Echo was up to, she punishes her by rendering her incapable of speaking any words except the last two or three she has heard someone else say. These she must repeat. Consequently, she speaks only "with mimick [mimic] sounds, and accents not her own."

Upon seeing Narcissus, she—like other maidens — cannot resist his charms and yearns to reveal to him her love. But, bearing the heavy burden of Juno's curse, she can only repeat his last words in a voice that sounds like his. When words he speaks reverberate back to him, he calls out to meet with whoever is mimicking him. Heartened, Echo approaches him and, by throwing her arms around him, communicates her love. However, Narcissus, proud and vain, coldly rejects her. He will not deign to occupy his time with this lowly maid. Thereafter, she pines away for his love until nothing is left of her except the sound of her mimicking voice. "Her bones are petrified, her voice is found / In vaults, where still it doubles every sound."

Meanwhile, another love-struck admirer seeks his love, but proud Narcissus ignores the suit. Frustrated and angry, the suitor prays to the gods, "Oh may he love like me, and love like me in vain!" The goddess of vengeance, known by the names of Rhamnusia /Nemesis, hears the prayer and decides to answer it. The occasion for the retribution comes when Narcissus is out hunting again and, hot and tired, decides to rest next to a pristine fountain surrounded by pleasant verdure and high trees that provide cooling shade. When he bends over the fountain to quench his thirst, he sees in the water a wondrous face and immediately falls in love with it, unaware that he is looking at himself.

(Excerpted from www.cummingsstudyguides.net/Guides3/Echo.html)

Questions for Reflection

1. Explain the prophesy of prophet Tiresias.
2. Why would Liriope make her son grow up avoiding any contact with rivers and lakes and among a group of masculine companions hunting in the mountains?
3. There are four most significant themes of the story. Please illustrate how they are reflected from the story respectively.
   (1) Male Abuse of Females
   (2) Unrequited Love
   (3) Vengeance
   (4) Excessive Pride

Text C Understanding Narcissism

What is narcissism?

True narcissism is not unhealthy. It is the part of us that smiles for the camera and enjoys both the spotlight and being around attractive people, and most would agree that these are positive things. The word narcissism in recent history has however seen it's meaning change to describe someone with Narcissistic Personality Disorder (NPD) which is a very different story. These days when someone is described as a narcissist (or we hear talk of narcissism) it usually describes someone who displays the symptoms of this personality disorder which include verbal abuse, aggression and defensiveness and a tendency to

manipulate and rely on (or "use") others while being charming or "playing for the crowd".

A different person when the crowd has gone home

Individuals with symptoms of NPD are first and foremost two-faced; the subject being charming and competitive in public while critical, rude, arrogant, sarcastic and aggressive in private; usually to the people who are closest to them and who give them the most love and care.

This person will pretend to operate from high standards, but in reality will be low in perfectionism, resulting in them being flakey, hypocritical or even an outright phoney or fake. They will not follow through on promises and will spend most of their energy and time seeking people who will adore them or who they can vent their aggression on, either directly by provoking fights or else by gossiping nastily about people behind their back.

Seduce and abandon

Whether sex is consummated or not there is often a pattern of seducing and abandoning lovers, friends or people they can attract as their "fans". Their lack of empathy and self interest, mixed with a particular cunning charm and ability to manipulate others makes them highly abusive to live with. They will think nothing of exploiting their partner financially, sexually or otherwise, while blaming their own weaknesses and shortcomings on this very same person; while at the same time hindering any attempt their partner may make to regain their sense of strength or self worth and get back on their feet or get on with their own life or get away. Narcissism (or more accurately NPD) is a disorder and not a disease. There is no blood test for narcissism and three different professionals may diagnose the same person in three different ways. Narcissism describes a pattern of behavior in an individual.

A selfish "child"

A narcissist is someone who never grew out of being a selfish child. They find it hard to share and even harder to share the limelight, always wanting to be the focus of attention. They invent stories to get what they want and pretend they are more important than they are and blame others for their own wrong doings. Narcissism flourishes in those who are charming and attractive, because this means they will get away with this behavior more easily. They may appear humble and very likable in public and may choose a less socially adept partner as their "foil". Narcissists will usually get angry or sulk (and feel very embarrassed) if they are seen to be wrong or have made a mistake, and like a child they might throw tantrums or rages and "rewrite history" instead of admitting their misdeeds.

The double life

Narcissists are always looking for attention. They are flirts and have constant crushes and real or fantasy affairs, they are very susceptible to becoming addicted to pornography and can be cyber-paths who have online affairs with numerous people who they manipulate and lie to. Narcissists often lead a "double life".

When narcissism has a hold of someone, they will feel VERY lonely and desperate for the affection of a "perfect" person who will be sympathetic and adore them. Sadly this "perfect" person is actually an illusion in the narcissist's mind, a tormenting fantasy that will make their life miserable and make them very hard on the people who they live with.

Steve and I beat the odds and overcame these problems in our marriage and hope that we can help you do the same. We host an online radio show called "The Love Safety Net" on Global talk radio with thousands of subscribers worldwide and have received countless testimonials from our readers. The advice that we offer in dealing with this disorder will also help anyone wanting to learn better life and relationship skills. Immaturity is rife in our community and is at the heart of this issue. We offer valuable and solid steps to help individuals and families to grow up and become more confident, happier and more secure.

(Excerpted from www.narcissism.com.au)

Questions for Reflection

1. Does your partner or family member or friend have narcissistic tendencies?
2. Do you suffer from narcissism?

Websites to Visit

http://winning-teams.com

This website provides links to information about some psychoanalyst knowledge about narcissism.

http://dh.0-6.com/MovView/3a96fb6b-653c-4186-b35f-bde4478393a5/

This website provides a short cartoon video clip telling the story of Echo and Narcissus

Movies to Watch

Hercules (1997)

Hercules is a 1997 American animated film produced by Walt Disney Feature Animation and released by Walt Disney Pictures. The thirty-fifth animated feature in the Walt Disney Animated Classics series, the film was directed by Ron Clements and John Musker. The film is based on the legendary Greek mythology hero Heracles (known in the film by his Roman name, Hercules), the son of Zeus, in Greek mythology.

Though Hercules did not match the financial success of Disney's early-1990s releases, the film received positive reviews, and made $99 million in revenue in the United States during its theatrical release and $252,712,101 worldwide.

Unit 14
Pygmalion

> In sculpture did ever anybody call the Apollo a fancy piece? Or say of the Laocoon how it might be made different? A masterpiece of art has in the mind a fixed place in the chain of being, as much as a plant or a crystal.
> ——R. W. Emerson

Unit Goals

- To be familiarized with the story of Pygmalion
- To understand the cultural heritage and influences of the story reflected from literary works
- To learn the useful words and expressions that describe the story of Pygmalion
- To improve language skills and critical thinking through the content of this unit

Before You Read

1. Which kind of art form are you most interested in? Please share your understanding of a certain form of art with the classmates.

Music

Drama

Literature

Architecture

Painting

Sculpture

A: I am most interested in the art form of _____, because:
1) _____
2) _____

2. The art of sculpture is a symbol of beauty and eternity, which is also an essential aspect of ancient Greek culture. Match the following pictures with the correct names, and identify which ones are Greek.

| Athena | The Thinker | Victory Samothrace | David | Discobolos | Aphrodite of Melos |

3. Please search the internet to get some knowledge about "heterophobia", and then share your findings with your classmates.

Start to Read

Text A Pygmalion

The story of **Pygmalion** and Galatea is found in Greek Mythology, and in the famous work "Metamorphoses", by the great Roman poet Ovid. Their love was so unique that it is difficult to define it. But from this legendary love story, one thing is clear, man can never love an inanimate object with as much passion as he loves a living, breathing being. Love gives rise to desire and without this passion any love remains unfulfilled.

Pygmalion was a master sculptor in the ancient city of Greece. All day he sculpted beautiful statues from huge pieces of rock. In fact, his creations were so wonderful that whoever saw them were mesmerized by their sheer artistic beauty and exact finish. Pygmalion himself was a fine and  handsome young man. He was liked by all men and women. Many women loved him for his great skill and looks.

But Pygmalion never paid attention to any of these women. He saw so much to blame in women that he came at last to abhor the sex, and resolved to live unmarried. He was a sculptor, and with his with wonderful skill he sculpted a beautiful ivory statue which was so lifelike that it was difficult to believe that it was lifeless at the first glance. The beauty was such that no living woman could compete with it. It was indeed the perfect semblance of a maiden that seemed to be alive, and only prevented from moving by modesty. His art was so perfect that it concealed itself and its product looked like the workmanship of nature. Pygmalion spent hours admiring his creation.

By and by Pygmalion's admiration for his own sculpture turned to love. Oftentimes he laid his hand upon it as if to assure himself whether it were living or not, and could not, even then, believe that it was only ivory. He caressed it, and gave it such presents as young girls love—bright shells and polished stones, little birds and flowers of various hues, beads and amber. He adorned his ivory maiden with jewels. He put raiment on its limbs, and jewels on its fingers, and a necklace about its neck. To the ears he hung earrings and strings of pearls upon the breast. Her dress became her, and she looked not less charming than when unattired. He laid her on a couch spread with cloths of **Tyrian** dye, and called her his wife, and put her head upon a pillow of the softest feathers, as if she could enjoy their softness. He gave the statue a name: "Galatea", meaning "sleeping love".

But what will be the consequence of falling in love with a lifeless ivory maiden?

The festival of **Aphrodite** was at hand—a festival celebrated with great pomp at **Cyprus**. Victims were offered, the altars smoked, and the odor of incense filled the air. When the festivities of Aphrodite started, Pygmalion took part in the ceremonies. He went to the temple of Aphrodite to ask forgiveness for all the years he had shunned her.

When Pygmalion had performed his part in the solemnities, he hesitantly prayed for a wife like his ivory virgin statue. He stood before the altar of Aphrodite and timidly said, "Ye gods, who can do all things, give me, I pray you, for my wife"—he dared not utter "my ivory virgin," but said instead—"one like my ivory virgin."

But Goddess Aphrodite understood what the poor man was trying to say. She was curious. How can a man love a lifeless thing so much? Was it so beautiful that Pygmalion fell in love with his own creation? So she visited the studio of the sculptor while he was away.

What she saw greatly amazed her, for the sculpture had a perfect likeness to her. In fact, it would not have been wrong to say that the sculpture was an image of Aphrodite herself.

Goddess Aphrodite was charmed by Pygmalion's creation. She brought the statue to life.

When Pygmalion returned to his home, he went before **Galatea** and knelt down before the woman of his dreams. He looked at her lovingly, with a lover's ardour. It seemed to him that Galatea was looking at her lovingly too.

For a moment, it seemed to Pygmalion that it was just a figment of his imagination. He rubbed his eyes and looked again. But no. There was no mistake this time. Galatea was smiling at him.

He laid his hand upon the limbs; the ivory felt soft to his touch and yielded to his fingers like the wax of **Hymettus**. It seemed to be warm. He stood up; his mind oscillated between doubt and joy. Fearing he may be mistaken, again and again with a lover's ardor he touches the object of his hopes. It was indeed alive! The veins when pressed yielded to the finger and again resumed their roundness. Slowly it dawned on Pygmalion that the animation of his sculpture was the result of his prayer to Goddess Aphrodite who knew his desire. At last, the votary of Aphrodite found words to thank the goddess. Pygmalion humbled himself at

the Goddess' feet.

Soon Pygmalion and Galatea were wed, and Pygmalion never forgot to thank Aphrodite for the gift she had given him. Aphrodite blessed the nuptials she had formed, and this union between Pygmalion and Galatea produced a son named **Paphos**, from whom the city Paphos, sacred to Aphrodite, received its name. He and Galatea brought gifts to her temple throughout their life and Aphrodite blessed them with happiness and love in return.

The unusual love that blossomed between Pygmalion and Galatea enthralls all. Falling in love with one's creation and then getting the desired object as wife — perhaps this was destined for Pygmalion. Even to this day, countless people and young lovers are mesmerized by this exceptional love that existed between two persons at a time when civilization was in its infancy.

(Excerpted from thanasis.com/pygmal.htm)

Proper Nouns

1. **Pygmalion** [pigˈmeiljən]：皮格马利翁，传说中的希腊雕塑家。
2. **Tyrian** [ˈtiriən]：提尔人，现黎巴嫩境内。
3. **Aphrodite/Venus** [ˌæfrəuˈdaiti]：阿芙罗狄蒂/维纳斯，爱与美女神。
4. **Cyprus** [ˈsaiprəs]：塞浦路斯。
5. **Galatea** [ˌgæləˈtiːə]：加勒提阿，皮格马利翁之妻。
6. **Hymettus** [haiˈmætəs]：叙米托斯山。
7. **Pathos** [ˈpeiθɔs]：帕索斯，皮格马利翁之子。

After You Read

Knowledge Focus

1. Fill in the blanks according to what you have learned from the text above.

1) Pygmalion was a _____, and had made with wonderful skill a statue of ivory.
2) He saw so much to blame in women that he came at last to abhor the sex, and resolved to _____.
3) Pygmalion admired his own work, and at last _____.
4) The festival of Aphrodite/Venus was a festival celebrated with great pomp at _____.
5) _____, who was present at the festival, heard Pygmalion and knew the thought he would have uttered.
6) Goddess Aphrodite was charmed by Pygmalion's creation. She _____.
7) For a moment, it seemed to Pygmalion that it was just a figment of his _____.
8) There was no mistake this time. Galatea was _____.
9) Pygmalion humbled himself at _____.
10) Aphrodite/Venus blessed the weddings she had formed, and from this union _____ was born.

Ancient Greek and Roman Mythology

2. Discuss the following questions with your partner.

1) What kind of person is Pygmalion? Provide some clues to support your argument.

2) Could you imagine the reasons for Pygmalion's aversion of women?

3) Is it possible for Pygmalion to fall in love with the other sculptors' works if they are as beautiful as his?

4) What kind of inner feeling did Pygmalion have when he uttered his wish to the goddess?

5) Why did Venus fulfill Pygmalion's dream?

6) What happened after Pygmalion got home?

Language Focus

1. Fill in the blanks with the words or expressions you have learned from the text.

abhor	resolved to	be mesmerized by	
compete with	fix ... on	ask forgiveness for	
be at hand	solemnities	yield to	ardor

1) I _____ advertising that is blatant, dull, or dishonest.

2) When we stood by the lake, we _____ the flashing colors of the fish. .

3) We will _____ nothing _____ unreasonable demands.

4) His political _____ led him into many arguments.

5) The examinations are close _____.

6) He reminded her that they had _____ stick together.

7) My handwriting cannot _____ my writing skills.

8) Loss and bereavement can remind you sharply of what can happen when in life you do not show your love and appreciation, or _____, and so make your loved ones.

9) I stand still, with my whole attention _____ the movements of her finger.

10) The Queen was crowned with all the proper _____.

2. Fill in the blanks with the proper form of the word in the brackets.

1) It requires great _____ (resolve) to choose an occupation against your parents' will, but it's your life after all.

2) No _____ (compare) should be made when it comes to the selection of a life partner.

3) She can's conceal her _____ (admire) to the young artist.

4) Being in such beautiful sceneries, no one could help admiring the _____ (create) of nature.

5) She found her husband very _____ (charm) when he focuses on his task.

6) The _____ (soft) of the silk well demonstrates the advancement of textile industry of China.

7) The traditional _____ (celebrate) of Chinese New Year formally started during the big dinner for the last day in the Lunar Calendar.

8) He has recently given _____ (utter) to his views.

9) The lovely _____ (round) of her face has gained a lot of attention for her.

10) His biggest enemy is his _____ when faced with difficulties.

3. **Fill in the blanks with the proper prepositions or adverbs that collocate with the neighboring words.**

   1) We can see a lot of realistic problems _____ this fictional work.
   2) Love gives rise _____ desire and without this passion any love remains unfulfilled.
   3) Once we observed that this giant image was sculpted _____ a single piece of rock, we felt stunted.
   4) Lots of fans loved him not only _____ his handsome appearance but his attractive temperament as well.
   5) He is a workaholic who hardly pays any attention _____ people around him once indulged in his own business.
   6) These old buildings were prevented _____ being torn down through the efforts of a group of researchers.
   7) When he laid his hands _____ the earth of his long-parted motherland, his eyes watered.
   8) Only miracles can bring this man-made plantation _____ life.

4. **Proofreading: The following passage contains ten errors. Each indicated line contains a maximum of one error. In each case, only ONE word is involved. Read the passage and correct the errors.**

   Sculpture is three-dimensional artwork created by shapes or combining hard materials—typical stone such as marble—or metal, glass, or wood. Softer (plastic) material can also be used, such as clay, textiles, plastics, polymers or softer metals. The term has been extend to works including sound, text and light.

   Materials may be worked by removing such as carving, or they may be assembled such as by welding, hardened such as by firing, or molded or cast. Surfacing decoration such as paint may be applicated. Sculpture has been described as one of the plastic arts because it can involve the usage of materials that can be molded or modulated.

   Sculpture is an important form of public art. A collection of sculpture in a garden set may be referred to as a sculpture garden.

   1) _____
   2) _____
   3) _____
   4) _____
   5) _____
   6) _____
   7) _____
   8) _____
   9) _____
   10) _____

Comprehensive Work

1. **Possible symptoms and causes of "*Gynephobia*" (the fear of woman)**

   Gynephobia: An abnormal, irrational and persistent fear of women. Sufferers experience anxiety even though they realize they face no threat.

   > "Gynephobia" is derived from the Greek "gyne" (woman) and "phobos" (fear). Alternate spelling: "gynaephobia." The prefix "gyne–" (or gyn–, gyno–, gynec–, gyneco–, gynaec–, or gynaeco–) enters into a number of biomedical terms such as, for examples, gynecology, gynecomastia (breast development in a male), and a gynecoid pelvis (a pelvis shaped like a woman's).

   Discuss with your team members, and try to determine some of the possible symptoms and causes of Gynephobia.

Ancient Greek and Roman Mythology

Gynephobia

Possible Symptoms	Possible Causes

Task:
Being a Self-developed Psychologist
Form groups of four students and discuss Gynephobia. Share your knowledge, understanding or personal experiences related to the phenomenon.

2. "Gender Discrimination" in western mythology
   In Bible stories, God created Eve, the first woman, from the ribs of Adam:

   After a certain period of time, God then sees that it is not good that Adam continue to remain alone — so He then creates the first woman Eve by causing a deep sleep to fall on Adam and then takes out one of his ribs.
   God literally creates the first woman from the rib of Adam. God meant for Eve to be a helper comparable to him and He then tells the both of them to be fruitful and multiply and to fill the earth and subdue it.

   Please compare the story of Genesis with the story of Pygmalion.

Questions for Discussion:
1) In the sense of sexual relations, what are the similarities and differences of the two stories?

2) Make some comments on the influences of the stories.

3. **Orally compose a story about a fastidious man's pursuit of a "perfect lady". The setting, the characters, and the plot of the story should be original, but the following words and expressions are required to be used.**

   abhor   perfectionism
   ardor   chauvinism
   despise   repel

endeavor   virginity
vain   modesty

Read More

Text B Bernard Shaw's *Pygmalion*

Based on classical myth, Bernard Shaw's *Pygmalion* plays on the complex business of human relationships in a social world. Phonetics Professor Henry Higgins tutors the very Cockney Eliza Doolittle, not only in the refinement of speech, but also in the refinement of her manner. When the end result produces a very ladylike Miss Doolittle, the lessons learned become much more far reaching. The successful musical *My Fair Lady* was based on this Bernard Shaw classic.

Two old gentlemen meet in the rain one night at Covent Garden. Professor Higgins is a scientist of phonetics, and Colonel Pickering is a linguist of Indian dialects. The first bets the other that he can, with his knowledge of phonetics, convince high London society that, in a matter of months, he will be able to transform the cockney speaking Covent Garden flower girl, Eliza Doolittle, into a woman as poised and well-spoken as a duchess. The next morning, the girl appears at his laboratory on Wimpole Street to ask for speech lessons, offering to pay a shilling, so that she may speak properly enough to work in a flower shop. Higgins makes merciless fun of her, but is seduced by the idea of working his magic on her. Pickering goads him on by agreeing to cover the costs of the experiment if Higgins can pass Eliza off as a duchess at an ambassador's garden party. The challenge is taken, and Higgins starts by having his housekeeper bathe Eliza and give her new clothes. Then Eliza's father Alfred Doolittle comes to demand the return of his daughter, though his real intention is to hit Higgins up for some money. The professor, amused by Doolittle's unusual rhetoric, gives him five pounds. On his way out, the dustman fails to recognize the now clean, pretty flower girl as his daughter.

For a number of months, Higgins trains Eliza to speak properly. Two trials for Eliza follow. The first occurs at Higgins' mother's home, where Eliza is introduced to the Eynsford Hills, a trio of mother, daughter, and son. The son Freddy is very attracted to her, and further taken with what he thinks is her affected "small talk" when she slips into cockney. Mrs. Higgins worries that the experiment will lead to problems once it is ended, but Higgins and Pickering are too absorbed in their game to take heed. A second trial, which takes place some months later at an ambassador's party (and which is not actually staged), is a resounding success. The wager is definitely won, but Higgins and Pickering are now bored with the project, which causes Eliza to be hurt. She throws Higgins' slippers at him in a rage because she does not know what is to become of her, thereby bewildering him. He suggests she marry somebody. She returns him the hired jewelry, and he accuses her of ingratitude.

The following morning, Higgins rushes to his mother, in a panic because Eliza has run away. On his tail is Eliza's father, now unhappily rich from the trust of a deceased millionaire who took to heart

Higgins' recommendation that Doolittle was England's "most original moralist." Mrs. Higgins, who has been hiding Eliza upstairs all along, chides the two of them for playing with the girl's affections. When she enters, Eliza thanks Pickering for always treating her like a lady, but threatens Higgins that she will go work with his rival phonetician, Nepommuck. The outraged Higgins cannot help but start to admire her. As Eliza leaves for her father's wedding, Higgins shouts out a few errands for her to run, assuming that she will return to him at Wimpole Street. Eliza, who has a lovelorn sweetheart in Freddy, and the wherewithal to pass as a duchess, never makes it clear whether she will or not.

(Exerpt from http://www.sparknotes.com/lit/pygmalion/summary.html)

Questions for Reflection

1. It has been said that *Pygmalion* is not a play about turning a flower girl into a duchess, but one about turning a woman into a human being. Do you agree?
2. What is the *Pygmalion* myth? In what significant ways has Shaw transformed that myth in his play? What are the effects?
3. If you were to create a sixth act to *Pygmalion*, who would Eliza marry? Or does she marry at all?

Text C The City of Paphos

For tourists who want to immerse themselves in culture, tradition and mythology, Paphos has so much to offer.

The history of Paphos is woven around the Greek Mythology and the goddess Aphrodite. Many variations of myths say that the town was named after Paphos, or Pafos, the son of Pygmalion and Aphrodite's ivory cult image. Other stories claimed Pafos was a daughter rather than a son, though whatever the story is, this stunning region is synonymous to beauty because of its association to the goddess Aphrodite.

According to Greek Mythology, Paphos is the birthplace of the goddess of love and beauty, Aphrodite. There are many versions of the story about Aphrodite but all of them agreed that Aphrodite's birth place is Paphos. One particularly interesting legend has it that Aphrodite was made from Ourano's seed when his son Cronus, cut his genitals off and threw them to the sea, then from the water's waves of foam, Aphrodite rose and washed to the shore carried by a giant scallop.

According to history, Paphos was the centre of the Aphrodite cult and pre-Hellenic fertility deities. In the twelfth century BC, the Mycenaean's built Aphrodite's temple in Paphos, which unfortunately does not stand anymore but remains dug from the site can be found in the nearby museum.

Like the legendary goddess Aphrodite, Paphos is an enchanting ancient town with stunning coastline and beautiful mountains and is a dream destination for tourists who have a thirst for culture and history as well as the love for beautiful beaches. Some holiday makers may consider Paphos a bit quiet but it offers a lot of the contemporary comforts that visitors can expect here. As part of the UNESCO world heritage site, is one of the most amazing and picturesque destinations in Cyprus and it has an added value of the Mediterranean weather that makes it an Eden for visitors all year round.

There are a lot of special places in Paphos that strengthen its close connection to the Greek Mythology. For the inquisitive mind, the whole region is a wonderful place that has so much to offer, beginning a Greek Mythology discovery with a visit to the House of Dionysus is our top recommendation. This was a roman villa dating to the 2nd century AD and here you will see an excellent mosaic pavement floors showing the scene from the Greek Mythology. It was named The House of Dionysus because it has many depictions of the God of Wine and the mosaic floors were accidentally discovered by farmers. The House of Dionysus is believed to have belonged to a wealthy Paphos citizen and the house has over 40 rooms. The original color of the limestone is still preserved in the mosaic flooring.

A fascinating second stop would perhaps be The House of Theseus, rather close to the house of Dionysus. The mosaic in this house is geometrically decorated and depicts mythological representations and especially worth seeing are the mosaic of "Theseus Killing the Minotaur" and "Achilles Birth". To the west of the House of Theseus is the House of Orpheus believed to be dating back to the 3rd century AD, plus there are three mythological representations worth seeing here. "The Hercules and the lion Nemea", the "Amazon" and the "Orpheus and his Lyre".

Paphos Odeon

After visiting the mosaics of Paphos, one might choose to head to the Paphos Odeon which is a small 2nd century Odeon built entirely from lime stone. The Paphos Odeon is located at the Paphos tourist area and during the summer months, musical and theatrical performances are held here. The remains of the building dedicated to the Greek God, Asklipeios, the Roman Agora and the ancient city wall are nearby and also worth checking out.

Aphrodites Rock

After having a fill of the old building and the remains related to Greek Mythology, you can head towards the sea and visit the Aphrodite's Rock (Petra Tou Romiou) which is located at the beautiful pebbled beach near Pissouri at the westernmost end of Paphos district. Aphrodite's Rock is a pair of rock formations that elegantly sit offshore and have been a source of inspiration for many poets and artists. The most famous work of art inspired by Aphrodite's Rock is Sandro Boticelli's "The Birth of Venus".

Legend tells that the rock itself is the place where Aphrodite surfaced from the sea naked which is from where the giant scallop shell carried her to the shore which means that the rock is the actual birth place of Aphrodite. Many believed, and perhaps still do, that if people swim around the rocks naked they would be blessed with eternal beauty so to swim around the larger of the two rocks three times, one might be blessed, however the surrounding area is a bit tricky and slightly dangerous and

not something recommended to moderate swimmers.

The Aphrodite Rock was not always given this name and was previously called Rock of the Greek or Petra Tou Romiou, still the local name for it. This is due to another legend that tells the story that the rock was thrown by a Byzantium soldier called Digenis Akritas. He was believed to have an enormous strength and it he threw the rocks at an invading Arabian pirates to protect island. In modern times, the rock was renamed Aphrodite's Rock to correlate with it Greek mythology origin.

Though Greek Mythology is the main theme for many tourist attractions in Paphos, or indeed Pafos, it has many more things to offer to holiday makers with its stunning beaches, spectacular and beautiful nature sites, and for young visitors it has a buzzing nightlife with bars and open air restaurants overlooking the sea.

(Excerpted from http://paphosholidayhomes.net/paphos-8.aspx\)

Questions for Reflection

1. Is the city of Paphos attractive to you as a tourist destination? Which aspect of Paphos is most impressive?
2. What is your dream destination? Why? Share it with your classmates.

Websites to Visit

http://library.thinkquest.org/23492/

This website provides links to information about ancient Greek sculpture.

http://www.tudou.com/programs/view/XJxJIHktfz8/

This website provides a short audio clip telling the story of Pygmalion.

Movies to Watch
Pygmalion (1938)

Pygmalion is a 1938 British film based on the George Bernard Shaw play of the same title, and adapted by him for the screen. It stars Leslie Howard and Wendy Hiller.

The film was a financial and critical success and won an Oscar for best screenplay and three more nominations. The screenplay was later adapted into the 1956 theatrical musical My Fair Lady, which in turn led to the 1964 film of the same name.

Unit 15

Eros/Cupid and Psyche

> Most people would rather give than get affection.
> ——Aristotle, Greek philosopher

Unit Goals

- To be familiarized with the story of Cupid and psyche
- To understand the cultural heritage and influences of the story reflected from literary works
- To learn the useful words and expressions that describe the story of Cupid and Psyche
- To improve language skills and critical thinking through the content of this unit

Before You Read

1. What is your attitude toward the external beauty of an individual? What kind of advantages and disadvantages does it have?

    A: I consider the external beauty of an individual as _____, because:
    (1) _____
    (2) _____
    (3) _____
    (4) _____

    A: Its advantages and disadvantages are:
    (1) _____
    (2) _____
    (3) _____
    (4) _____

2. Love between man and woman is an eternal theme in all kinds of art forms, yet it remains such a complicated and confusing matter that people are always questioning. Here are some commonly accepted elements about love listed. Please share your understanding about them with your classmates.

The Positives	The Negatives
Passion	Impertinence
Warmth; Sense of security	Entanglement; Jealousy

Loyalty	Betrayal
Eternity	Caprice

3. Please describe and comment on the following carton picture..

Start to Read

Text A Eros/Cupid and Psyche

Once upon a time there was a king with three daughters. They were all beautiful, but by far the most beautiful was the youngest, **Psyche**. She was so beautiful that people began to neglect the worship of **Venus**, the goddess of love and beauty. Venus was very jealous. Shaking her ambrosial head with indignation, she exclaimed, "Am I then to be eclipsed in my honors by a mortal girl? In vain then did that royal shepherd, whose judgment was approved by **Zeus/Jupiter/ Jove** himself, give me the palm of beauty over my illustrious rivals, **Athena/ Minerva/Pallas** and **Hera/Juno**. But she shall not so quietly usurp my honors. I will give her cause to repent of so unlawful a beauty."

Venus asked her son Cupid (the boy with the arrows) to make Psyche fall in love with a horrible monster. **Eros/Cupid** prepared to obey the commands of his mother. There are two fountains in Aphrodite/Venus's garden, one of sweet waters, the other of bitter. Eros/Cupid filled two amber vases, one from each fountain, and suspending them from the top of his quiver, hastened to the chamber of Psyche, whom he found asleep. He shed a few drops from the bitter fountain over her

lips, though the sight of her almost moved him to pity; then touched one side of her body with the point of his arrow. At the touch she awoke, and opened eyes upon Eros/Cupid (himself invisible) which so startled him that in his confusion he wounded himself with his own arrow. Heedless of his wound his whole thought now was to repair the mischief he had done, and he poured the balmy drops of joy over all her silken ringlets.

Despite her great beauty no-one wanted to marry Psyche. Her

parents consulted an oracle, and were told that she was destined to marry a monster, and they were to take her to the top of a mountain and leave her there. The west wind took her and wafted her away to a palace, where she was waited on by invisible servants. She had not yet seen her destined husband. He came only in the hours of darkness, and fled before the dawn of morning, but his accents were full of love, and inspired a like passion in her. She often begged him to stay and let her have a look at him, but he would not consent. On the contrary, he charged her to make no attempt to see him, for it was his pleasure, for the best of reasons, to keep concealed. "Why should you wish to behold me?" he said. "Have you any doubt of my love? Have you any wish ungratified? If you saw me, perhaps you would fear me, perhaps adore me, but all I ask of you is to love me. I would rather you would love me as an equal than adore me as a god."

Although her invisible husband was kind and gentle with her, and the invisible servants attended to her every desire, Psyche grew homesick. When her husband came one night, she told him her distress, and at last drew from him an unwilling consent that her sisters should be brought to see her.

So calling Zephyr, she acquainted him with her husband's commands, and he, promptly obedient, soon brought them across the mountain down to their sister's valley. They embraced her and she returned their caresses. "Come," said Psyche, "enter with me my house and refresh yourselves with whatever your sister has to offer." Then taking their hands she led them into her golden palace, and committed them to the care of her numerous train of attendant voices, to refresh them in her baths and at her table, and to show them all her treasures. The view of these celestial delights caused envy to enter their bosoms, at seeing their young sister possessed of such state and splendor, so much exceeding their own.

They asked her numberless questions, among others what sort of a person her husband was. Psyche replied that he was a beautiful youth, who generally spent the daytime in hunting upon the mountains. The sisters, not satisfied with this reply, soon made her confess that she had never seen him. Then they proceeded to fill her bosom with dark suspicions. "Call to mind," they said, "the Pythian oracle that declared you destined to marry a direful and tremendous monster. The inhabitants of this valley say that your husband is a terrible and monstrous serpent, who nourishes you for a while with dainties that he may by and by devour you. Take our advice. Provide yourself with a lamp and a sharp knife; put them in concealment that your husband may not discover them, and when he is sound asleep, slip out of bed bring forth your lamp and see for yourself whether what they say is true or not. If it is, hesitate not to cut off the monster's head, and thereby recover your liberty."

Psyche resisted these persuasions as well as she could, but they did not fail to have their effect on her mind, and when her sisters were gone, their words and her own curiosity were too strong for her to resist. So she prepared her lamp and a sharp knife, and hid them out of sight of her husband. When he had fallen into his first sleep, she silently got up and with her lamp discovering that her husband was not a hideous monster, but the most beautiful and charming of the gods, with his golden ringlets wandering over his snowy neck and crimson cheek, with two dewy wings on his shoulders, whiter than snow, and with shining feathers like the tender blossoms of spring. As

she leaned the lamp over to have a nearer view of his face a drop of burning oil fell on the shoulder of the god, startled with which he opened his eyes and stared at her; then, without saying one word, he spread his white wings and flew out of the window. Psyche, in vain endeavoring to follow him, fell from the window to the ground. Eros/Cupid, looking at her as she lay in the dust, stopped his flight for an instant and said, "O foolish Psyche, is it thus you repay my love? After having disobeyed my mother's commands and made you my wife, will you think me a monster and cut off my head? But go; return to your sisters, whose advice you seem to think preferable to mine. I inflict no other punishment on you than to leave you forever. Love cannot dwell with suspicion." So saying he fled away, leaving poor Psyche prostrate on the ground, filling the place with mournful lamentations.

Psyche roamed about looking for her husband, and eventually in desperation approached his mother, Venus. Still angry, the goddess set various tasks for Psyche, all of which she passed, with a bit of help from ants and river gods.

At last Cupid found out what was going on, then as swift as lightning penetrating the heights of heaven, he presented himself before Zeus/Jupiter/Jove with his supplication. Zeus/Jupiter/Jove lent a favoring ear, and pleaded the cause of the lovers so earnestly with Aphrodite/Venus that he won her consent. On this he sent Hermes/Mercury to bring Psyche up to the heavenly assembly, and when she arrived, handing her a cup of ambrosia, he said, "Drink this, Psyche, and be immortal; nor shall Eros/Cupid ever break away from the knot in which he is tied, but these nuptials shall be perpetual."

Thus Psyche became at last united to Eros/Cupid, and in due time they had a daughter whose name was Pleasure.

The fable of Eros/Cupid and Psyche is usually considered allegorical. The Greek name for a butterfly is Psyche, and the same word means the soul. There is no illustration of the immortality of the soul so striking and beautiful as the butterfly, bursting on brilliant wings from the tomb in which it has lain, after a dull, groveling caterpillar existence, to flutter in the blaze of day and feed on the most fragrant and delicate productions of the spring. Psyche, then, is the human soul, which is purified by sufferings and misfortunes, and is thus prepared for the enjoyment of true and pure happiness.

In works of art Psyche is represented as a maiden with the wings of a butterfly, alone or with Eros/Cupid, in the different situations described in the allegory.

(Excerpted from http://ancienthistory.about.com/cs/grecoromanmyth1/a/mythslegends4.htm)

Proper Nouns

1. **Psyche** ['psaiki]：普塞克，爱神丘比特之妻。
2. **Venus** ['vi:nəs]：维纳斯，爱与美的女神。
3. **Zeus/Jupiter/Jove** [zju:s]：宙斯，众神之神。
4. **Athena/Minerva/Pallas** [ə'θi:nə]：雅典娜，智慧女神。

5. **Hera/Juno** [ˈhiərə]: 赫拉，仙后。
6. **Eros/Cupid** [ˈiərɔs]: 丘比特，爱神。

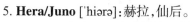
After You Read

Knowledge Focus

1. Fill in the blanks according to what you have learned from the text above.

1) Once upon a time there was a king with three daughters. They were all beautiful, but by far the most beautiful was _____.
2) Venus was very jealous about Psyche's beauty, because _____.
3) Venus asked _____ to make Psyche fall in love with a horrible monster.
4) There are two fountains in Aphrodite/Venus's garden, one of _____, the other of _____.
5) Psyche opened eyes upon Eros/Cupid (himself invisible) which so startled him that in his confusion _____.
6) Psyche's parents consulted an oracle, and were told that she was destined to marry _____.
7) _____ took her and wafted her away to a palace, where she was waited on by _____.
8) Because of jealousy, Psyche's sisters proceeded to fill her bosom with _____.
9) When Psyche silently got up, with her lamp, she discovered that her husband was not a hideous monster, but _____.
10) Cupid, as swift as lightning penetrating the heights of heaven, presented himself before _____ with his supplication.

2. Discuss the following questions with your partner.

1) Why is Venus so angry about Psyche's beauty? What has she done wrong?
2) Why has Cupid failed to fulfill Venus' command?
3) What kind of feelings did Psyche have when she was first put into the palace?
4) Why did her sisters prompt Psyche to kill her husband?
5) Why was Psyche so compunctious after her husband left her?
6) How did Psyche become immortal?
7) What is the modern meaning of the name "Psyche"?

Language Focus

1. Fill in the blanks with the words or expressions you have learned from the text.

jealous	ambrosial	with indignation	move ... to pity
consult	acquaint ... with	supplication	
celestial	satisfied with	inflict ... on	

1) A wise old man with rich life experiences is always a good source you can _____.
2) Are you _____ his explanation?

Ancient Greek and Roman Mythology

3) Othello was a _____ husband.
4) Don't _____ your ideas _____ me.
5) Everyone longs for the _____ food that fructifies the soul, the mind, the heart.
6) My last _____ of all, is this: For you, and for any dear to you, I would do anything.
7) She was _____ by the young beggars because of their miserable experiences.
8) It is the courtesy to _____ him _____ your arrival as he regard himself as your friend.
9) The distance between two _____ bodies is often measured by the unit of light year.
10) His face reddened _____.

2. Fill in the blanks with the proper form of the word in the brackets.

1) He is such a terrible husband that his constant _____ (neglect) put her wife in unbearable miseries.
2) Confidence is good, but it becomes _____ if it carries to an excess. (vain).
3) _____ (mortal) is the ultimate state that human beings have pursued for thousands of years.
4) This is the _____ (honor) moment for her to stand on the splendor stage in front of all the audiences.
5) Several days after watching the movie, he can still feel the _____ (horrible) when thinking about the scenes.
6) Some of the beggars are not _____ (pity) at all.
7) The ways in this small town can be very _____ (confusion) sometimes.
8) The chief motif of this science fiction is a(n) _____ (vision) mantle, which can provide unlivable power to the owner.
9) After the tiresome project, the only thing she wanted is a _____ (fresh) holiday.
10) There are _____ (number) products in the super market.

3. Fill in the blanks with the proper prepositions or adverbs that collocate with the neighboring words.

1) No one knows how successful he will be in the future, but he has already revealed unbelievable potentials _____ far.
2) Venus, the goddess _____ love and beauty, was worshiped by lots of mortals.
3) It is hard to resist the feeling when you truly fell in love _____ some one.
4) Every qualified soldier is ready to obey all the commands _____ his senior officer.
5) He poured the balmy drops of joy _____ all her silken ringlets.
6) When he arrived at home, he found that he was waited _____ by his wife and children.
7) For a well educated man, it is the necessary social etiquette to be gentle _____ ladies.
8) Happiness can be obtained only when one knows to be satisfied _____ what he/she has already got.

4. Proofreading: The following passage contains ten errors. Each indicated line contains a maximum of one error. In each case, only one word is involved. Read the passage and correct the errors.

In Roman mythology, Cupid is the god for desire, affectionate and erotic love. He 1) _____
is often portrayal as the son of the goddess Venus, with a father rarely mention. 2) _____
His Greek counter is Eros. Cupid is also known in Latin as Amor. 3) _____
Although Eros appears in Classic Greek art as a slender winged youth, during the 4) _____
Hellenistic period he was increasingly portrayed as a chatty boy. During this time, 5) _____
his iconography required the bow and arrow that remain a distinguishing attribute. 6) _____
A person, or even a deity, who is shout by Cupid's arrow is filled with 7) _____
uncontrollable desire. The Roman Cupid maintains these characteristics, which 8) _____
continue in the depiction of multiple cupids in both Roman art and the later 9) _____
classical tradition of Western art. 10) _____

Comprehensive Work

1. Sharing Ideas: "*Jealousy*"

Many people feel jealous from time to time. Jealousy is easy to deal with, once you understand what it is teaching you. Here are some pointers on working through your emotions and feelings of jealousy.

Understand the emotions. Jealousy is a combination of fear and anger: fear of losing something and anger that someone is "moving in on" something that you feel belongs only to you.
Allow yourself to actually "feel" emotions in a healthy way. When you start feeling jealous, ask yourself: Is it more fear-based or more anger-based? Recognize which part of your body is being affected.
Communicate your feelings. Sharing your true feelings with someone without blaming them can create a deep sense of connection between the two of you and open up a dialogue about the path of your relationship.
Identify what your jealousy is teaching you. Jealousy can alert you to what you want and what is important to you. If you are jealous of someone talking to a friend of yours, personal relationships may be important to you.
...
...
...
...

Ancient Greek and Roman Mythology

Questions for Discussion:

1) Do you think the advice abobe in overcoming jealousy will work? How useful do you think they can be?

2) Could you provide more tips on overcoming jealousy? Provide your reasons.

2. Role–play

Form groups of 8—10 students and prepare a 10-minute play on the story of Cupid and Psyche. Try to be creative as long as they are reasonable imagination.

3. Compose a speech stating your personal opinion about love. The following words and expressions are required to be used.

passion	entanglement
impertinence	loyalty
passion	betrayal
sense of security	eternity
jealousy	caprice

Read More

Text B Voluptas and The Kharites

Kharites, also commonly known as the Graces, were three goddesses of grace, beauty, adornment, mirth, festivity, dance and song. A number of "younger Kharites" presided over the other pleasures of life, including play, amusement, banqueting, floral decoration, happiness, rest and relaxation.

The Kharites were attendants of the goddesses Aphrodite and Hera. One named Kharis, was the wife of Hephaistos. Another, Pasithea, was married to Hypnos (Sleep).

The three Kharites were usually depicted in classical sculpture and mosaic as three naked women, holding hands and dancing in a circle. They were sometimes crowned with myrtle and held sprigs of myrtle in their hands.

In Roman mythology, Voluptas or Volupta was the beautiful daughter born from the union of Cupid and Psyche. She is one of the Kharites, or Three Graces, and is known as the goddess of "sensual pleasures" whose Latin name means "pleasure" or "bliss".

Some Roman authors mention a goddess named Volupia, who had a temple near the Romanula gate at Rome and was likely the same as Voluptas.

In Greek Mythology, she is called Hedone. Her opposites are the

Algea, or pains. Algea is used by Hesiod in the plural as the personification of sorrows and grief, which are there represented as the daughters of Eris, Greek goddess of strife.

The beloved legend of Cupid & Psyche tells of how the female Psyche fell in love with her invisible lover Cupid. It is an age-old tale of love tested and regained. The tale, it's full name The Marriage of Cupid & Psyche, ends in rejoice, when the union of the two lovers gives birth to a beautiful daughter, known as Voluptas.

She is recognized as one of three graces from Ancient Greece - Voluptas being the word meaning pleasure.

Little is known from ancient records about the legend of Voluptas - up until now there have been no known poems dedicated to her beauty, and also no specific artworks. There are only the cusoriest of mentions, perhaps several lines in a poem, or her necessitated presence in Three Graces works.

Which seems very incredible, given the popularity of the myth of Cupid & Psyche — a beautiful daughter, combining the ethereal beauties of two eternal lovers, should give rise to all manner of artistic and literary creation.

There is a modern poem singing to the beauty of Voluptas:

Voluptas, born of the soul, breathed into life by passion
Daughter of the earth and sky
Voluptas, in a shower of white stars
Pleasure, a blossom in her golden hair

Voluptas, the glowing edge of a dove's wing
The sea shell's song, the voice of twilight
A pearl formed in secret, made of pain
Softened by tenderness

Maiden f heaven, stars in the folds of her skirts
Gliding bare-foot along the sands of longing
Weeping in her sleep, soothed by caresses
Voluptas, roses at her feet, daughter of love

Goddess, bending near to touch the earth
Called forth into existence, a sapping of light
A feather from Cupid's wings
Stirred the River Styx, to flow to Voluptas

Psyche's heart, touched by the gods' compassion
Warmed, supple to Cupid's advances
Brought into the world a daughter, Voluptas
As beautiful as the dawn

Voluptas, a sister to the Graces of humankind
A poetess, and lover of beauty
Borne on the pinions of angels
Afloat on the drew of the sea

Gathered by foamy waves to the bosom of the shore
Asleep on sun-lit rocks
Adrift in the clouds, a bluebird singing forever
Her songs of the soul

(Excerpted from *http://www.voluptas.info/*)

Questions for Reflection

1. What is the significance of the existence of Voluptas as the last god on Olympus?

Text C Beauty and Beast

As Bruno Bettelheim notes in *The Uses of Enchantment, Beauty and the Beast* is a variant of *Cupid and Psyche*.

The rich merchant not only has three daughters but also three sons who have little to do with the story. All the girls are good-looking, particularly the youngest who becomes known as Little Beauty. The sisters are vain and jealous of Beauty who is by contrast modest and charming and wishes to stay with her father.

All of a sudden the family loses its money and is forced into a poorer lifestyle which makes life more difficult all around and exaggerates the differences between Beauty and her sisters. Beauty and the three brothers throw themselves into working for their new life while the sisters are bored. The father takes a trip in the hopes of regaining his wealth, and the older sisters demand he bring them expensive garments. Beauty asks simply for a rose.

The father is unsuccessful in his attempt to regain his wealth and in despair, wandering in the forest, is trapped in a snow storm. He comes upon a seemingly deserted palace where he finds food and shelter for the night. In the morning he wanders into the garden where he sees the perfect rose for Beauty. Upon plucking it, a hideous Beast appears and says that for his thievery he must die. The father begs for his life and, the Beast agrees to let him go if one of his daughters will take his place. If she refuses, then he must return to die himself. The Beast gives him a chest filled with gold and sends him home. This treasure enables the older daughters to make fashionable marriages. On giving Beauty the rose, her father cannot help but tell her what happened. The brothers offer to slay the Beast but the father knows that they would die in the process. Beauty insists on taking her father's place, and so she returns with him to the Beast's palace where he reluctantly leaves her.

In a dream Beauty sees a beautiful lady who thanks

her for her sacrifice and says that she will not go unrewarded. The Beast treats her well; all her wishes are met by magic. He visits her every evening for supper and gradually Beauty grows to look forwards to these meetings as a break to the monotony of her life. At the end of each visit the Beast asks Beauty to be his wife, which she refuses although agreeing never to leave the palace. Beauty sees in the magic mirror that her father is desperately missing her and asks that she might return to visit him. The Beast assents on the condition that she return in seven days, lest he die.

The next morning she is at home. Her father is overjoyed to see her but the sisters are once again jealous of Beauty, her newly found happiness and material comfort with the Beast. They persuade Beauty to stay longer, which she does, but on the tenth night she dreams of the Beast who is dying. Wishing herself back with him, she is transported back to the castle where she finds the Beast dying of a broken heart. She realizes that she is desperately in love with the Beast and says that she would gladly marry him. At this the Beast is transformed into a prince, the Father joins them at the palace and the sisters are turned into statues until they own up to their own faults.

The Prince and Beauty live happily ever after because their "contentment is founded on goodness."

(Excerpted from www.balletmet.org/Notes/StoryOrigin.html)

Questions for Reflection

1. What are the similarities and differences of the two tales?
2. What themes can you see from the tale of Beauty and Beast?
3. What do you think of the type of "Beauty and Beast" relationship in real life?

Websites to Visit

http://www.voluptas.info/

This website provides specific information about the goddess of pleasure and some original artistic works.

http://dh.0-6.com/MovView/3a96fb6b-653c-4186-b35f-bde4478393a5/
This website provides a short video clip telling the story of Cupid and Psyche.

http://tripwow.tripadvisor.com/tripwow/ta-00d1-2786-e292
This website provides a slide show telling the story of Cupid and Psyche.

Ancient Greek and Roman Mythology

Movies to Watch
Beauty and the Beast (1997)

Beauty and the Beast is a 1991 American animated musical film produced by Walt Disney Animation Studios and released by Walt Disney Pictures. The story is based on the fairy tale La Belle et la Bête by Jeanne-Marie Le Prince de Beaumont and get some ideas from the 1946 film of the same name. It centers on a prince who is transformed into a Beast and a young woman named Belle whom he imprisons in his castle. To become a prince again, the Beast must love Belle and win her love in return.

Key to Exercises

Unit 1

Knowledge Focus

1. Solo Work: Decide whether the following statements are true or false.
   1) T 2) T 3) T 4) T 5) F 6) F 7) T 8) F 9) F 10) T

Language Focus

1. Please explain the following words/phrases with the help of dictionary.

   1. **tantalize:** to tease or torment (a person or an animal) by the sight of sth that is desired but cannot be reached.
      Tantalus was a king in an ancient Greek story who had to stand up to his chin in water under a fruit tree, but was unable to reach either the water to drink or the fruit to eat.
   2. **a Herculean effort:** needing a lot of strength and determination in order to be achieved.
      in ancient Roman stories, Hercules was a hero known for his very great strength and for performing twelve very difficult and dangerous jobs known as the Labours of Hercules.
   3. **a Sisyphean task:** a task that is endless and ineffective.
      As a punishment from the gods for his trickery, Sisyphus was made to roll a huge boulder up a steep hill, but before he could reach the top of the hill, the rock would always roll back down, forcing him to begin again.
   4. **a Procrustean bed:** a scheme or pattern into which someone or something is arbitrarily forced.
      In Greek mythology Procrustes, "the stretcher", was a rogue smith and bandit who physically attacked people, stretching them, or cutting off their legs so as to make them fit an iron bed's size. In general, when something is Procrustean different lengths or sizes or properties are fitted to an arbitrary standard.
   5. **to open Pandora's box:** to do or start something that will cause a lot of other problems.
      Pandora's box is an artifact in Greek mythology. The "box" was actually a large jar given to Pandora, which contained all the evils of the world. When Pandora opened the jar, the entire contents of the jar were released, but for one — hope.
   6. **Midas touch:** if someone has the Midas touch, everything they do is successful and makes money for them.
      In ancient Greek stories, Midas is a king who was given the power to change everything he touched into gold. He soon realized this would not bring him happiness, when he found that even his food and drink changed into gold as soon as he touched them.
   7. **Achilles heel:** Someone's Achilles heel is the weakest point in their character or nature, where it is easiest for other people to attack or criticize them.
      The ancient Greek hero Achilles was dipped as a baby into the river Styx to protect him, but the part of his heel he was held by did not get wet, and so remained unprotected.
   8. **on an Odyssey:** to be on a long journey with a lot of adventures or difficulties.
      The Odyssey is an epic poem attributed to Homer recounting the longitude wanderings of Odysseus.
   9. **hear a siren:** to hear a warning message.
      Sirens were a group of women in ancient Greek stories, whose beautiful singing made sailors sail towards them into dangerous water.

10. Titanic: a large British passenger ship which was people considered impossible to sink, but which hit an iceberg in the Atlantic Ocean on its first journey in 1912, and as a result sank, killing more than 1500 of its passengers.

Titans were a family of giants in Greek mythology born of Uranus and Gaea and ruled the earth until overthrown by the Olympian gods

2. Fill in the blanks with the words or expressions you have learned from the text.

1) personified	2) allusions	3) stomach	4) treatise	5) uplift
6) infidelities	7) sulkiness	8) suffused	9) scoffed	10) distaste

3. Fill in the blanks with the proper form of the word in the brackets.

1) mythological	2) appreciative	3) disastrously	4) suspicion	5) unanswerable
6) spirituality	7) legendary	8) scornful	9) virtuous	10) humanity

4. Fill in the blanks with the proper prepositions or adverbs that collocate with the neighboring words.

1) to/with	2) in	3) with	4) after	5) up
6) in	7) in/through ... for	8) for	9) as	10) for

5. Proofreading: The following passage contains TEN errors. Each indicated line contains a maximum of ONE error. In each case, only ONE word is involved. Read the passage and correct the errors.

Greek mythology is the body of myths and legends <u>belonged</u> to the ancient Greeks, <u>concerned</u> their gods and heroes, the nature of the world, and the origins and significance of their own cult and ritual <u>practice</u>. They were a part of religion in ancient Greece. Modern scholars refer to, and study the myths <u>for</u> an attempt to throw light <u>in</u> the religious and political institutions of Ancient Greece, its civilization, and ∧ <u>gain</u> understanding of the nature of myth-making itself.

Greek myth <u>attempt</u> to explain the origins of the world, and details the lives and adventures of a <u>widely</u> variety of gods, goddesses, heroes, heroines, and mythological creatures. It has exerted an <u>intensive</u> influence on the culture, the arts, and the literature of Western civilization and <u>remain</u> part of Western heritage and language. Poets and artists from ancient times to the present have derived inspiration from Greek mythology and have discovered contemporary significance and relevance in these mythological themes.

1) belonging

2) concerning

3) practices

4) in

5) on

6) to

7) attempts

8) wide

9) extensive

10) remains

Unit 2

Knowledge Focus

1. Solo Work: familiarize yourself with gods and goddesses by filling out the following form.

Ancient Greek and Roman Gods

GREEK NAME	ROMAN NAME	ROLE IN MYTHOLOGY
Athena	Minerva	Virgin goddess of arts, craft and war
Demeter	Ceres	Goddess of corn or of the earth and fertility
Hera	Juno	Goddess of marriage and protector of married women
Hestia	Vesta	Virgin goddess of the hearth and hearth fire
Poseidon	Neptune	God of the sea and also god of earthquakes and of horses
Zeus	Jupiter, Jove	Supreme god and ruler of Olympus. Lord of the Sky, the Cloud-gatherer, the Rain-god and Zeus the Thunderer

2. Solo Work: Match each figure with its description according to what you have learned from the text above.
   1) E; I   2) A; G   3) F; J   4) B   5) C   6) D; H

Language Focus

1. Fill in the blanks with the words or expressions you have learned from the text.
   1) citadel   2) principal   3) categorize   4) composition   5) susceptible to
   6) omnipotent   7) gracious   8) trickery   9) overthrow   10) distinguishing

2. Fill in the blanks with the proper form of the word in the brackets.
   1) disagreement   2) survival   3) Association   4) expectation   5) recognize
   6) rocky   7) respectable   8) religious   9) separation   10) depiction

3. Fill in the blanks with the proper prepositions or adverbs that collocate with the neighboring words.
   1) into   2) on   3) to   4) of   5) in
   6) up   7) of   8) into   9) to   10) with

4. Proofreading: The following passage contains ten errors. Each indicated line contains a maximum of one error. In each case, only one word is involved. Read the passage and correct the errors.

   Zeus — King of the gods and ruler of the universe from his throne on Mount Olympus. <u>Original</u> a god of the sky and storm, thunder and lightning, he also <u>become</u> patron of kingship and government, law and custom, the patriarchal lord of the status quo. He is depicted <u>like</u> a powerfully built bearded man of middle <u>aged</u>, often <u>grasped</u> a thunderbolt or lightning flash, <u>attending</u> by his messenger the eagle and his sacred tree the oak.

   Zeus/Jupiter has a less exalted aspect, however. He is also an insatiable lecher, pursuing nymphs and mortal women and boys, and seducing or raping them in various <u>form</u>,

   1) Originally
   2) becomes
   3) as
   4) age
   5) grasping
   6) attended

   7) forms

thus fathering many heroes and heroines and founding many of the great royal and noble families of mythology. His sexual exploits have provided <u>endlessly</u> material for artists and poets, who ∧ tended to treat them in a lighthearted spirit. Ovid, observing the spectacle of the lord of the universe transformed <u>to</u> a bull and mooing his love for Europa, comments wryly that 'majesty and love go ill together'.

8) endless
9) have
10) into

Unit 3

Knowledge Focus

1. Solo Work: familiarize yourself with gods and goddesses by filling out the following form.

Ancient Greek and Roman Gods

GREEK NAME	ROMAN NAME	ROLE IN MYTHOLOGY
Aphrodite	Venus	Goddess of love and beauty
Apollo	Apollo	God of youth, music, prophecy, archery and healing
Ares	Mars	God of war
Artemis	Diana	Virgin goddess of childbirth and of wild animals; goddess of hunting and the chase
Hephaestus	Vulcan	God of fire and metalworking
Hermes	Mercury	herald and messenger of the gods, known for his invention and for theft

2. Solo Work: Match each figure with its description according to what you have learned from the text above.
   1) F 2) D; G 3) A 4) C 5) B 6) E

Language Focus

1. Fill in the blanks with the words or expressions you have learned from the text.
   1) delivery 2) crumble 3) murderous 4) guardian 5) Archery
   6) notable 7) attribute 8) notorious 9) infancy 10) chase

2. Fill in the blanks with the proper form of the word in the brackets.
   1) invention 2) Origin 3) contradiction 4) numerous 5) persuasion
   6) confrontation 7) supervision 8) musical 9) popularity 10) beauty

3. Fill in the blanks with the proper prepositions or adverbs that collocate with the neighboring words.
   1) as 2) to 3) with 4) from 5) with
   6) on 7) on 8) in 9) to/towards 10) out

4. Proofreading: The following passage contains ten errors. Each indicated line contains a maximum of one error. In each case, only one word is involved. Read the passage and correct the errors.

Plato, in the *Symposium*, declared that there are two Aphrodites: "Common Aphrodite", <u>god</u> of ordinary love and sex, and "<u>Heaven</u> Aphrodite", Aphrodite Urania, a potent spiritual force. This is a philosopher's concept rather ∧ a genuine myth, but it does suggest the goddess's range of personalities. <u>On</u> one extreme is the goddess of the universal cycle of life. Common Aphrodite, on the other hand, is the embodiment of human love, and can be regarded in ∧ many ways as love can be: as something rapturous, or kind and <u>cared</u>, or wantonly lustful, or elegantly frivolous, or cruel. She ∧ married to Hephaestus/ Vulcan, but continually unfaithful to him; her <u>principle</u> lover is Ares/Mars, but she also has human lovers, <u>with</u> whom Adonis is the most famous. The opposite in most ways of chaste Artemis/Diana, she is like her in her harsh punishment of those who offend <u>on</u> her and her values; the most famous example is the tragedy of Hippolytus and Phaedra.

1) goddess
2) Heavenly
3) than
4) At
5) as
6) caring
7) is
8) principal
9) of
10) against

Unit 4

Knowledge Focus

1. Solo Work: Fill in the blanks according to what you have learned from the text above.
   1) Hades; Persephone   2) Cronus; Rhea   3) Acheron; Cocytus; Lethe; Phlegethon; Styx
   4) Erebus; Tartarus   5) cMinos; Rhadamanthys; Aeacus
   6) Cerberus   7) Thanatos; Hypnos; Morpheus
   8) Pomegranate seeds   9) Perses; Asteria   10) Hecate
2. Solo Work: Match each figure(s) with its description according to what you have learned from the text above.
   1) C 2) F 3) A 4) H 5) D 6) G 7) E 8) B

Language Focus

1. Fill in the blanks with the words or expressions you have learned from the text.
   1) distinction 2) decreed 3) compromise 4) depicts 5) connivance
   6) barren 7) poisonous 8) conspire against 9) exceptional 10) possession
2. Fill in the blanks with the proper form of the word in the brackets.
   1) invasion 2) initiation 3) fertility 4) renewal 5) description
   6) inhabitant 7) seasonal 8) reservation 9) geographical 10) forgetful
3. Fill in the blanks with the proper prepositions or adverbs that collocate with the neighboring words.
   1) into 2) for 3) at 4) to 5) of
   6) out 7) to 8) with 9) on 10) away

4. Proofreading: The following passage contains ten errors. Each indicated line contains a maximum of one error. In each case, only one word is involved. Read the passage and correct the errors.

Later writers usually place the underworld underneath the earth, where it can be <u>reach</u> by various passages: Orpheus <u>ascends</u> through a cave at Taenarus in southernmost Greece, Aeneas through the sibyl's cavern near Lake Avernus in Italy. Its boundary is marked <u>on</u> the river Styx, the "hateful river", by whose black and poisonous water the gods swear their most <u>breakable</u> oaths. The spirits of the newly dead wait on its bank to be ferried across by Charon, the filthy and churlish old boatman. The fare is <u>a</u> obolus, a small coin; those who lack <u>of</u> the coin, or have not been properly buried, are doomed ∧ wait in limbo on the banks of the Styx. On the other side, the boundaries of the underworld are marked ∧ by five rivers: Styx, Acheron ("sorrowful"), Cocytus ("wailing"), Phlegethon ("fiery"), and Lethe ("forgetful"); those who drink <u>in</u> Lethe forget their former lives and identities. The entrance <u>of</u> the underworld, or the gate of Hades' palace, is guarded by the fearsome three-headed (or, more extravagantly, fifty-headed) hell-hound Cerberus.

1) reached
2) descends

3) by

4) unbreakable

5) an
6) of
7) to

8) out

9) from
10) to

Unit 5

Knowledge Focus

1. Solo Work: Matching. Draw a line to match the Greek god or creature with the description.
   1) c   2) d   3) a   4) e   5) b   6) i   7) g   8) j   9) f   10) h
2. Solo Work: True or False. Identify the following statements, please correct the false ones.
   1) T   2) F   3) F   4) F   5) F   6) T   7) F   8) F   9) F   10) T

Language Focus

1. Fill in the blanks with the words or expressions you have learned from the text; change the form when necessary.
   1) diverse   2) version   3) associates   4) grant   5) identify
   6) immortal   7) honor   8) panic   9) descend   10) minor
2. Fill in the blanks with the proper form of the words in brackets.
   1) embody   2) gossiped   3) Eternity   4) destined   5) relate
   6) worship   7) Pursuing   8) creature   9) reject   10) dwell
3. Fill in the blanks with the proper prepositions or adverbs that collocate with the neighboring words.
   1) to   2) at   3) at   4) with   5) in
   6) at   7) for   8) at   9) of, of   10) with, with

4. Proofreading: The following passage contains ten errors. Each indicated line contains a maximum of one error. In each case, only one word is involved. Read the passage and correct the errors.

    Aethra and her father begged Theseus to go to Athens <u>on</u> sea, for horrible robbers and bandits inhabited <u>in</u> the road, but Theseus was bold and went overland. ... Theseus started walking again. Not much farther he saw a giant man <u>held</u> a battle-ax on the side of the road. "I am Sciron and these are my cliffs. To pass you must wash my feet <u>like</u> a

toll!" the man said. "What would happen if I <u>did</u>?" replied Theseus. "I will chop off your head with this ax, and don't think that puny little twig you're carrying will save you, you're absolutely ... WRONG!!!!" Sciron yelled.

    So Theseus sat down <u>but</u> started to wash

Sciron's feet. Theseus looked over the side of the cliff, there was a monstrous turtle <u>on</u> the bottom. Then Theseus knew that this was the Sciron <u>what</u> kicked people off the cliff <u>which</u> a man-eating turtle waited. <u>Where</u> Sciron's foot came towards him, Theseus jerked aside and hurled Sciron off the cliff.

1) by
2) ~~in~~
3) holding
4) as
5) didn't

6) and

7) at
8) that
9) where
10) When

Comprehensive Work

1. Translation. Read the story—*The Apple of Discord*, and then retell it in English.

The Apple of Discord

    The wedding of Peleus and the sea-goddess Thetis were held and all gods were invited. But the absence of one goddess was clearly noticeable. It was Eris, the goddess of discord. As she planted seeds of discord wherever she went, it was natural that her presence at the ceremony was not desirable. She had good reason to feel angry. So she decided to make fun of the group at the party. Eris slipped into the hall after the couple left and rolled on the floor a golden apple, having the words, "For the fairest." It caused a violent quarrel among the three goddesses, Hera, Athena and Aphrodite. Zeus found it advisable to send them before a shepherd boy on Mt Ida, Paris by name, for judgement. Hermes, the messenger, took the apple in his hand and led the goddesses away.

    Paris was son of Priam, king of Troy. As his mother dreamed at his birth that she was bearing a piece of burning wood, the babe was regarded as representing the destruction of the city itself. To save the kingdom from possible disaster, the parents had the helpless infant left on top of Mt Ida to die. However, he survived his ill fate. Brought up by the herdsmen, he became a strong, handsome lad. He was secretly united with Oenone, a fair and faithful mountain fairy maiden. On this particular day, as he was taking care of his sheep on the mountainside, the youth was surprised to see four human beings standing before him. Hermes told him about his mission and left. The three holy beauties then competed with each other, showing themselves up before the shepherd. Hera promised to make him king of Asia. Athena undertook to help him get imperishable fame in war; whereas Aphrodite offered to secure for him the love of the most beautiful woman in the world. The primitive instinct of the boy thus moved, Aphrodite won the prize, and the other two goddesses left in anger and became deadly enemies of Troy.

Unit 6

Knowledge Focus

1. Guess who in the Greek mythology am I?

   1) Chaos   2) Gaia   3) The Furies   4) Cronus
   5) Zeus   6) Prometheus   7) Pandora   8) Deucalion

2. Complete the family tree of Greek gods.

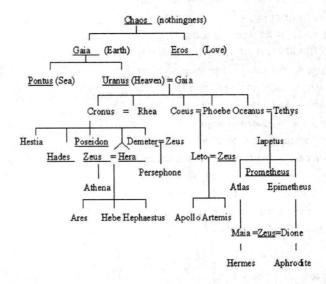

Language Focus

1. Fill in the blanks with the words in the bank; there's no need to change the form of any of them.

   1) objected   2) retreat   3) plotted   4) chaos   5) conflicting
   6) save   7) ultimate   8) exile   9) spare   10) grief

2. Complete the sentences with right verb phrases selected from the text; change the form of the verbs when necessary.

   1) took up   2) take your side   3) trick (the brain) into feeling
   4) feeds on   5) spring up

3. Fill in the blanks with the proper prepositions or adverbs that collocate with the neighboring words.

   1) to   2) into   3) at   4) out   5) with   6) on

4. Proofreading: The following passage contains ten errors. Each indicated line contains a maximum of one error. In each case, only one word is involved. Read the passage and correct the errors.

That evening when the courtiers sat <u>feasted</u>	1) feasting
in the palace and the minstrel arose to sing,	
Iobates bade him tell the tale of Phaethon, <u>which</u>	2) who
tried to equal the immortals by driving the	
chariot of the sun. Then as the minstrel's tale	
came to an end, and Phaethon fell from heaven	
in a trail of gleaming fire, the king turned to his	
chief guest and drank a toast to him, <u>said</u>, "Tell	3) saying
me, Bellerophon, do you think that Phaethon	
was wise? He aspired <u>to ∧ like</u> a god, and though	4) be

218

he failed, his end was glorious, but he has become a hero of song. Would you not rather try some impossible feat and die than rest content at the knowledge that there were things you dared not do?"

"I dare do all things," answered the young Bellerophon, with his blue eyes sparkled. "I dare even mount to Olympus and battle with the gods. What matter if I fail? I shall still die a hero because of I aimed for mighty deeds."

"Then do a deed for me," Iobatess leaned forward quickly. "Rid me of the monster that no man in my kingdom dares to face. Kill me the Chimera." ...

As Bellerophon said goodnight to his host, both men were well pleased. To Iobates it seemed most likely that the Chimera would kill Bellerophon and accomplish the desire of King Proitos. If not, however, at most the kingdom of Lycia would be rid of the dreadful beast. Bellerophon at his side was glad at the thought of the great adventure. In his mind was already a plan by which he might approach the monster. He hoped to capture first the horse, Pegasus, and with his aid to conquer the Chimera.

5) and

6) with

7) sparkling

8) of

9) least

10) on

Unit 7

Knowledge Focus

1. Answer the following questions according to what you learn from the text.
   1) D 2) D 3) B 4) D 5) C 6) Echo; himself 7) D 8) C 9) A 10) B

Language Focus

1. Fill in the blanks with the words you have learned in the text.
   1) shelter   2) yield   3) consent   4) approach   5) advances
   6) disguise   7) trait   8) sting   9) condemn   10) bridge
2. Fill in the blanks with the proper form of the words in brackets.
   1) consequently 2) resemblance 3) transformation 4) arrogant   5) combination
   6) division   7) rejecting   8) interfered   9) interpretation 10) unfulfilled
3. Fill in the blanks with the proper prepositions or adverbs that collocate with the neighboring words.
   1) in   2) in   3) after   4) for
   5) up   6) up   7) up   8) to

4. Proofreading: The following passage contains ten errors. Each indicated line contains a maximum of one error. In each case, only one word is involved. Read the passage and correct the errors.

    King Acrisius of Argos was uncertain in battle and <u>unluck</u> in the hunt. "My daughter, Danae, grows tall and ripe," he said to himself one day. "Her eyes fog over when I speak to her. She is ready for <u>the</u> husband, but am I ready for a son-in-law? I dislike the idea and always have. A son-in-law will be a younger man <u>wait</u> for me to die so he can take the throne. Perhaps he will even try to hasten that sad event. But she is ready and princesses must not be spinsters ... a grave decision ... I shall consult <u>on</u> the oracle." He sent to the oracle at Delphi, and <u>a</u> messenger returned with this prophecy: "Your daughter will bear a son who will one day kill you."

    "The Pythoness' auguries are supposed to be accurate," he thought. "<u>And</u> are they? What if I were <u>slay</u> my daughter now while she is still childless; how then <u>can</u> she have a son to kill me? But, must I kill her to keep her childless? ..."

    Thereupon he shut the beautiful young girl in a brass tower which he had specially built <u>by</u> no doors and only one tiny window. The tower was surrounded by high walls and guarded by sentries and savage dogs. Here Acrisius locked his daughter away, and so murderous was his temper in those days that no one dared ask him <u>who</u> had become of the laughing young girl.

1) unlucky

2) a

3) waiting

4) ~~on~~

5) the

6) But

7) to ∧ slay

8) could

9) with

10) what

Text C
True or False.
1) T 2) T 3) F 4) T 5) F 6) F 7) T 8) T

Unit 8

Knowledge Focus

1. Solo Work: Decide whether the following statements are true or false.
   1) T 2) F 3) F 4) T 5) F 6) F 7) F 8) F 9) F 10) F

Language Focus

1. Fill in the blanks with the words or expressions you have learned from the text.
   1) retrieve   2) evade   3) talked ... into ...   4) locate   5) motif
   6) dispose of   7) partial   8) disguise   9) make peace with   10) oracle

2. Fill in the blanks with the proper form of the word in the brackets.
   1) inheritance   2) descent   3) unwelcome   4) invisibility   5) forcibly
   6) reconciliation   7) Herculean   8) intervention   9) fearless   10) monstrous

3. Fill in the blanks with the proper prepositions or adverbs that collocate with the neighboring words.
   1) out   2) of   3) by   4) in
   5) by ... with 6) by/at   7) with ... against 8) on ... with

4. Proofreading: The following passage contains ten errors. Each indicated line contains a maximum of one error. In each case, only one word is involved. Read the passage and correct the errors.

After his labors Hercules married Deianeira, the daughter of King Oeneus. The couple did not live happily ever after, although. One day in their travels Hercules and Deianeira had to cross a river swelling by floods. Hercules swam across but left his wife to be ferried across by a centaur boatman, who attempted to rape Deianeira. Hercules then shot the centaur by one of the arrows poisoned with the Hydra's blood.

The dead centaur extracted his revenge by offering Deianeira his blood, promising that it would act as a love ointment to keep her husband faithful to her.

One day Deianeira began to doubt that Hercules was interested in another woman. So she gave Hercules a shirt on which she had spread some of the dying centaur's blood. When Hercules put on the shirt the poisoning blood began to do its work, burning Hercules' meat to the bone. Hercules could not die. So he built himself a funeral pyre. He spread his lionskin cloak on the pyre and laid down on it. The flames burned up the moral part of him, while the immortal part descended to Mount Olympus, where Zeus set him among the stars.

1) though
2) swollen

3) with

4) dying

5) √

6) poisoned
7) flesh

8) lay
9) mortal
10) ascended

Unit 9

Before You Read
3) Answer to Napoleon's riddle: the French Cock
4) Unlike the Greek sphinx which was a woman, the Egyptian sphinx is typically shown as a man. In addition, the Egyptian sphinx was viewed as benevolent in contrast to the malevolent Greek version and was thought of as a guardian often flanking the entrances to temples.

Knowledge Focus
1. Solo Work: Decide whether the following statements are true or false.
   1) T 2) F 3) F 4) T 5) F 6) T 7) T 8) F 9) T 10) F
2. Match each figure with its description according to what you have learned in the text.
   1) e 2) h 3) a 4) b 5) c 6) d 7) f 8) g

Language Focus
1. Fill in the blanks with the words or expressions you have learned from the text.
   1) pilgrimage   2) ward off   3) yoke   4) bestowed   5) machinations
   6) interlude   7) credited   8) invulnerable to 9) lineage   10) banished

Ancient Greek and Roman Mythology

2. Fill in the blanks with the proper form of the word in the brackets.
   1) rightful   2) invulnerable   3) parentage   4) incomprehensibly
   5) Exhilaration   6) contradictory   7) devotee   8) Predictably
   9) tragedian   10) prophetically

3. Fill in the blanks with the proper prepositions or adverbs that collocate with the neighboring words.
   1) on   2) into   3) of   4) on   5) in
   6) for   7) in   8) to ... in 9) in   10) at ... for

4. Proofreading: The following passage contains ten errors. Each indicated line contains a maximum of one error. In each case, only one word is involved. Read the passage and correct the errors.

King Aeetes' most valuable possession was a golden ram's fleece. When Jason and the crew of the Argo arrived Colchis seeking the Golden Fleece, Aeetes was willing to relinquish it and set Jason a series of seemingly impossible tasks with the price of obtaining it. Medea fell in love with Jason and agreed to use her magical to help him, in return with Jason's promise to marry her.

    1) at
    2) unwilling
    3) as
    4) magic
    5) for

Jason fled in the Argo after obtaining the golden fleece, taking Medea and her young brother, Absyrtis, with him. King Aeetes pursued them. In order to delay the pursuit, Medea killed her brother and cut his body into pieces, scattered the parts behind the ship. The pursuers had to stop and collect Absyrtis' dismembered body in order to give it properly burial, and so Jason, Medea and the Argonauts escaped.

    6) yonger
    7) scattering
    8) proper

After the Argo returned safely to Iolcus, Jason's home, Medea continued using her sorcery. She returned the youth of Jason's aged father, Aeson, by cutting his throat and filling his body with a magical potion. She then offered to do ∧ same for Pelias the king of Iolcus who had usurped Aeson's throne. She tricked Pelias' daughters into killing him, but left the corpse without any youth-restoring potion.

    9) restored
    10) the

Unit 10

Knowledge Focus

1. Fill in the blanks according to what you have learned from the text above.
   1) Eris
   2) dominion over the whole world, offered certain victory in every battle, the most beautiful woman in the world: Helen, a daughter of Zeus
   3) Paris   4) his heel   5) unfavorable winds   6) the Trojans
   7) Ajax   8) Athena   9) Odysseus   10) serpents

Key to Exercises

2. Read the text again and put the following sentences into the correct order.
8 3 5 10 2 4 9 6 1 7

Language Focus

1. Fill in the blanks with the proper forms of words or expressions you have learned in the text.

1) succumbed   2) capacity   3) ensued from   4) formidable   5) cunning
6) ploy   7) stench   8) appease   9) impartial   10) opted

2. Fill in the blanks with the proper form of the word in the brackets.

1) reputedly   2) entertains   3) furious   4) reservations   5) disembarking
6) penetrated 7) vulnerable   8) impregnable 9) ingenious   10) atrocity

3. Fill in the blanks with the proper prepositions or adverbs that collocate with the neighboring words.

1) at   2) at   3) of   4) on
5) into 6) with 7) at

4. Proofreading: The following passage contains ten errors. Each indicated line contains a maximum of one error. In each case, only ONE word is involved. Read the passage and correct the errors.

Passage	Corrections
<u>As</u> the rise of modern critical history, Troy and the Trojan War were consigned to the realms of legend. In <u>1870s</u>, however, the German archaeologist Heinrich Schliemann excavated a hill, called Hisarlik by the Turks, near <u>town</u> of Chanak (Çanakkale) in north-western Anatolia.	1) with 2) the ∧ 3) the ∧
There he discovered the <u>ruin</u> of a series of ancient city, <u>dated</u> from the Bronze Age to the Roman period. Schliemann declared one of these cities—at first Troy I, later Troy II—<u>be</u> the city of Troy, and this identification was widely accepted at that time. After Schliemann, the site was further excavated <u>with</u> the direction of Wilhelm Dörpfeld (1893-1894) and later Carl Blegen (1932-1938). In 1988 excavations were resumed by a team of the University of Tübingen under the direction of Professor Manfred Korfmann. The question of Troy's status in the Bronze Age world <u>had</u> been the subject of a <u>sometime</u> acerbic debate between Korfmann and the Tübingen historian Frank Kolb in 2001-2002. <u>Remainings</u> found in the ditch were dated to the late Bronze Age, the alleged time of Homeric Troy.	4) ruins 5) dating 6) to ∧ 7) under 8) has 9) sometimes 10) Remains

Comprehensive Work

2. Translate the following paragraph into Chinese.

珀琉斯和忒提斯(阿喀琉斯的父母)举行婚礼时邀请了众神,唯独忘了请不和女神厄里斯。厄里斯因此感到愤怒,向客人扔了一个金苹果,上面刻着"属于最美者"。 赫拉、阿佛洛狄忒和雅典娜都认为苹果理应属于自己。宙斯不愿意处理这件棘手的事情,就让她们去艾达山找英俊的牧羊少年帕里斯(特洛伊王子)评判苹果的归属。于是女神们来到他面前。赫拉许诺给他权利和财富,雅典娜许诺让他在战争中赢得荣誉和美名,阿佛洛狄忒许诺让他娶最美丽的女子为妻。每个女神都试图通过施加影响让他做出

有利于自己的评判。帕里斯决定支持阿佛洛狄忒，把金苹果给了她。这样，他就得罪了另外两个女神。

Read More
Text B

Questions for Reflection

2. Fill in the blanks about Mount Ida in Asia Minor according to what you read in the text above.
   1) Zeus   2) Aphrodite   3) Aeneas   4) shepherd   5) nymphs
   6) Paris   7) the Trojan War   8) Poseidon   9) the Greeks

Multiple choice

Please decide on the best choice from the four choices marked A., B., C., and D..
1. A.   2.C.   3. D.   4. B.   5.A.   6.B.

Unit 11

Knowledge Focus

1. Fill in the blanks according to what you have learned from the text above.
   1) Iphigenia   2) Clytemnestra   3) Athena   4) Cyclops Polyphemus
   5) song   6) death shroud   7) twelve axes   8) Cumaean Sibyl
   9) she wolf   10) Rea Silvia

2. Solo Work: Decide whether the following statements are true or false.
   1) F   2) F   3) T   4) F   5) F   6) F   7) T   8) F   9) F   10) T

Language Focus

1. Fill in the blanks with the proper forms of words or expressions you have learned in the text.
   1) impious   2) thrust   3) fumbled   4) antidote   5) on the verge of
   6) caressed   7) enamored   8) avenge   9) convince   10) egregious

2. Fill in the blanks with the proper form of the word in the brackets.
   1) insane   2) unleashed   3) immortal   4) treacherous   5) seductive
   6) wagged   7) inciting   8) intervene   9) eliminated   10) vindicated

3. Fill in the blanks with the proper prepositions or adverbs that collocate with the neighboring words.
   1) at   2) down   3) on   4) in
   5) on   6) in   7) on   8) to

4. Proofreading: The following passage contains ten errors. Each indicated line contains a maximum of one error. In each case, only ONE word is involved. Read the passage and correct the errors.

   <u>At</u> Ithaca, Penelope is having difficulties. Her   1) In
   husband has been gone for 20 years, and she does
   not know for sure whether he is <u>living</u> or dead.   2) alive
   Odysseus arrives, at last, <u>complete</u> alone. Upon   3) completely
   landing, he is <u>disguising</u> as an old man in rags by   4) disguised
   Athena. Odysseus is welcomed by his old
   swineherd, Eumaeus, who does not recognize him,
   but still treats him well.

   His faithful dog, Argos, is the first <u>recognize</u>   5) to ∧
   him. <u>Aging</u> and decrepit, the dog does its best to wag   6) Aged

its tail, <u>and</u> Odysseus, not wanting to be found out, pays him no attention. The disconsolate dog <u>died</u>. The first human to recognize him is his old wet nurse, Euryclea, who knows him well enough to see through the rags, recognizing <u>with</u> him by an old scar on his leg received when hunting boar. His son, Telemachus, does not see through the disguise, <u>and</u> Odysseus reveals his identity to him.

7) but
8) dies

9) ~~with~~

10) but

Comprehensive Work

2. Translate the following paragraph into Chinese.

奥德修斯的船队离开特洛伊后,首先在柯孔涅斯人的都城伊斯马洛斯登陆。在那里他们同当地居民发生了小规模冲突。每条船都有六个人阵亡。他们扬帆离开后又遇到了风暴,在海上漂了九天九夜,到了食忘忧果民族的国家。在那儿,他们受到热情款待,吃了他们给的忘忧果。吃了这些食物的后果是忘了家乡,渴望留在那个国家。奥德修斯用武力把这些人拖上船,甚至不得不把他们绑在船中的固定座椅上。

Read More
Text B

Questions for Reflection

Multiple choice
Please decide on the best choice from the four choices marked A., B., C., and D..
1. A.   2. B.   3. C.   4. D.   5.A.

Text C

Questions for Reflection

True or False.
1) F   2) F   3) T   4) T   5) T   6) F

Unit 12

Knowledge Focus

1. Fill in the blanks according to what you have learned from the text above.
   1) Eros/Cupid   2) love   3) leaden shaft   4) crime   5) Artemis/Diana
   6) Delphos   7) form   8) wreaths   9) Armstrong   10) Adonais
2. Solo Work: Decide whether the following statements are true or false.
   1) F   2) F   3) F   4) T   5) F   6) T   7) T   8) F   9) T   10) F

Language Focus

1. Fill in the blanks with the proper forms of words or expressions you have learned in the text.
   1) meddle with   2) lavished   3) rejoined   4) alluding to   5) elated

6) fawned   7) bold   8) tempted   9) rederssed   10) kindled

2. Fill in the blanks with the proper form of the word in the brackets.

1) malice   2) repelled   3) blunt   4) abhor   5) charmed
6) entreated   7) virtues   8) feeble   9) darted   10) embraced

3. Fill in the blanks with the proper prepositions or adverbs that collocate with the neighboring words.

1) about   2) with   3) with   4) up
5) with   6) into   7) upon   8) to

4. Proofreading: The following passage contains ten errors. Each indicated line contains a maximum of one error. In each case, only ONE word is involved. Read the passage and correct the errors.

<u>As</u> the most Hellenic of all gods, Apollo apparently was <u>foreign</u> origin, coming either from somewhere north of Greece or from Asia. Traditionally, Apollo and his twin, Artemis, <u>are</u> born <u>in</u> the isle of Delos. From there Apollo went to Pytho (Delphi), <u>he</u> slew Python, the dragon that guarded the area. He established his oracle by taking <u>in</u> the guise of a dolphin, leaping aboard a Cretan ship, and <u>forced</u> the crew to serve him. Thus Pytho was <u>named</u> Delphi after the dolphin (delphis), and the Cretan cult of Apollo Delphinius superseded that previously established there by Earth (Gaea). During the Archaic period (8th to 6th century BC), the fame of the Delphic oracle spread as far as Lydia in Anatolia and <u>achieving</u> pan-Hellenic status. The god's medium was the Pythia, the local woman over fifty years old, who, under his inspiration, delivered oracles in the main temple of Apollo.

1) Though
2) of ∧
3) were
4) on
5) where ∧
6) on
7) forcing
8) renamed
9) achieved
10) a

Comprehensive Work

3. Translate the following paragraph into Chinese.

    达佛涅是阿波罗的第一个意中人。他们不是偶然恋爱,而是厄洛斯/朱庇特的残忍行为造成的。阿波罗看见一个小孩在玩弓箭,由于他刚战胜了一个海怪正深感自豪,就对小孩说:"小朋友,你拿着兵器干什么呀?放下他,像我这样的人才配玩这些兵器。"这个小孩其实是阿佛洛狄忒的儿子。听了这些话他反驳说:"阿波罗,你的箭可以用来射别的东西,但是我的箭要射你。"说完这些话,他就抽出两支不同性能的箭,一支是点燃爱情之火的金箭,另一支是熄灭爱情之火的铅箭。他用第一支箭射中阿波罗的心脏,用第二支箭射中女神达佛涅。于是阿波罗对达佛涅产生了强烈的爱情,而达佛涅却非常厌恶爱情,她喜爱在森林中游玩。许多神向她求爱,但她都拒绝了,只喜欢在林中打猎,根本不考虑爱情和结婚的事。

Text B

> Questions for Reflection

Multiple choice
Please decide on the best choice from the four choices marked A., B., C., and D..
1. D. 2. C. 3. A. 4. B. 5.A.

Text C

> Questions for Reflection

Decide whether the following statements are true or false.
1) T 2) F 3) F 4) T 5) F 6) T

Unit 13

> Knowledge Focus

1. Fill in the blanks according to what you have learned from the text above.

   1) wood nymph   2) many love affairs   3) taking away her voice
   4) Leiriope of Thespia   5) the woods   6) overjoyed
   7) cursed Narcissus   8) Ameinius   9) Artemis   10) a flower

> Language Focus

1. Fill in the blanks with the words or expressions you have learned from the text.

   1) in repetition of   2) amuse   3) are worthy of   4) out making money
   5) in frustration   6) shun   7) passion for   8) fall in love with
   9) rebuff   10) vain

2. Fill in the blanks with the proper form of the word in the brackets.

   1) attendance   2) pursuit   3) companionship   4) startling
   5) hasty   6) habitual   7) hunting   8) spiritual
   9) indifference   10) consumption

3. Fill in the blanks with the proper prepositions or adverbs that collocate with the neighboring words.

   1) by   2) in   3) of   4) for
   5) with   6) through   7) upon   8) of

4. Proofreading: The following passage contains ten errors. Each indicated line contains a maximum of one error. In each case, only one word is involved. Read the passage and correct the errors.

   Narcissus is a genus of mainly hardy, mostly spring-flowering, <u>natively</u> to Europe,   1) native
   North Africa, and Asia. There are also
   several Narcissus <u>specie</u> that bloom in   2) species
   the autumn. Though Hortus Thira <u>city</u> 26 wild   3) cities
   species, Daffodils for North American
   Gardens cites between 50 <u>or</u> 100 including   4) and
   species <u>varying</u> and wild hybrids. Through   5) variants
   taxonomic and genetic research, it ˇ speculated   6) is
   that over time this number will probably

continue to be <u>refining</u>. Daffodil is a common English name, sometimes used now for all <u>variations</u>, and is the chief common name of horticultural prevalence used by the American Daffodil Society. The range <u>for</u> forms in cultivation has been <u>heavy</u> modified and extended, with new variations available from specialists almost every year.

7) refined

8) varieties

9) of

10) heavily

Unit 14

Knowledge Focus

2. Fill in the blanks according to what you have learned from the text above.
   1) master sculptor   2) live unmarried   3) he fell in love with his work
   4) Cyprus   5) Venus/Aphrodite   6) brought the statue to life
   7) imagination   8) smiling at him   9) at the Goddess' feet   10) Paphos

Language Focus

1. Fill in the blanks with the words or expressions you have learned from the text.
   1) abhor   2) were mesmerized   3) yield ... to ...   4) ardour   5) at hand
   6) resolved to   7) compete with   8) ask for forgiveness   9) fixing on   10) solemnities

2. Fill in the blanks with the proper form of the word in the brackets.
   1) resolution   2) comparison   3) admiration   4) creation   5) charming
   6) softness   7) celebration   8) utterance   9) roundness   10) timidity

3. Fill in the blanks with the proper prepositions or adverbs that collocate with the neighboring words.
   1) from   2) to   3) from   4) for
   5) to   6) from   7) upon   8) into

4. Proofreading: The following passage contains ten errors. Each indicated line contains a maximum of one error. In each case, only one word is involved. Read the passage and correct the errors.

   Sculpture is three-dimensional artwork created by <u>shapes</u> or combining hard materials — <u>typical</u> stone such as marble—or metal, glass, or wood. Softer (plastic) <u>material</u> can also be used, such as clay, textiles, plastics, polymers <u>or</u> softer metals. The term has been <u>extend</u> to works including sound, text and light.

   Materials may be worked by <u>removing</u> such as carving, or they may be assembled such as by welding, hardened such as by firing, or molded or cast. <u>Surfacing</u> decoration such as paint may be <u>applicated</u>. Sculpture has been described as one of the plastic arts because it can involve the <u>usage</u> of materials that can be molded or modulated.

   Sculpture is an important form of public art. A collection of sculpture in a garden <u>set</u> may be referred to as a sculpture garden.

   1) shaping
   2) typically
   3) materials
   4) and
   5) extended

   6) removal

   7) Surface
   8) applied
   9) use

   10) setting

Unit 15

Knowledge Focus

1. Fill in the blanks according to what you have learned from the text above.
   1) the youngest, Psyche
   2) people began to neglect the worship
   3) her son Cupid
   4) sweet waters; bitter
   5) he wounded himself with the arrow
   6) a monster
   7) The west wind; invisible servants
   8) dark suspicions
   9) the most beautiful and charming god
   10) Zeus/Jupiter/Jove

Language Focus

1. Fill in the blanks with the words or expressions you have learned from the text.
   1) consult
   2) satisfied with
   3) jealous
   4) inflict ... on
   5) ambrosial
   6) supplication
   7) moved to pity
   8) acquaint with
   9) celestial
   10) with indignation

2. Fill in the blanks with the proper form of the word in the brackets.
   1) neglect
   2) vanity
   3) Immortality
   4) honorable
   5) horror
   6) pitiable
   7) confusing
   8) invisible
   9) refreshing
   10) numerous

3. Fill in the blanks with the proper prepositions or adverbs that collocate with the neighboring words.
   1) by
   2) of
   3) with
   4) of
   5) over
   6) on
   7) with
   8) with

4. Proofreading: The following passage contains ten errors. Each indicated line contains a maximum of one error. In each case, only one word is involved. Read the passage and correct the errors.

   In Roman mythology, Cupid is the god <u>for</u> desire, <u>affectionate</u> and erotic love. He is often <u>portrayal</u> as the son of the goddess Venus, with a father rarely <u>mention</u>.

   His Greek <u>counter</u> is Eros. Cupid is also known in Latin as Amor.

   Although Eros appears in <u>Classic</u> Greek art as a slender winged youth, during the Hellenistic period he was increasingly portrayed as a <u>chatty</u> boy. During this time, his iconography <u>required</u> the bow and arrow that remain a distinguishing attribute. A person, or even a deity, who is <u>shout</u> by Cupid's arrow is filled with uncontrollable desire. The Roman Cupid <u>maintains</u> these characteristics, which continue in the depiction of multiple cupids in both Roman art and the later classical tradition of Western art.

   1) of
   2) affection
   3) portrayed
   4) mentioned
   5) counterpart
   6) classical
   7) chubby
   8) acquired
   9) shot
   10) retains

Bibliography

[1] Burn, Lucilla.(2003) *Greek Myth*. The British Museum Press.

[2] Daly, Kathleen N. (2009) *Greek and Roman Mythology A to Z*, Third Edition. Chelsea House

[3] Graf, Fritz(1993). *Greek Mythology: An Introduction*. Translated by Thomas Marier. Baltimore: Johns Hopkins University Press.

[4] Grant, Michael(1962). *Myths of the Greeks and Romans*. London: Weidenfeld and Nicolson.

[5] Graves, Robert(1993). *The Greek Myths*. 2 vols. Baltimore: Penguin Books.

[6] Hard, Robin.(2004) *The Routledge Handbook of Greek Mythology*. Routledge.

[7] Harris, Stephen L., and Platzner, Gloria. (2001) *Classical Mythology*. 3d ed. Mountain View: Mayfield Publishing Company.

[8] Kerényi, C(1960). *The Heroes of the Greeks*. New York: Grove Press.

[9] Kerenyi, C. (2002) *The Gods of The Greeks*. Thames & Hudson.

[10] Mark P.O. Morford, Robert J. Lenardon (2003) *Classical Mythology*, 7th ed. Oxford University Press.

[11] Mayerson, Philip. (2001) *Classical Mythology* in Literature, Art, and Music. Focus Publishing.

[12] Powell, Barry B. (2004) *Classical Myth*. Pearson Education, Inc.

[13] Roman, Luke & Monica Roman.(2010) *Encyclopedia of Greek and Roman Mythology*. Facts On File, Inc.

[14] Ruck, Carl A. P., and Danny Staples.(1994) *The World of Classical Myth: Gods and Goddesses. Heroines and Heroes*. Durham, N.C.: Carolina Academic Press.

[15] 伯恩斯.(2010) 古希腊罗马神话传说. 上海:上海世界图书出版公司.

[16] 杰西·M·塔特洛克.(2010) 希腊罗马神话. 北京:中央编译出版社.

[17] 毛利群等.(2009) 希腊神话中的主神. 上海:复旦大学出版社.

[18] 施瓦布.(2010)希腊古典神话——经典译林. 南京:译林出版社.

[19] 陶洁等译. (2008) 希腊罗马神话:英汉对照. 北京:中国对外翻译出版公司.

[20] 王磊.(2010) 希腊罗马神话欣赏. 上海:上海外语教育出版社.

[21] 杨俊峰. (2004) 古典神话与西方文学. 沈阳:沈阳出版社.

[22] 郑振铎. (2010) 希腊神话与英雄传说. 北京:新世界出版社.

[23] Ancient Greek Mythology: www.mlahanas.de/Greeks/GreekMythology.htm

[24] Classical Myth: http://wps.prenhall.com/hss_powell_classical_4/

[25] Greek Mythology: www. greekmythology.com

[26] Greek Mythology: http://www.theoi.com/

[27] Greek Mythology Gods: www.greek-mythology-gods.com/

[28] Greek & Roman Mythology: http://bama.ua.edu/~ksummers/cl222/

[29] Olympians— Greek Mythology:

[30] www.greekmythology.com/Olympians/olympians.html

[31] The Age of Fable: Stories of Gods and Heroes: http://www.bartleby.com/181/

[32] Theoi Greek Mythology: http://www.theoi.com/

[33] Mr. Dowling's Greek Mythology Page: www.mrdowling.com/701-mythology.html